Known Violin Makers

by

John H. Fairfield

～

*With my compliments
and best wishes for
sucess in the violin
business.*

Robert Ames

PREFACE

I am offering this publication as a guide and reference book for those interested in instruments of the violin family and their makers. Though there are many such books available, most of the authoritative works are either antiquated or written in a foreign language and there seems to be very little American literature on this subject. In view of the fact that in the course of the last century instruments of most European makers have been brought to this country, it seems to me that this is an opportune time to publish a book stressing the value of these instruments on the American market. I have given a short outline of the life and work of the more important makers. Many European makers who have only achieved local fame but are scarcely known in this country are not listed, while others whose names are popular in America are treated in more detail.

An entire section of this book is devoted to modern American craftsmen. Their number is steadily increasing and I think it is important that they become more widely known to the American public. The biographical notes given herein come direct from these various makers and the prices quoted are the ones they themselves have placed on their works.

The valuation of the old makers, as I have given it, and the description of their work refer to genuine examples and such instruments have been sold for the prices listed.

It must be remembered that an exceptional violin may by far surpass the average work of its maker, while he at times produced others at a lesser cost of labor and material which do not come up to his usual standard, and this partly accounts for the wide range in the prices of one individual maker.

For my knowledge and experience in the violin business I am deeply indebted to Mr. J. C. Freeman, an internationally known authority on old violins, under whom I have served for twenty years. The violin world is well acquainted with Mr. Freeman as the foremost expert in this country.

I have asked Mr. Freeman to write a short reminiscence of his life which I am sure will be of great interest, as it shows, at the same time, the development of the rare violin business in this country since 1889.

For historical data I consulted "Die Geigenmacher" by Freiherr v. Lütgendorff and "Dictionnaire Universel des Luthiers" by René Vannes. Other valuable information was obtained from publications of W. E. Hill & Sons, The Rudolph Wurlitzer Company, "The Strad" and other magazines.

To Miss Linda Hellmann I offer my appreciation for the valuable assistance she has rendered me in the necessary research and preparation of the manuscript.

CONTENTS

VIOLIN REMINISCENCES

by

JAY C. FREEMAN

Mr. Fairfield, who has been associated with me in the violin department since 1922, has asked me to recount, at not too great length, something from my early experience as it relates to the development of the violin business in this country. This I am glad to do in the hope it may prove to be of some interest to at least a few of the many readers of his book.

Because of poor health as a boy of 17 years, I was forced to leave high school in Chicago to live in the "grand open spaces" of Texas and what was then known as Indian Territory, now Oklahoma, and soon found myself a pony rustler and later a cow-puncher on the then 80,000 acre R-S ranch in the Cheyenne country, 7 miles West of Fort Supply.

We had a Negro cook named Joe who fiddled at night in the ranch-house for the boys to dance. He could reel off "Arkansas Traveler," "Turkey in the Straw" and many other tunes in what seemed to me then to be the acme of perfection. I soon was taking lessons from Joe on the side and after a fashion learned how to hold the violin and bow and to play, by ear of course, Joe's repertoire, so that in a short time I was able to relieve my teacher at the Saturday night fandangoes.

Those dances were stag affairs and often wild ones. After the round-up season was over and the men returned to headquarters after several weeks absence on the range, the Saturday night dance was the one all-important event the men looked forward to, and Joe had to fiddle for anywhere from ten to twenty cow-punchers in high heel boots and jingling spurs to dance. And dance they did, without let-up, from dusk until the wee-small hours of Sunday morning. The fiddler's job required a lot of endurance and a substitute was welcome. That is where "Chicago the Kid" as I was called, came in, and I was happy.

After about 18 months, I took a better job on the Box T ranch in the Texas pan-handle, but alas, there I found neither a Joe or a fiddle to relieve the daily monotony. So, after the lapse of six months or so, I decided to return to Chicago and take up violin study in earnest.

Thus it happened that in the summer of 1887 I was apprenticed to a Chicago violin-maker, named August Heck, who for $500.00 agreed to teach me how to make violins, while at the same time I began to take violin lessons. My first teacher was Baron De Vey, pupil of Wieniawski, an erratic but enthusiastic teacher. Later I went to S. E. Jacobson, a really great teacher, pupil of Ferdinand David.

For the next few years I lived violins. I read every book I could find on the history of violin making. I was fascinated by the story of violin development in Italy and early violin music and violinists, all of which developed concurrently. I came to the decision that my future career was to be not that of a professional violinist, to which I at first aspired, but a collector and dealer in rare violins.

VII

How this was to come about I did not then know; nevertheless it came, for on March first 1889, I entered the employ of Lyon & Healy as violin-salesman at the then munificent salary of $10.00 per week.

I soon found I could sell, but that there were no good violins for me to sell. There were at that time mighty few good instruments in the West, or in the East either, for that matter. I saw a great country developing, as yet slowly, musically speaking, but one which would eventually demand the best the world afforded. I came to the conviction that it was to be possible for me to supply the needed instruments with the aid of the financial power of the firm and the complete confidence they reposed in me.

The result was that on March 14, 1890, a year after I entered their employ, and then earning the princely salary of $30.00 per week, I sailed from New York for Southampton on the S.S. Werra, with Mr. Robert B. Gregory, Vice President of Lyon & Healy, who was en route to Leipzig and Markneukirchen to buy musical merchandise of all kinds, for in those days everything in musical merchandise was imported. My mission was to study and learn as much as I could and to buy the violins, violas and cellos which were to form the beginning of a Lyon & Healy Collection.

We reached London on a cold rainy Saturday night and put up at the First National Hotel on Holburn. My room was cold and damp and I asked to have a fire made in the grate, and was told that the wind wasn't blowing from the right direction and therefore it was not possible. I don't remember ever having been more thoroughly congealed than that night. Very few if any London hotels at that time had "central heating" plants. So, as far as a grate fire was concerned, I could freeze, until the wind shifted.

Arriving in London, my first desire was to visit the Wardour Street district, locating the famous violin-shops I had read so much about, for almost all of them were located there and on Soho Square, and they were of far greater interest to me at that time than Westminster, the National Museum or the Tower of London.

Next day I met William and Arthur Hill. Alfred, being absent on the continent, I met for the first time some days later in Hammig's shop in Leipzig. Thus began a warm friendship which endured until Alfred's death in April 1940; he was the last of the brothers to pass on.

I made the acquaintance also of Geo. Hart, Senior and Junior, John Beare, Withers and many others. In Paris I met Silvestre, Gand and Bernardel, Serdet and other luthiers. In Germany, Wm. H. Hammig and his better half Frau Hammig in Leipzig, Emil Hamma in Stuttgart and — of most importance to me — August Riechers, Berlin, who was, with Hammig, the most dependable expert in Germany. In the week or two I was in Berlin he gave me much valuable advice and information, for which I have always been grateful. It was the same every subsequent trip I made. All these good friends seemed sincerely interested to help me train my eye and ear in the most subtly difficult of all callings in which I was engaged.

Returning to Chicago after three months abroad, I was faced with the problem of cataloguing and disposing of the instruments I had purchased. I wrote the descriptions of the 200 to 300 instruments and we issued the first violin catalogue to be published in the United States. This was in the fall of 1890.

Most were sold out in the following year and, in 1892, I made my second trip and thereafter, until 1914, I made regular expeditions visiting nearly every violin dealer on the continent this side of Russia and as far South as Sicily and North to Scotland and Denmark. On my return from each trip I catalogued the instruments I had bought. Between European trips I did a great deal of traveling selling instruments and also buying here and there a Stradivari or Guarneri.

The most important purchase ever effected in this country up to that time I made in 1900, when I bought the famed Hawley Collection from the late Ralph Granger in San Diego, California. I wrote the Hawley Brochure, which was published by Lyon & Healy in 1902 at $3.00 and now brings £6. in London. The edition was about sold out by the time it was off press.

During my 1908 trip I accumulated convincing evidence that satisfied our U. S. Treasury Department that European nations regarded antique violins as "works of art and of educational value," as required by the Dingley Tariff Act. On returning to Chicago, I went to see our Customs attorney, Mr. Achkoff, and laid before him the facts I had gathered. He left immediately for Washington and obtained a favorable ruling entitling antique violins to free entry, and nearly every violin I had purchased that trip came in free. Since that time, all antique violins (i.e., made prior to the year 1801) have paid no duty, where previously a tax of 40% on the purchase price was levied. As a result of this ruling we have in the United States today the major portion of existing 16th-18th century good Italian, French and other instruments.

In the Fall of 1920, I accepted the invitation of Messrs. Rudolph, Howard and Farny Wurlitzer to come to New York and take full charge of their violin department, and thus began a new phase of my business experience which proved to be most happy for me. It gave me a much broader field under far more favorable conditions than I had known in Chicago, where, after the death of Mr. P. J. Healy and other heads of the business, things were changed.

The collection I found in New York had recently been made by Mr. Rudolph H. Wurlitzer, and many of its finest instruments were sold by 1923. That summer I had a letter from an old acquaintance in Glasgow, Mr. R. S. Waddell, who owned a number of very fine violins, including the Betts Stradivari, 1704, and the Le Duc Joseph Guarneri, 1743. He intimated he might sell. I caught the first steamer I could and went straight to Glasgow and, after several days of battling with a very canny Scot, I bought for Wurlitzer all thirteen instruments. I think this transaction gave me greater personal satisfaction than any other I ever made.

A far larger transaction took place in May 1929, when we purchased the Wanamaker Collection. Financially this was undoubtedly the most important in the history of violins. It involved enough violins, violas, 'cellos and string basses to equip a symphony orchestra with the finest Cremona, Venetian and other 17th and 18th century instruments.

Between these two very important deals I had another which gave me great satisfaction, for I finally beat a London house to the "kill." In the Fall of 1926 I was called on at my hotel in London by the executors of the estate of the late Capt. Murray of Galashiels, Scotland, who wanted to sell his quartet of Stradivarii. "Barkus was willin'," but they couldn't make delivery it later transpired, because a Wardour Street dealer, having them in his keeping because he hoped to get them, left town so that he would not be forced to give them up. I sailed for New York without them. Negotiations continued, and finally they arrived on this side and we bought them. Among them was the Ex Gibson Stradivari viola, 1728, a very beautiful cello and two first class violins.

All these wonderful instruments, and many others, have found new owners, here and abroad, and I take some satisfaction in the thought that the vision I had as a youth and the hope to see my country the possessor of the world's finest instruments has been fulfilled.

New York, June 1942.

JAY C. FREEMAN
Violin Expert
Curator and Manager of the
Wurlitzer Collection

SELECTION OF AN INSTRUMENT

This book was written to aid and guide the person, whether student, amateur, or professional artist, in selecting an instrument, and it covers the different points to be considered in making such a selection, namely, the price, model and measurements, tone and physical condition. Hearing of the high prices paid for old violins would lead one to believe that it costs a fortune to acquire a good instrument. This is not necessarily so. A good old violin, viola or cello can be bought for as little as $150.00.

Before selecting an instrument, the purchaser should acquire a general knowledge of the subject, learn what to expect and how to select. The ideal tone is generally found in old instruments, but there are many new ones, well broken in, which sound excellent and are better than an inferior old instrument. The purchaser should know the better makers in the class he is looking for and have an idea of what a fair price should be. This book gives a brief history of known makers, indicates their ranking and furnishes many interesting points helpful to the serious player, amateur or collector.

The value of an instrument is made up of the quality of its tone, workmanship, appearance and physical condition. When seeking tone and tone quality alone, do not look for a famous name, unless you can afford to pay for it. There are many instruments on the market with excellent tone, well worth considering, although most likely unknown to the average musician.

Many players find it difficult to select the instrument that has just the quality of tone they desire. After the purchase is made, they discover certain faults and regret they did not choose another. It is important that the instrument vibrates freely to assure maximum quality and volume of tone. It is hard to play an instrument that responds slowly, and quick passages can not be executed satisfactorily on it, especially in the higher register. There should be no noticeable changes in the volume of tone when passing from one string to the next; all should be equal. The instrument should be tested for perfect double notes, thirds, sixths, octaves, etc., also for three- and four-part chords.

The carrying power is very important in large concert halls. An instrument that sounds loud under the ear does not necessarily carry well. Generally a solid, mellow tone is preferred for solo work and a strong, brilliant tone for orchestra.

Any instrument must be correctly adjusted before it is tried. The neck must be set at the right angle so that the slope of the fingerboard and the height of the bridge are right. The string length, i.e., the distance from the fingerboard nut to the center of the bridge should correspond to the dimensions of the instrument. For example, if the stop of a violin (from the upper edge to the notch in the soundhole) is 7⅝", the string length should be just under 13". In violas and cellos, there are so many sizes that it would be necessary to measure the individual instrument to ascertain the correct string length. The thickness of the strings should be gauged to suit each particular instrument. Usually a heavy gauge is required with a short string length, a thin gauge with a long string length.

The testing should be done in a place where the tone is dampered by drapes, rugs, plenty of furniture and tapestry. If an instrument sounds well in such a room, it should be satisfactory anywhere. Any instrument sounds well where there are hard floors, much glass and little furniture.

When selecting an instrument, have someone help you — someone whom you have heard play and whose style you know. In this way you can hear the instrument from a distance and also have the opportunity of the listener's comment. All wood instruments are affected by dampness and will not sound at their best in rainy or humid weather.

It does not matter whether you have a $15.00 or a $1000.00 instrument, it should be correctly adjusted and cared for.

CARE OF THE INSTRUMENT

If a peg sticks, do not use pliers or yank the peg with force. You are likely to break the button off or damage the pegbox, and I have even seen scrolls snapped off. A repair of this nature is costly. Rather have a violin maker move the peg, and no damage will occur.

If a peg is hard to turn, or jumps, it should be treated with a peg composition, which is not expensive and can be used safely. This should be done at least four or five times a year. Many people use chalk and soap, but it is inadvisable unless you know exactly how to do it. Too much chalk makes the peg bind and too much soap makes it slip.

When lubricating the pegs, release the tension on one string at a time and bring the string up to pitch before proceeding with the next. If the pressure on all strings is released completely, the bridge will move and the soundpost most likely fall.

The fingerboard should be examined at least once or twice a year. The constant wear of the strings on the board causes "railroads" or ruts and when they become deep, the strings hit the sides of these ruts and start to buzz. The fingerboard should then be redressed. If it is warped, due to climatic changes, it also needs attention, and unless a violin repairer can reshape it, a new fingerboard is necessary.

The bridge should be adapted to the quality of wood of the particular instrument for which it is chosen. A violin with a top of fibrous narrow grain and harder texture should have a soft wood bridge, whereas a top of broad grain and softer texture should have a harder bridge. Some violins sound better with a thin bridge and some with a thick bridge, depending upon the thickness of the top and back. The width of the feet of the bridge depends on the distance between the soundholes and the position of the bass bar. The worst thing on the market is a cheap bridge sold over the counter, with the advocation of fitting it yourself. Ready-made bridges can be purchased, but since the arching is different on every instrument and the wear from the pressure of the bridge changes the contour of the table, it is impossible to find one that fits perfectly. The only thing to do is to have a violin maker fit a bridge to the individual instrument.

Due to the expansion and contraction of the wood, most instruments require two bridges, a summer and a winter bridge.

The strings, when tuned, naturally pull the bridge forward toward the fingerboard and bring it into a slanting position in which, under the intense pressure, it may easily buckle or warp. To avoid this, from time to time the top of the bridge should be straightened; use both hands, one to push it back into its natural position, while the other prevents it from going too far or falling. If the bridge is allowed to lean forward, it will shorten the string length and thereby change the positions on the fingerboard. A bridge snapping down on the table may split the belly from top to bottom, and a big repair bill follows.

The soundpost is the soul of the instrument and this is what really governs the quality and evenness of tone on all four strings. The selection of wood, the thickness and the correct position are very important. To adjust it is a job for an expert and should never be attempted by the player, whether he has a fine instrument or a cheap one. If the post is too tight it will mar the inside of the table and choke the tone. In time the pressure will cause cracks in the table or back.

The tailpiece-gut should be replaced before it wears thin or perspiration makes it rot. Should it break while playing it is apt to cause serious trouble. The sudden release of pressure may split the top or cause the player to drop the instrument. When tuning, keep the head turned away, for a string might break and hit the eye and thus cause blindness. Such a thing has happened.

The chinrest must be selected by the individual player so that his chin will hold the instrument firm and in the proper position, leaving the left hand free from the weight of the instrument. This will increase accuracy and diminish fatigue. A wrongly fitted chinrest is apt to cause serious throat trouble.

A bow should be rehaired at least every two months if in continuous use, and it is cheaper to use hair of the best grade because it seldom breaks, though it wears smooth from use. Have this done only at a reliable place. In the last twenty years I have seen many beautiful and expensive bows ruined by inexperienced violin makers or repairers. About one out of ten old bows seen have a split frog, mutilated by careless workmen. It should not cost over $1.50 anywhere in the United States to have a bow rehaired, cleaned and adjusted in the very finest manner.

When the bow is not in use it should be completely loosened and all the pressure taken off the stick. If left tight, the camber of the bow, i.e., its curve, straightens and the playing value is *lost*.

Rosin is a very important item. There are many grades of rosin on the market but the majority of them are poor. A fine grade of rosin can be purchased at a reasonable price. Some of the better brands are Hill AB, Grip-All, Bernardel, Black American, Hart, Sherman, etc. Rosins of this quality do not powder too much and will not slip or slide. The most expensive rosin is cheap in the end.

The instrument should be kept clean at all times. Do not let dust and rosin accumulate on the top, because this dulls the tone. Wipe the strings all the way down with a rag slightly dampened with alcohol. This will remove rosin and perspiration and allow the strings to vibrate freely. Caution, use alcohol sparingly and do not let it touch the table, for it may dissolve the varnish and leave spots which cannot be taken out.

There are high grade cleaning preparations on the market; an excellent one is made by W. E. Hill & Sons, London. It preserves the varnish, gives a beautiful luster and keeps the instrument in a healthy condition.

Never leave your instrument exposed. Always keep it in its case, away from the heat. Wrap it in a silk cloth and place it near the floor, not in a closed closet or high up in the room where the air is too dry. Warm air has a tendency to dry out the glue and pulverize it. When the sides are unglued, have them closed immediately. This is a small expense if done at once. Have your instrument examined at least twice a year by a reputable man or firm, of which there are many in the United States. For this service no charge should be made unless actual work is done.

Advice on Repairs. If your instrument is sounding poorly and you cannot discover the cause of the trouble, have it examined by an expert, not a person looking just for a repair job. Many violin makers will tell you immediately that the top must be removed, a new bass bar is needed, the top is too thin, the back need strengthening, or the neck is wrong. This may be true, but in many cases such a major job is not necessary and would not improve, but might harm, the tone of your instrument. The writer, who is a lover of fine instruments, does not believe in such repairs unless they are positively necessary. A list of many of the finest professional violin makers and repairers who would gladly give their honest advice will be found in the American section of this book.

European Makers

ACHNER, MICHAEL — *Worked between 1764 and 1773, member of a large family of violin makers in Wallgau, Bavaria.*

Not a well known maker and of the lower class. His instruments, usually covered with a brown to dark red-brown varnish, have sold from $125.00 to $300.00.

ACTON, WILLIAM J. — *B. 1848 in Woolwich, London, d. 1931.*

Son of the violin maker A. W. Acton. His instruments are known for their large tone. He generally followed a pattern similar to Stradivari, selecting the finest wood and making his own varnish. He did all of his work himself and had no apprentices, and was an expert bow-maker, too.

ALBANI, MATTHIAS — *Bolzano, or Bozen (Latin: Bulsani). B. about 1620, d. about 1712.*

Most likely he was a pupil of Jacobus Stainer, the greatest Tyrolean maker. The work of his earlier period is purely Tyrolean in style and shows Stainer's influence. Later he changed to Italian principles. During his lifetime, his instruments were considered next to those of Amati and Stainer. He was one of the finest craftsmen, selecting his woods with the greatest care. The varnish is generally brown or red-brown and has the qualities of the old Italians. His models are usually rather high arched, with wide sides. On many instruments the head is carved in a form of a dragon's or man's head. The tone is exceptionally good, particularly in instruments of the last period of his life. Violins, violas and cellos: $750.00 to $3000.00.

> *Label:* Matthias Albanus fecit / Bulsani in Tyroli 16....
> (and others)

ALBANI, JOHANN MICHAEL — *Graz, Austria. B. about 1677, d. 1730.*

Son of Matthias. Many fine examples of the work of this famous maker are still in existence today, mostly cellos. He worked quite differently from his father. The purfling is set farther in, the corners are wider and the scrolls more heavily cut. Rather high arching. Varnish of very good texture, generally yellow or red brown. He was very careful in selecting his woods. Many of his instruments were quite thin and had to be strengthened. Prices: $1000.00 to $3000.00.

ALBANI, JOSEPH — *Bozen, Tyrol. B. 1680, d. 1722.*

He learned his trade from his father, Matthias, and worked for him a number of years. Very few instruments bear his original label, but it is possible that he used his father's. He followed the models of the old Italian masters. His selections of wood are good. He used a yellow-brown and red-orange varnish. Prices: $500.00 to $850.00. Exceptional specimens much higher.

> *Label:* Josephus filius Matth. Albani / me fecit Bulsani in
> Tyroli / Anno 17....

ALBANI, NICOLAS — *Mantua, Italy. Worked between 1763 and 1770.*

His instruments are built on a large pattern and covered with a reddish varnish. The wood is not always the best, but the tone is powerful. Very few of his instruments exist today.

ALBERT, CHARLES FRANCIS — *B. 1842 in Freiburg, Germany, d. 1901 in Philadelphia, Pa.*

He had his own business in Philadelphia, made fine instruments and was considered one of the better American makers. He used American wood and generally built his instruments on a large flat model. He made many copies of the great old masters such as Stradivari, Guarneri, etc. His son, Charles F. Albert, b. 1869, succeeded him in business. Violins, violas and cellos range from $100.00 to $250.00.

ALBERTI, FERDINAND — *Worked in Milan, Italy, 1737 to about 1760.*

Little is known of this maker. He generally followed flat models. His wood is well selected. The tone of his instruments is rather small, but very pleasing. He usually used a red brown varnish. Prices: $500.00 to $650.00.

ALBRECHT, JOHANNES — *Krems, Austria. B. 1766, d. 1828.*

A fair maker though not of any great importance. Prices: $75.00 to $100.00.

ALDRIC, JEAN FRANÇOIS — *B. in Mirecourt, France, 1765, d. 1843.*

He had his own business in Paris about 1785. A follower of the French school. Some of his instruments are exceptionally fine and are considered almost the equal of Nicolas Lupot. Many of them are copied from original Stradivaris. His varnish is red and red-brown, generally very thick. He was also a very clever repairer as well as a dealer. Violins, violas and cellos range from $350.00 to $750.00.

> *Label:* Rue de Seine No. 71, près celle de Bussy / ALDRIC
> / luthier à Paris. an 18.... (and others)

ALLETSEE, PAUL — *Munich, Germany. B. about 1670, d. about 1735.*

A master craftsman in his work as is shown in his instruments, especially viol d'amours. Wood of fine selection, good quality varnish, light yellow, sometimes dark red. The heads are generally cut in the form of a lion's head. Handsome workmanship. Prices: $350.00 to $600.00.

> *Label:* Paulus Alletsee hof-/ Lauten und Geigen / macher
> in München 17.... (and others)

AMATI, ANDREA — *Cremona, Italy. B. about 1535, d. (according to Hill) before 1581.*

Founder of the famous Cremona school of violin making. His models are medium high arched, with narrow sides and wide sound-holes. He used excellent wood and mostly slab cut maple backs. The varnish is generally golden brown. Prices: $3000.00 to $7500.00.

AMATI, ANTONIO — *Cremona, Italy. B. about 1555, d. before 1630. Eldest son of Andrea.*

Worked together with his brother Girolamo (Hieronymus) who probably was the more skillful workman. Their work excelled earlier makers and the tone was greatly improved by the introduction of the so-called "grand pattern." The varnish is a golden brown or golden orange. Prices: $4000.00 to $7500.00, violas and cellos as high as $12,500.00.

> *Label:* Antonius & Hieronymus Fr. / Amati Cremonesi
> Andrea F. 16.... (and others)

AMATI, NICOLO — *Cremona, Italy. B. 1596, d. 1684. Son of Girolamo.*

He is considered the greatest master of his family. He followed his father's small models and also the "grand pattern." The dimensions are larger and the tone bigger, the wood well selected and the thicknesses properly calculated. The varnish is very flexible and generally a rich yellow-brown to golden red. His earlier instruments have a very sweet and pleasing tone but not the large tone of the "grand patterns." Prices: $3000.00 to $ 7500.00.

Label: Nicolaus Amatus Cremonen. Hieronymi / Fil. ac
Antonij Nepos Fecit 16.... (and others)

AMBROSI, PETRUS — *Worked in Brescia and Rome, Italy, between 1712 and 1748.*

Little known, though some very fine specimens of his work are still in existence. Violins: $600.00 to $800.00; violas $800.00 to $1000.00.

Label: Petrus Ambrosi Fecit / Brixiae 17....

ANDRES, DOMENICUS — *Worked in Bologna, Italy, between 1740 and 1750.*

Known as an amateur maker, following the early Italian school. He probably made only a small number of instruments as very few have been seen. His work is excellent, the color of the varnish reddish brown. Prices: $600.00 to $1000.00.

ANTONIAZZI, GAETANO — *Cremona, Italy. B. 1823, d. in Milan 1897.*

His instruments are well made. He copied many of the old masters, but the varnish is only fair, usually golden red. Prices: $350.00 to $600.00.

ANTONIAZZI, RICCARDO — *Son of Gaetano.*

He is little known and made but few instruments. Those seen are very good. Prices: $250.00 to $400.00.

ANTONIAZZI, ROMEO — *B. in Cremona 1862. Also a son of Gaetano.*

Took over his father's shop. Made copies of the great makers, including Guadagnini and Pressenda. His workmanship is very good, the tone quality excellent. The varnish is generally yellow-orange or red-orange. Prices: $250.00 to $600.00.

Label: Antoniazzi Romeo Cremonese / fece a Cremona
l'anno 19....

ARLOW, HEINRICH — *Worked in Brünn, Czechoslovakia, 1850-65.*

A pupil of Sawicki in Vienna. He made very few, but good instruments, generally Stradivari models, and used a red-brown varnish. Prices: $300.00 to $350.00.

ARTELLI, GIUSEPPE ANTONIO — *Milan, Italy, about 1765.*

A little known maker. His work resembles Testore and probably some of his instruments now bear Testore labels. They are well made and the tone is quite good. Prices: $400.00 to $800.00.

ASCENSIO, VINCENZO — *Worked in Madrid, Spain, between 1775 and 1790.*

A monk who made and repaired violins. His work is fair, the tone small but very mellow. Prices: $500.00 to $850.00.

AUBERT, CLAUDE — *Troyes, France. Active from 1765 to 1790.*

Not an important maker but a few of his instruments are known. They are valued up to $300.00.

AUDINOT, NESTOR DOMINIQUE — *Paris, France. B. 1842, d. 1920.*

Surpassed all other members of this violin making family. He worked for his father and later for Seb. Vuillaume, whose successor he became in 1875. He made very many violins and quite a few bows. His wood is not always of the best quality, the varnish varies from yellow-brown to dark red-brown, and most of his instruments are built on a large masculine pattern. They range in price from $150.00 to $250.00.

BAADER (BADER) — *Commercial makers of violins in Mittenwald, Bavaria, up to the present time.*

Their instruments, copies of the old masters, have been sent all over the world. The selections of wood are very plain, the work well done, the varnish very hard and chippy and generally yellow. For cheap instruments they have a fine tone. The older ones, of which there are many still in existence, have sold from $75.00 to $100.00; the later commercial copies from $25.00 to $75.00.

BAGATELLA, ANTONIUS — *Padua, Italy. B. 1755, d. 1829.*

A literarily and musically versed man, the author of a book first published in 1786 which elaborates on principles of the old school of violin-making. Only a few of his instruments have ever been seen.

BAILLY, PAUL — *Mirecourt, France. B. 1844, d. 1907.*

He served his apprenticeship in Mirecourt, worked for François Vuillaume and later for J. B. Vuillaume in Paris. Back in Mirecourt in 1892, he worked for different large violin houses of Paris and

London. For some time he was established in America, but in 1898, he returned to Paris. He copied many of the famous Stradivari violins. His work is excellent and his instruments are especially good for orchestra. He generally used a chestnut brown or orange-red oil varnish. After his death, his daughter, Jenny, took over the business. Prices: $250.00 to $500.00.

BAIRHOFF, GIORGIO — *Naples, Italy, late 18th century.*

His instruments are especially known for their large tone, though the workmanship is not equal to some of the old masters. Selected copies are quite in demand. He generally followed the Stradivari pattern but also copied other masters. The arching is usually rather high, the varnish a golden red or brown color. Prices: $500.00 to $1000.00.

Label: Giorgio Bairhoff fecit / Napoli 17___ (Initials in double circle)

BAJONI, LUIGI — *Milan, Italy. Second part of 19th century.*

Known mostly for his fine basses. He worked on the large pattern and used excellent wood. Violins priced at about $300.00, violas at $500.00, and basses from $600.00 to $850.00.

BALDANTONI, GIUSEPPE — *Ancona, Italy. B. 1784, d. 1873.*

He worked as a mechanic and violin maker and made about 200 instruments. They are a good flat model, the varnish mostly yellow-brown. Those seen are excellent in workmanship and quality of tone. Prices: $700.00 to $1000.00.

Label: Joseph Baldantoni Anconae / fecit Anno 18___

BALESTRIERI, TOMMASO — *Mantua, Italy. B. about 1735-40, d. 1790.*

Strongly influenced by Pietro Guarneri and Stradivari. His instruments are very highly thought of for their fine workmanship, tone and beauty. He worked mostly on a large pattern, the edges very wide, the scroll of masculine cut, the selections of wood excellent, the varnish yellow to rich red-orange. He also made a few violas and cellos. Prices of violins and violas: $2500.00 to $4500.00. Some of his exceptionally fine instruments sold as high as $8000.00.

Label: Thomas Balestrieri / Cremonensis / Fecit Mantuae anno 17.... (and others)

BANKS, BENJAMIN — *Salisbury, England. B. 1727, d. 1795.*

A pupil of Peter Wamsley and one of the finest English makers. He followed mostly the "grand pattern" of Amati and some of the other Cremonese makers. Was known as the "perfect workman" because of the exactness of measurements and beauty of workmanship and varnish. The color is usually a light yellow-brown, sometimes a dark red. He also made violas and cellos. Many of his instruments have been found with Italian labels and were sold as such. Prices: $450.00 to $850.00.

BARBÉ, TÉLESPHORE AMABLE — *B. 1822 in Dijon, France, d. 1892 in Mirecourt.*

He served his apprenticeship under Derazey, worked for Remy, Gand, Jacquot and others and particularly for J. B. Vuillaume. He made very few instruments of his own but those seen are quite well done. He generally followed the Stradivari patterns and used a red-brown varnish (more red than brown). He had a cousin Auguste Barbé, who was a bow-maker. Prices $250.00 to $450.00.

BARTL — *Family of violin makers in Vienna, Austria.*

The best among them was Michael Andreas, 18th century. Their instruments are not particularly good and sell from about $100.00 to $150.00.

BASSOT, JOSEPH — *Paris, France. B. 1738 in Mirecourt, d. about 1810.*

His early work was not very good but in his later years he improved considerably. His varnish is yellow-brown, sometimes with a tint of red. Prices: $250.00 to $500.00.

BAUSCH, LUDWIG — *Leipzig, Germany. B. 1805, d. 1871.*

Known mostly as a maker of bows of fairly good quality. They range in price from $35.00 to $150.00. His son, Ludwig, took over the shop and carried on after his father's death, also as a bow maker. Many cheap commercial bows bear this brand.

BAUSCH, OTTO — *Leipzig, Germany. B. 1841, d. 1875.*

Younger brother of Ludwig II. Made mostly bows ranging from $35.00 to $65.00, but also some violins. Those seen sold as high as $450.00.

BELLONE, PIETRO ANTONIO — *Milan, Italy, late 17th century.*

A little known maker, but the instruments seen are excellent. Brown amber varnish. Prices: $600.00 to $1000.00.

BELLOSIO, ANSELMO — *Venice, Italy. B. about 1715, d. 1785.*

A pupil of Sanctus Seraphin. He is not equal to his master and his instruments are not as valuable. Some are excellent, others quite inferior. Exceptional specimens have sold from $1000.00 to $3000.00. He used a wine-red and red-brown varnish.

> *Label:* Anselmus Bellosius Fecit / Venetiis 17....

BENOÎT, EUGÈNE — *Worked in Brussels, Belgium, about 1750.*

Little is known of this maker. A few of his instruments have been seen. His workmanship is fine. He used selected wood and the models are usually on the larger pattern. The varnish is generally dark brown. Prices: $250.00 to $450.00.

BENOÎT, PIERRE — *Worked in Châlons-sur-Saône, France, around 1900.*

A carpenter and violin repairer who also made some instruments which are not of any great value however. He followed the larger flat patterns of the French school and usually used a brown or red-brown varnish. Prices: $100.00 to $200.00.

BENTI, MATTEO — *Brescia, about 1580.*

Probably a pupil of Maggini. His instruments are little known. They are fairly well made but not very desirable from a player's point of view on account of the model, and sell for about $150.00.

BERETTA, FELICE — *Como, Italy, worked from 1758 to 1789, approximately.*

It is said that he was a pupil of Giuseppe Guadagnini. His instruments are little known but a few are exceptionally well made. Yellow varnish. Prices: $350.00 to $850.00.

> *Label:* Felice Beretta alievo di Giuseppe Guadagnini / fece
> in Como l'Anno 17....

BERGONZI, CARLO — *Cremona, Italy. B. 1683, d. 1747.*

One of the great contemporaries of Stradivari and Guarneri. Little is known about the years of his apprenticeship and his early working life, although many books state he was one of Stradivari's best pupils. His most prolific period was between 1730 and 1735. It is said that he took over Stradivari's business after the death of Francesco and Omobono Stradivari. His model, the arching and setting of the soundholes, purfling and even the interior work show more likeness to Guarneri than Stradivari. Also the texture of the varnish is more like that used by Guarneri. Some instruments show that it was put on either too rapidly or too thickly. The colors are red-brown and orange-red. He selected the very finest of woods and left it amply strong. The tone is powerful and of excellent quality. The value of his instruments has increased immensely in recent years, probably more so than any other maker's. Prices: $6,000.00 to $12,000.00; some exceptional specimens higher.

Label: Anno 17.... Carlo Bergonzi / fece in Cremona (and others)

BERGONZI, MICHEL ANGELO — *Cremona, Italy. B. 1722, d. about 1765.*

He was not as fine a craftsman as his father, Carlo, although his instruments are well liked and the wood and varnish are of fine quality. Some have brought as much as $5,000.00, but they are generally priced around $2,000.00.

BERGONZI, NICOLA — *Worked in Cremona, Italy, about 1760-96.*

Eldest son of Michel Angelo. His instruments on the average are made better than his father's. Yellow amber varnish, sometimes with a tint of orange. Prices: $1,800.00 to $4,000.00.

His younger brothers were Zosimo (1750-1777) and Carlo II (1758-1838), whose work is little known.

Label: Nicolaus Bergonzi / Cremonensis faciebat / Anno 17....

BERNARDEL, AUGUSTE SEBASTIEN PHILLIPE — *Mirecourt, France. B. 1798, d. 1870.*

In 1820, he went to Paris and worked for Nicolas Lupot. He also worked for Gand. Later, he had his own shop in Paris and in 1859 he was joined by his sons and retired from business in 1866. He was one of the most skillful makers of his time. His instruments were made of selected fine wood for tone, and are very well liked, especially for orchestra. His sons were Ernest (1826-99) and Gustave (1832-1904). Gustave worked for Eugene Gand and in 1892 became the successor of the firm of Gand & Bernardel, originally founded by Nicolas Lupot. He followed the Lupot style of work; his instruments are very well made. He only used oil varnish, light reddish brown. He was succeeded by Caressa & Français. Fine copies by either maker sell from $250.00 to $500.00.

BERNARDEL, LÉON — B. in Paris 1853.

Served his apprenticeship in Mirecourt, France, and worked for Gand & Bernardel from 1870 to 1898. He then established his own shop. He was known as a good maker, used Stradivari, Lupot and Gand models and always an oil varnish.

BERTOLOTTI, GASPARO — Called da Salò, after the place of his birth on the Lake Garda, Italy. B. 1542, d. 1609.

He was the founder of the Brescian school of violin making and one of the originators of the violin in its present form. The shape of his instruments differs from that of modern ones in that the arching is fuller, the soundholes are cut almost perpendicular and very narrow, the middle bouts longer and the corners quite short. He very often used pearwood for his scrolls. The varnish is beautiful, a dark red-brown color, sometimes a golden red-orange. For modern playing, his violas are unquestionably the best. They are very much in demand, not only for their beauty but for their quality and power. They are usually very large in pattern (17½") and probably the finest violas ever made, but only a few are left. Gasparo da Salo never dated his instruments and any found with a date are only copies. Violins: up to $8,000.00; Violas: $5,000.00 to $12,000.00.

> Label: Gasparo da Salò, In Brescia.

BERTUCCI, F. M. — Rome, Italy. B. 1897.

His work is fairly good, the model flat, the varnish golden yellow or brown. Prices: $250.00 to $400.00.

BETTS, JOHN EDWARD — London, England. B. 1755, d. 1823.

A pupil of Richard Duke in London. He employed skilled workmen such as Panormo, Fendt, Carter, and his nephew Edward, to make copies of the old Cremonese masters. He was a clever dealer and a fine connoisseur of Italian instruments and some very excellent copies of Amati were created in his shop. His woods are carefully selected and mostly varnished in a deep dull yellow color. Prices: $350.00 to $850.00.

BIANCHI, NICOLO — B. 1796 in Genoa, Italy, d. 1881 in Nice.

A pupil of some Italian master, possibly of Pressenda. He worked first in Aix, France, then from 1845 to 1868 in Paris, from 1868 to 1872 in Genoa and afterwards in Nice. Some of his instruments are well made, though not of exceptional quality. They are varnished in various shades of red. Prices: $250.00 to $500.00.

BIMBI, BARTOLOMEO — *A Florentine maker who worked in Siena, Italy, about 1750-69.*

He followed a small pattern, with high arching. His varnish is generally orange with a tint of red, and of good quality. His instruments are finely made and possess good tone. Prices: $400.00 to $600.00.

BISIACH, LEANDRO — *Milan, Italy. B. 1864, d. 1914.*

A pupil of Antoniazzi. A well-known modern maker who enjoyed great fame even during his life time. He had studied in Cremona and presumably had bought tools and photographs of the recipe for the varnish used by Stradivari. His violins range in price from $250.00 to $500.00. He had two sons, Carlo, established in Florence, and Andrea, in Milan. The original house is still in existence under the direction of Giacomo and Leandro Bisiach, grandsons of Leandro, senior.

BLANCHARD, PAUL FRANÇOIS — *B. 1851, d. 1915.*

Worked at Marseille, France, later for Silvestre and also for A. Darte and J. B. Vuillaume. In 1876, he opened his own shop in Lyon. An excellent maker, using only the finest wood. His models are generally flat and the varnish a rich red-amber. He copied mostly the famous classic makers. Prices: $350.00 to $750.00.

BOGNER, AMBROSIUS JOSEPH — *Prague, Czechoslovakia. B. 1752, d. 1816.*

This maker's model is medium flat, the wood used not too good, the varnish very brittle and of a dark brown color. It has, like that of most Viennese instruments, turned darker with age. Prices: $200.00 to $300.00.

BOHMANN, JOSEPH — *B. 1848 in Bohemia.*

Came to the United States in 1873 and established himself in Chicago, Ill.. He used Canadian wood, imitated many of the old Italian masters. Oil varnish, mostly of yellow amber color. He also made bows. Instruments are priced from $200.00 to $350.00.

BOIVIN, CLAUDE — *Worked in Paris, France, about 1725-60.*

Little known as a violin maker, as he made chiefly guitars and violas. Well made instruments have been seen, with good quality wood and yellow-brown dull varnish of dry texture. Prices: $250.00 to $600.00.

BOLLER (or POLLER), MICHAEL — *Worked in Mittenwald, Germany, about 1740-1800.*

His violins are well-made and possess good tone. He used excellent patterns and a yellow-brown varnish. Prices: $200.00 to $250.00.

BOLLINGER, JOSEPH.

An Austrian maker of the early 19th century. Prices: $75.00 to $250.00.

BOQUAY, JACQUES — *B. in Lyon, France; worked in Paris about 1700-1736.*

A fine French maker whose style is very similar to that of Claude Pierray. The models he used are mostly small, the varnish brown or red-brown, sometimes with a tint of yellow. Some of his instruments, especially his cellos, are very well-made and bring good prices. Violins, $350.00 to $850.00; cellos as high as $1000.00.

BORELLI, ANDREA — *Worked in Parma, Italy, about 1720-46.*

Little known, but violins of excellent quality have been seen, built on large patterns, with good yellow to red-brown varnish. Prices: $500.00 to $850.00.

BORGIA, ANTONIO — *Milan, Italy, around 1769.*

His name has been found in many violins not made by him. He is otherwise little known. Varnish medium brown, style of Testore. Prices: $450.00 to $700.00.

BOUMEESTER, JAN — *Amsterdam, Holland. B. 1629, d. 1681.*

One of the best Dutch makers of the 17th century. The majority of his instruments are built on a large pattern, with medium arching. Many have probably been sold as Italian. Excellent yellow or reddish-yellow varnish. Prices: $600.00 to $850.00.

BRANDILIONI (BRANDIGLIONI), FILIPPO — *Worked in Brescia about 1790-1800.*

Little known. His work is similar to Mittenwald schools. Medium arching, varnish generally brown with slight tint of red. Priced about $350.00.

BRANDINI, JACOPO — *Worked in Pisa, Italy, about 1789-1807.*

The quality of his instruments, especially the varnish, is very good, though all are not equally handsome. He also made some fine violas. Prices: $350.00 to $850.00.

BRANDSTAETTER, MATHAEUS IGNAZ — *Worked in Vienna, Austria, about 1791-1851.*

His instruments, though beautiful, are tonally not always very good. He is little known in this country. Yellow-brown varnish. Prices: $250.00 to $500.00.

BRETON, JOSEPH FRANÇOIS—*Worked in Mirecourt, France, about 1740-99.*

His labels, however, are marked Paris. His instruments are very similar to those of another François Breton who also worked in Mirecourt about the same time. In fact both makers are on a more or less equal standing. He used a broad, flat pattern, Stradivari model. The workmanship is good. The color of the varnish is usually medium brown. Some violas made by him have been seen with red-brown varnish. Instruments by both these makers are either labelled or branded "Breton breveté." Prices are from $200.00 to $350.00.

BUCHSTETTER, GABRIEL DAVID — *Worked in Regensburg and Stadt am Hof, South Germany, about 1752-71.*

He was considered one of the finest German makers of his time. His instruments are narrow and have a flat arching. Neat workmanship. The varnish is usually yellow-brown unless darkened by age. Prices: $200.00 to $450.00.

BULL, OLE — *Bergen, Norway.*

A well known violinist, who also made some instruments. He tried to improve the tone of the violin, but his experiments were not very successful. There are hundreds of violins branded on the back "Ole Bull" which are only the very cheapest commercial instruments, worth $10.00 to $15.00.

BUSAN, DOMENICO — *Worked in Vicenza and Venice, Italy, between 1740 and 1780.*

His violins are built on a large pattern. He also made some fine violas but is chiefly known for his basses. Red-brown varnish. Basses sell as high as $750.00; Violins, up to $1000.00.

BUSSETTO, GIOVANNI MARIA (del) — *Worked in Cremona and Brescia, Italy, about 1640-81.*

Very few of his instruments are known, but those seen are excellent. The model is nice, medium arched, the varnish yellow-brown. His instruments have sold from $1000.00 to $1500.00.

BUTHOD — *Mirecourt, France. B. 1810, d. 1889.*

He worked for Vuillaume, then opened a large factory: Husson, Buthod & Thibouville. For factory instruments they are well made, mostly varnished in a deep red-brown. Broad flat pattern. The tone is big but not mellow. Prices: $60.00 to $100.00.

CALCANIUS, BERNARDO — *Worked in Genoa, Italy, about 1710-50.*

His instruments are exceptionally well made, of very handsome wood. He followed the Stradivari model almost exclusively and used a beautiful yellowish red or orange varnish. His scrolls are small and very gracefully cut. Prices: $750.00 to $1800.00.

Label: Bernardus Calcanius / fecit Genuae Anno 17__

CALVAROLA, BARTOLOMMEO — *Worked in Bologna and Bergamo, Italy, about 1750-67.*

His violins are fair, some show excellent workmanship, patterned after Ruggeri. The scrolls are poorly cut. Usually used yellow varnish. Prices: $300.00 to $500.00.

CAMILLI, CAMILLO — *Mantua, Italy. B. about 1704, d. 1754.*

Believed to be a pupil of Zanotti, and to a certain extent, he followed his style, but his instruments are of slightly smaller size and rounder arching. The design of his soundholes, which are usually set almost straight, is his own. He used the finest wood and worked with greatest care. The varnish is a light wine-red or pinkish yellow color. His instruments are well liked for their carrying power and beautiful mellow quality. Most of them are a little short in the stop and string length. Prices: $1500.00 to $3500.00.

Label: Camillus de Camilli / fecit in Mantova 17__ (also manuscript)

CAMPOSTANO, ANTONIO — *Worked in Milan, Italy, about 1699-1710.*

He followed the style of Grancino. The selections of wood are quite good. His instruments are well cut and of excellent quality. The varnish is usually yellow-brown. He also made some basses and viols. Prices: $275.00 to $350.00.

CAPPA, GIOFFREDO — *Saluzio, Italy. B. 1644, d. 1717.*

He was a pupil of Nicolo Amati, and his work shows Amati's influence. He made different sized violins, the larger ones being the better. The tone of these is exceptionally fine. He also made cellos, with high arching. The varnish is usually a golden yellow, sometimes more yellow-brown. Many of his instruments have been mis-labelled and the original labels used in cheaper instruments. Prices: $1000.00 to $2000.00; some exceptional specimens have sold as high as $3000.00.

Label: Iofredvs Cappa Fecit / Salvtvs Anno 16....

CARCASSI — *A family of violin makers in Florence.*

The best known is *Lorenzo* who, with his brother, formed the firm of Lorenzo and Tomaso Carcassi. His instruments are dated between 1735 and 1776. He also worked on his own. His work is very well done, and the tone exceptionally fine. Medium high arching, golden yellow to dark brown varnish. Lorenzo's instruments sell for $850.00 to $1350.00; the finest specimens of Lorenzo and Tomaso sold as high as $2500.00.

Label: Lor.° E Tom.° Carcassi / in Firenze nell'Anno 17....
/ all'Insegna del Giglio.

CARDI, LUIGI — *Verona, Italy.*

A maker of the 19th century, known mostly for his violas. Some have sold up to $500.00.

CARESSA, FELIX ALBERT — *Paris, France. B. 1866 in Nice, d. 1939.*

Pupil, and later, manager of Gand & Bernardel; successor of Gustave Bernardel. His instruments are not very well known, as he made only very few. He worked mostly on Stradivari and Lupot patterns. These instruments sold for about $350.00; those made under the name of Caressa & Français at $100.00 to $300.00 for violins, $150.00 to $250.00 for violas.

CARLETTI, CARLO — *A modern Italian maker who has his shop in Pieve di Cento near Bologna, Italy.*

He generally follows a Stradivari model. His instruments are well made but do not equal the best among modern makers. Light brownish red varnish. Priced about $250.00.

CARTER, JOHN — *Worked in London about 1780-90.*

He was one of the best workmen of John Betts under whose name were sold many of his violins and cellos. A very clever imitator of the old masters. Exceptionally fine work. His instruments are priced up to $400.00.

CASINI (CASSINI), ANTONIO — *Modena, Italy. B. about 1630, d. after 1705.*

A well-known maker of his time. He made a very large number of violins, cellos and basses. The models are small, well cut, the varnish mostly chestnut brown. The tone is fair but not large. Prices: $250.00 to $500.00.

CASTAGNERI, ANDREA — *Worked in Paris, France, about 1730-60.*

Son and pupil of Giovanni Paolo Castagneri. He was a little known but excellent maker. His instruments are built on a small pattern and after the model of Stradivari. Fine workmanship, the varnish usually brown tinged with red. Many instruments found today with his label are not genuine. His name is one of the most abused of that period. Authentic violins are priced from $350.00 to $750.00; his violas as high as $600.00.

Label: Andrea Castagneri nell / Pallazzo di Solffone, Pariggi 17....

CASTELLANI, PIETRO — *Florence, Italy. Late 18th century, d. in 1820.*

A guitar maker who also made some fine violins and cellos. Dark red varnish. Cellos bring as much as $800.00.

CASTELLO, PAOLO — *Worked in Genoa, Italy, about 1750-80.*

His work is fair though not exceptional and his wood is not always the best. Some of his fine violins sell up to $1500.00.

Label: Paulus Castello fecit / Genuae 17....

CAVALLI, ARISTIDE — *Cremona, Italy. B. 1856.*

Little is known of this maker, though his instruments have sold up to $600.00. However, many imitations are on the market bearing copies of his label.

CELANI, EMILIO (called The Turk) — *Worked in Ascoli Piceno, Italy, first part of the 19th century.*

Not well known. His label has been used in many Italian violins not of his make. Prices of originals: $150.00 to $300.00.

CERIN, MARCO ANTONIO — *Worked in Venice, Italy, about 1780 to 1825.*

Most likely a pupil of Bellosius. His work is very well done, the model mostly after Stradivarius. Used handsome wood and yellow or orange-brown varnish. He also made excellent basses. Violins, $500.00, exceptional copies as high as $1800.00; basses up to $850.00.

Label: Marcus, Antonius Cerin, Alumnus / Anselmii Belosii fecit Venetiae An 17....

CERUTI, GIOVANNI BAPTISTA — *Cremona, Italy. B. 1755, d. 1817.*

Pupil and successor of Lorenzo Storioni. His work is typical of the Cremonese school, on the patterns of Amati, Guarneri and Stradivari. His varnish varies in color; many instruments are of a golden yellow color, others dark red or reddish brown. He is not rated as high as other Cremona makers but his instruments are excellent. Prices: $800.00 to $2500.00.

Label: Jo: Baptista Ceruti Cremonensis / fecit Cremonae An 18....
G B C in circle

CERUTI (CERUTTI), GIUSEPPE — *Cremona, Italy. B. about 1787, d. 1860.*

Son of Giovanni Baptista Ceruti. He worked on small patterns, used handsome, well selected wood. The varnish is golden orange. He did not have the reputation of his father, but his instruments have been priced up to $1200.00.

Label: Josephus Cerutti filius Joannis Baptis / tae Cremonensis fecit Anno 18....

CERUTI, ENRICO — *Cremona, Italy. B. 1808, d. 1883.*

Son of Giuseppe and the last violin maker of his family. He made a great number of violins and also some very good cellos. As a more modern maker, he is better than the average. Violins: $350.00 to $600.00; Choice specimens of his cellos as high as $1500.00.

Label: Enricus Ceruti fecit / Cremonae Anno 18.... E.F.C.
(and others)

CHANOT — *A large family of violin makers in Mirecourt, France. Its most prominent member was Georges. B. 1801, d. 1883.*

He was one of the best French makers of the 19th century. He had great knowledge of the old Italian schools from which he copied. His workmanship is excellent, the varnish generally a shaded orange-red. The tone is very big and has a beautiful quality. His brother was François. Prices: $500.00 to $650.00.

Label: Georges Chanot, à Paris / Quai Malaquais Année 18.... G C in circle

CHANOT, GEORGES — *B. 1830 in Paris, d. 1893 in London.*

Son and pupil of Georges Sr.. About 1850, he went to London to work for Charles Maucotel and later went into business for himself. He was one of the best London makers of that time. He followed his father's models and varnish very closely. Prices: about $500.00. His son George Adolphe, b. 1855, d. 1923, studied under his uncle, Joseph Chardon, serving also under his grandfather, George Chanot, in Paris. Very few of his instruments are in existence.

CHAPPUY, NICOLAS AUGUSTIN — *B. about 1730, d. 1784.*

Worked in Paris until the middle of the 18th century, then returned to Mirecourt, his home town. His violins are considered very good in quality. He used spirit varnish, mostly yellow or brown, sometimes shaded. Many violins bearing his label are not original, for dealers have often used his name on cheaper French instruments to make them more readily saleable. Genuine Chappuy violins are exceptionally well-made and range in price from $350.00 to $600.00.

CHARDON, JOSEPH MARIE — *B. 1843 in Paris, d. 1930.*

Pupil and son-in-law of Georges Chanot whose business he took over about 1870. Later his son, Georges, joined him. He made some very excellent instruments, used finely selected wood. The tone quality is good and very large. His best instruments have been priced as high as $900.00.

CHAROTTE — *A large family of violin makers in Mirecourt, France.*

The earliest was *Charles François,* who established his business in 1721 and worked also in Nancy. *Joseph Charotte* (1798-1849), an apprentice of Aldric, branded his instruments "Charotte à Paris," although he never worked in Paris. Most of his violins are on the Strad model, with light yellow varnish. Others are red-brown. He also made cellos and basses. Prices range from $200.00 to $500.00. The house was later taken over by Georges Apparut (b. 1877).

CHARLES, JEAN — *Worked in Marseille, France, last part of the 18th century.*

He was a pupil and nephew of Guersan, not very well known. Made violins as well as cellos, and the latter sold up to $600.00.

CHEVRIER — *A large family of violin makers in Mirecourt, France, 18th and 19th centuries.*

The oldest were *Nicolas, Joseph,* and *Victor,* who operated the factroy of Thibouville Lamy in Mirecourt, known for their commercial violins. Prices: $150.00 to $300.00.

CHIOCCHI (CIOCCHI), GAETANO — *Padua, Italy. B. 1814, d. about 1880.*

Little is known of this maker. Possibly he was a pupil of Giuseppe Ceruti. Made very few violins. Selections of wood good, varnish yellow-brown to golden. One superb specimen dated 1879 was in the style of Gagliano, the scroll gracefully cut, the varnish a beautiful golden brown, workmanship excellent, medium arching. Average prices: $250.00 to $400.00, exceptional examples up to $700.00. Many instruments bear his name which are not original.

CLARK, A. B. — *Richmond, Va. Worked about 1880-1890.*

An American maker, not well known. He probably made not over 100 instruments. Fair workmanship. He used old American wood and followed the Cremonese models. His instruments sold as high as $150.00.

CLAUDOT — *Large family of violin makers in Mirecourt, France, of the 18th and 19th centuries.*

The best known is Charles; others are Augustin, Paul, Pierre, Jean Baptiste, Charles II and III, Félix and François. They all worked on the same style, generally Stradivari model, large pattern. Prices: $150.00 to $400.00.

CLÉMENT, JEAN LAURENT — *A maker of Mirecourt origin, worked in Paris between 1783 and 1847.*

He followed the Italian style, selected very good wood and generally used a dark red to reddish brown varnish. Many apprentices and workmen were employed in his shop. Prices: $150.00 to $450.00.

COLETTI, ALFRED — *B. 1878 in Vienna, Austria.*

Studied under C. H. Voigt and became the successor of Joseph Hamberger in 1905. His instruments, made of excellent old wood and well constructed, possess good tone. The varnish is usually a light red color with a brownish tint. Prices: $200.00 to $450.00.

COLLIN-MÉZIN, CHARLES JEAN BAPTISTE — *B. 1841 in Mirecourt, France, d. 1923.*

He was established in Mirecourt but also worked in Paris 1855-57. He was a member of a large family of violin makers, including Claude Nicolas, Charles and Jean Nicolas. His instruments, very well-made, are of the broad pattern and generally varnished in a red-brown color. Prices: $150.00 to $250.00.

COLLIN-MÉZIN — *A company formed by members of this family in Mirecourt, 1870.*

They worked commercially, on mass production, and hundreds of instruments were sold in the United States. They are typical Mirecourt work, the varnish generally a heavy red-brown. Violins sell for as much as $200.00, the better grade cellos up to $350.00.

COMUNI, ANTONIO — *Worked in Piacenza, Italy, about 1820-23.*

A maker of no great importance although some of his instruments have been priced as high as $500.00. His name has been used promiscuously and is found in violins not of his make.

Label: Antonius Comuni / fecit Placentiae Anno 18....

CONTRERAS, JOSEPH — *Madrid, Spain. B. about 1710, d. about 1780.*

He is one of the best-known Spanish makers and ranks very high but is probably underestimated today. He worked in the style of J. B. Guadagnini and Stradivari. His varnish is usually golden amber or reddish-orange. His son took over the business but never equalled the work of his father. Prices: $750.00 to $1200.00.

COSTA, FELIX MORI — *Worked in Parma, Italy, about 1804-12.*

He was not a maker of great repute, but made good instruments. His varnish is generally reddish-brown, sometimes yellow-brown. Prices: $600.00 to $800.00.

Label: Felix Mori Costa / Fecit Parmae / anno 18....

COSTA, GIOVANNI BAPTISTA — *Venice, Italy, about 1770.*

He may have been a pupil of Sanctus Seraphin, because the work of these two makers is very similar. Costa's violins are very rare; probably many have been sold as Sanctus Seraphins. They are priced from $500.00 to $750.00.

COUTURIEUX, N. — *Worked in Toulon, France, about 1840-50.*

A good maker, working after the style of D. Nicolas. He probably learned his trade in Mirecourt. Used fine wood and worked on a large pattern. The workmanship is good, the varnish a deep dark red, sometimes yellow. His violins are branded N C. Prices range from $100.00 to $150.00.

CRASKE, GEORGE — *England. B. 1797, d. 1888.*

A pupil of Wm. Forster and of Thomas Dodd. He was established in many different places—Bath, Leeds, Sheffield, Birmingham and last in Manchester and Stockport. He made a large number of violins, violas and cellos, also some basses. His workmanship is fine and the tone quality almost like that found in good Italian instruments. The color of the varnish is mostly medium red-brown. W. E. Hill & Sons bought out his shop after his death. Quite a few of his violins are in this country. Hill placed a label in the instruments they sold which reads: "Made by George Craske, b. 1797, d. 1888, sold by W. E. Hill & Sons, London." Prices today: $250.00 to $400.00.

CROSS, NATHANIEL — *Worked in London, England, about 1700-1751.*

One of the better-known makers of the English school. He followed the patterns of Stainer. The varnish is generally light yellow. About 1715, he went into partnership with Barak Norman. A good many of these instruments, which are branded with the initials N C placed over a cross, are in England. Those seen here are quite exceptional and would bring at least $500.00.

CROWTHER, JOHN — *Worked in London, England, beginning in 1755, d. about 1810.*

He worked mostly for dealers and made very few instruments under his own name. They are well done, following the English school. Price about $350.00.

CUYPERS, JOHANNES — *B. in Dornick, 1724, worked in The Hague, Holland, d. 1807.*

He usually followed the Stradivari model of the later period, but he had his own characteristic soundholes and scroll. His work is exceptionally well-done, the wood beautiful, the varnish good but rather thick and usually light golden brown. The tone is strong and heavy. Prices: $750.00 to $1200.00.

Jean François Cuypers, son and pupil of Johannes, and Johannes Bernardus, youngest son of Johannes, were also violin makers, but they are little known and not of great importance.

DALINGER, SEBASTIAN — *Worked in Vienna, Austria, 1768 to about 1809.*

He is one of the better Viennese makers, used handsome wood and followed Stainer models. His scrolls, sometimes carved in the form of a lion's head, are usually made of pear wood. The varnish is generally dark brown, sometimes yellow, and of very good quality. He also made violas and cellos. Prices: $250.00 to $500.00.

DALLA CORTE, ALFONSO — *Worked in Naples, Italy, in the 19th century.*

He made very good copies of the old masters, including violas. He used a yellow to yellow-orange varnish. Many Italian violins have been baptized Dalla Corte when dealers did not know what else to call them. Prices: $400.00 to $650.00.

DALLA COSTA, PIETRO ANTONIO — *Native of Alba, worked in Treviso, Italy, about 1700 to 1768.*

Supposed to have worked also in Venice and Mantua. Possibly a pupil of Goffriller and Seraphin. His selections of wood are fine and he followed the style of Nicolo Amati and Stradivari, also Antonio and Hieronymus Amati. His quality of varnish is excellent, the color generally being orange or red-brown. Not many original violins by Dalla Costa are in existence; many bear fake labels. He is rated very high, especially as a maker of cellos. Prices: $850.00 to $2500.00.

Label: Pietro Antonio dalla Costa / fece in Treviso Anno 17....

DALL'AGLIO, GIUSEPPE — *Worked in Mantua, Italy, about 1795 to 1840.*

A maker whose name has been abused by inserting reproductions of his label in violins which are not his work. He was an excellent craftsman and his instruments command good prices. Many of his violins are built after the style of Camillus Camilli, high arched, with rich yellow or golden red varnish. He also made some good violas. Prices: $500.00 to $1000.00.

Label: Joseph Dall'Aglio Fecit / Mantuae 18.... (and others)

DARCHE, NICOLAS — *Aachen, Germany. B. about 1815 in Mirecourt, d. 1873.*

He served his apprenticeship in Mirecourt, France, and about 1840 opened his own shop in Aachen. He copied the old masters. The varnish is generally thick, the color red or brown, and of very good quality. His cellos are finished especially fine. Prices range from $500.00 to $1000.00.

He had two brothers, Charles François and Joseph, who both worked for N. F. Vuillaume in Brussels, Belgium. They were quite good makers but did not surpass their elder brother.

DARTE, AUGUSTE — *B. in Paris, France, 1830, d. in Mirecourt, 1892.*

He was a pupil of Nicolas Vuillaume and for a short time worked for J. B. Vuillaume. He became one of Nicolas Vuillaume's workmen in 1865 and later his successor. He worked on various models, preferably Strad. His instruments are finely made and possess good tone. They are branded inside and on the shoulder button. Spirit varnish. Prices up to $300.00.

DAVIDSON, PETER — *B. 1834 in Scotland, d. about 1910.*

Came to the United States of America in 1886 and established himself at Louisville, Ga.. Little is known of his violins, but he was the author of a very good book on violin making: "Construction, Dictionary of Violin Makers, and Lists of Violin Sales," published in London 1881.

DEARLOVE, MARK WILLIAM — *B. about 1800 in England, d. 1865.*

Established himself in Leeds. His instruments are fairly well-made, the varnish is golden brown. Prices: $250.00 to $500.00.

DE COMBLE, AMBROISE — *Worked in Tournay, Belgium, about 1740-85.*

A well-known Flemish maker. He followed the Italian style but was not too careful about his workmanship. A few excellent instruments have been seen. The varnish is generally red to red-brown. The tone is quite good. Prices: $400.00 to $1000.00.

Label: Fait à Tournay par / Ambroise De Comble 17—

DECONET, MICHAEL — *Worked in Venice about 1752-95.*

During the last period of his life he worked in Padua. He followed the Cremona school, although his varnish, which is yellow-brown or red-brown, is very similar to Montagnana's, whose pupil he may have been. He selected his wood very carefully and is considered an excellent maker. His model, medium arched, is generally on the style of Peter Guarneri. He also made fine violas and cellos. Prices: $900.00 to $2,500.00.

Label: Michael Deconet Fecit / Venetiis Anno 17... (and others)

DEGANI, EUGENIO — *B. about 1840 in Montagnana, Italy.*

He was a son of Domenico Degani who was a lute, mandolin and violin maker of lesser importance. About 1885, he established himself in Venice. He worked on his own models and his varnish is exceptionally good, the color generally yellow-brown. Many of his instruments are used professionally today. He also made some very fine cellos. Prices: $300.00 to $650.00. (For Giulio Degani, son of Eugenio, refer to American Section.)

DELEPLANQUE, GERARD J. — *Worked in Lille, France, between 1755 and 1790.*

He is not very well known for his violins, more so for his lutes and guitars. His workmanship is good, the varnish generally yellow-red. Prices: $250.00 to $350.00.

DELUNET, AUGUSTE LEON — *Member of a large family of violin makers in Mirecourt, France. B. 1867, d. 1939 in Norwood, N. J.*

He worked in his father's shop until the age of 17, then was taken to London by W. E. Hill & Sons, where he worked as a repairer of fine old instruments for 33 years. In 1921, after one year's stay in the employ of R. S. Williams in Toronto, Canada, Mr. J. C. Freeman of the Wurlitzer Co. of New York, persuaded him to come and work for them as an expert repairman. From 1924 until his death, he was in business for himself. He enjoyed a fine reputation and hundreds of professional musicians came to him from all parts of the United States. He made very few instruments, but these are excellent in workmanship, covered with a red-brown varnish. They sold for $350.00.

DE PLANIS, AUGUST — *Genoa, Italy, last part of the 18th century.*

His work is fairly well liked. He used good models and usually a red-brown varnish. Prices: $150.00 to $400.00.

DERAZEY, JEAN JOSEPH HONORÉ — *B. 1794, d. 1883.*

Served his apprenticeship in Mirecourt and Paris, France. He later operated his own shop, made many instruments and employed a large staff of workmen. His work is typical of the French school, following chiefly a flat Stradivari model. He used good wood and generally a yellowish-brown varnish. Prices: $125.00 to $300.00. His instruments are branded.

He had a son, Justin Amédée (1839-90), who took over his business. He did not equal his father's work; his varnish being brittle and poor. His instruments have sold up to $200.00. Both made violas and cellos.

DESPINE (D'ESPINE), ALEXANDER — *Worked in Turin about 1823-42.*

A pupil of Pressenda but little known. He was an exceptionally fine maker, used well selected wood and worked mostly on a small pattern. His varnish, generally a medium wine-red, is of excellent quality. Judging from some examples seen, he ranks with the better semi-modern Italian makers. Prices: $1000.00 to $1500.00.

> *Label:* Alessandrus d'Espine Fecit / Taurini anno Domini 18....
> (and others)

DE VITOR, PETRUS PAULUS — *Worked in Brescia, Italy, about 1738-40.*

Only very few of his instruments are known. He had an excellent varnish, usually a beautiful red color. Otherwise his work is fair but not outstanding. High arching. Prices: $250.00 to $500.00.

DIDELOT, DOMINIQUE — *Worked in Mirecourt, France, about 1820.*

He followed the usual French flat model and large pattern. Dark red-brown varnish. He is not very well known in this country, but made many good instruments. Prices: $100.00 to $150.00.

DIDION, GABRIEL — *Worked in Mirecourt, France, about 1860-80.*

He made many instruments but very few are seen in this country. He used a red-brown varnish, sometimes a medium brown, with a slight tint of yellow. Workmanship is very good, the selections of wood excellent. Prices: $100.00 to $250.00.

DIEHL, NIKOLAS — *Hamburg, Germany. B. 1779, d. 1851.*

Member of a large family of violin makers, son of Martin. Their instruments, including violas and cellos, are all made in the same general style and range in price from $150.00 to $300.00.

DIENER, FRANZ — *Graslitz, Bohemia. B. 1790, d. 1866.*

Son of Joseph Diener. Made many instruments, on a commercial basis. They are well made and usually varnished brown. Violins, $100.00 to $150.00; cellos, up to $350.00.

DIEUDONNÉ, AMÉDÉE DOMINIQUE — *B. 1890 in Mirecourt, France.*

An apprentice of G. Bazin and later workman under Darche in Brussels. Has conducted his shop in Mirecourt since 1920. He is already famous for his excellent workmanship. He is very skillful in producing copies of the old Cremonese models and uses only the best materials. The varnish is yellowish red to vivid red. His violins have sold in this country for $75.00 to $150.00, specials as high as $300.00; his violas for $85.00 to $200.00; his cellos for $250.00 to $600.00.

DODD, EDWARD — *B. 1705 in Sheffield, England, d. 1810 in London.*

He started as a violin maker, but later changed his career and became a bow maker. He is a member of a large family of violin and bow makers, of which the most important are Thomas and John Kew.

DODD, THOMAS — *B. about 1760 in Sterling, England, d. about 1820.*

He began violin making in 1776 and also made bows. In 1798, he established himself in London. Two of his workmen were Bernhard Fendt and John Lott. His violins are not very well known, but his cellos are famous. The selections of wood are excellent. He made a very beautiful, rich, transparent golden red varnish. He copied all the famous old masters. His cellos range in price from $900.00 to $1800.00.

DODD, JOHN KEW — *B. 1752 in Sterling, England, d. 1839 in Richmond, in a workhouse.*

He enjoyed the reputation of being the most popular bow maker in England at that time. His bows are exceptionally well made, the balance exceedingly fine and they are beautiful specimens to look at. He made some of his sticks a little short. He never hired any workmen and thus kept his secret of cutting the sticks to himself. The color is generally chocolate brown, although some are plain brown. His bows, violin, viola, and cello range in price from $85.00 to $250.00.

DOERFFEL — *Klingenthal, Saxony.*

Makers of violins and lutes during the 17th and 18th centuries. Prices: $50.00 to $100.00.

DOETSCH, MICHAEL — *Berlin, Germany. B. 1874.*

Pupil of Kohlbacher. He is a very fine imitator and many of his instruments have been sold for "old masters." Some of these copies, which are worth only up to $350.00, have brought as much as $750.00 to $1000.00.

DOLLING — *Commercial makers in Markneukirchen, Germany, 19th century.*

Their varnish varies and their instruments are not exceptionally well made. Prices: $50.00 to $100.00.

DOLLENZ, GIOVANNI — *Trieste, Italy, d. about 1850.*

Possibly a pupil of Storioni. He made violins, violas and cellos, also some bows. Excellent workmanship. He usually used a yellowish red varnish. He is one of the many makers whose names have been used promiscuously when instruments could not be identified. Originals sell from $300.00 to $500.00. He had a son, Giuseppe, also a violin maker, d. 1889.

Label: Giovanni Dollenz, fecit / in Trieste Anno 18 ... (and others)

DROUIN, CHARLES — *Mirecourt, France.*

Member of a family of violin makers of the 19th century. Their instruments are well made, the selections of wood good. They made some excellent cellos.

DROUIN, LOUIS — *One of the above family, migrated to the United States about 1915, d. 1938.*

He was well known as a good repairer. His instruments sold for about $500.00.

DUCHESNE (DUCHÊNE), NICOLAS — *B. in Mirecourt, France, date unknown.*

Worked from 1742 to 1772, the latter part of this period in Paris. His model is flat, with rather high ribs, large scroll and long soundholes. The varnish is reddish brown or dark yellow. Sweet tone. His instruments are branded: Nicola Duchesne a Paris.

DUIFFOPRUGCAR, see TIEFFENBRUCKER.

DUKE, RICHARD — *Worked in London, England, about 1750-1780.*

One of the better English makers. He originated his own models, similar to Stainer, high arched, long pattern. His workmanship is superb, the tone very soft and mellow. The varnish is yellow and of good quality; he used a special stain before applying it. He made excellent copies of Stradivari and Amati, his instruments are usually branded on the back over the top block. His name is often found in poorly made instruments which are not his work. Originals are priced at $250.00 to $500.00.

He had a son, Richard Jr., who worked in the same style, but his instruments are not to be compared with his father's in workmanship or value.

DUNCAN, ROBERT — *Worked in Aberdeen, Scotland, about 1740-62.*

Ordinary work, high model, similar to Stainer. He used an oil varnish which is generally yellow-brown. Not many of his instruments have been brought to this country. Prices: $200.00 to $350.00.

Label: Robert Duncan Maker / Aberdeen, 17....

DURFELL, J. GOTTLOB — *Altenburg, Germany, about 1775.*

He made violins as well as some basses. The model is generally high arched. Dark brown varnish of poor quality. The tone, however, is quite good. Prices: $75.00 to $125.00.

DVORAK, JOHANN BAPTIST — *Prague, Czechoslovakia. B. 1825, d. 1890.*

His masters were some of the best makers in Vienna and Prague. His work is quite good. Generally used a yellow-brown varnish which during the course of years, has turned much darker. Also made some cellos and violas. Prices: $200.00 to $300.00.

DYKES, GEORGE L. — *Leeds, England. B. 1884.*

A son of the well-known violin dealer Harry Dykes, in whose shop he learned his trade. He also worked for Paul Bailly. His instruments are well known in the British Isles, but there are not very many in the United States. He copied Stradivari and Guarneri, though not very successfully. His instruments are worth about $250.00.

EBERLE, JOHANNES UDALRICUS — *Prague, Czechoslovakia. B. 1699, d. 1768.*

A pupil of Edlinger. He generally followed the Stainer model. His workmanship is excellent and his instruments very handsome. The varnish is generally red or brown, seemingly on a yellow ground. He is one of the finest representatives of the Prague school and his instruments sell from $250.00 to $500.00.

Label: Joannes Udalricus Eberle, / fecit Pragae 17.... (and others)

EBERLE, MAGNUS — *Worked in a suburb of Vienna, Austria, about 1803-35.*

His instruments are not as well known as those of Johannes but are quite good. His varnish is a heavy dark red. Prices up to $400.00.

Label: Magnus Eberle fecit / W. Neostadi 18....

EBERLE, TOMASO — *Worked in Naples, Italy, about 1760-1792.*

His work, superb in all parts, is very much like that of Nicolo Gagliano and he was probably a pupil of one of the Gaglianos. The scrolls are quite differently cut and the soundholes graceful. The wood is of excellent selection, the varnish of fine quality, red-brown to yellowish brown. The original labels of many of his instruments have been removed and replaced by reproductions of more famous makes. He also made some fine violas. Prices: $800.00 to $1500.00.

Label: Thomas Eberle, / fecit Neap. 17.... (and others)

EDLINGER, THOMAS — *Augsburg, Germany; earliest date recorded 1656, d. 1690.*

A skillful maker. He generally used high archings, brown varnish, well-selected wood and the tone is powerful. Very few of his instruments have been seen in this country. Prices $200.00 to $350.00.

Label: Thomas Edlinger / Lauten und / Geigenmacher in
Augsburg 16.... (and others)

ELLERSIECK, ALBERT — *B. 1843 in Magdeburg, Germany.*

Established himself in Rostock 1878, later transferred his shop to Greiz and finally to Berlin. He favored a large Stradivari model. Used both spirit and oil varnishes. He enjoyed a great reputation as a maker and has been awarded many medals for his fine craftsmanship. He was an honorary member of the Academy of Art & Science in Brussels, Belgium. Few of his instruments have been seen in this country.

ELLERSIECK, HELMUTH — *See American section.*

ENDERS, F. & R. — *Markneukirchen, Saxony.*

A commercial house originating from Grossbreitenbach, still in existence. They employed many workers in their own shops and also bought instruments from outside makers. They made excellent copies of Gagliano, Vuillaume, Amati, Stainer and others and generally branded their instruments F.&R.E. Commercial violins without their names are priced at $25.00 to $75.00; better instruments with their brands at $75.00 to $200.00.

ENEL, CHARLES — *Son of Jules. B. 1880 in Mirecourt, France.*

Apprentice under Grillon and G. Bazin, worked for Léon Mougenot, later for Deroux and others in Paris. Established his own business there in 1909. His instruments, which are made of finely selected wood and covered with a flexible, reddish brown varnish, have been sold up to $500.00.

ERNST, FRANZ ANTON — *Gotha, Germany. B. 1745, d. 1805.*

He was originally a violinist, but later learned the trade of violin making. He worked mostly on the Stradivari models and was very successful. Prices: about $250.00.

EURY, NICOLAS — *Worked in Paris about 1810-30.*

An excellent bow maker, a rival to François Tourte. Most of his bows are stamped "Eury." The color is usually a rich red-brown. Many of his fine bows have tortoiseshell frogs, mounted with gold. They are priced from $150.00 to $700.00.

FABBRICATORE, GENNARO — *Worked in Naples, Italy, about 1788 to 1830.*

Member of a Neapolitan family of violin, lute and guitar makers. His instruments are fairly well made, though not exceptional. He used a medium flat model and generally a light red-brown varnish. Prices $200.00 to $500.00.

Label: Gennaro Fabricatore / Anno 18.... Napoli / Strada
S. Giacomo N.37.

FABRIS, LUIGI — *Venice, Italy; earliest date recorded 1852, d.*
about 1872.

His work was the average of the period. He used red varnish of
fair quality. A maker whose name has been connected with instruments of unknown origin which dealers baptized as his. Originals
have sold from $250.00 to $500.00.

Label: Luigi Fabris fecit / Venezia l'anno 18....

FAGNOLA, HANNIBAL — *Established in Turin, Italy, 1890.*

His shop is still in existence. A very clever maker, followed
the style of Pressenda, Rocca, Guadagnini and others and his varnish
is a red color typical of Pressenda. His instruments are not as fine
as the makers he copied, but some have excellent tone. Prices: $150.00
to $350.00.

FAROTTI, CELESTE — *Milan, Italy. B. 1864, d. 1925.*

Established his business in 1900. Good modern workmanship.
Flat Stradivari model. Soundholes usually large. The varnish is
orange-red to golden brown. He also made some nice cellos. Prices:
$250.00 to $600.00.

FENT, FRANÇOIS — *Worked in Paris, France, about 1765-91.*

One of the best Parisian makers of his time. He studied the
Italian schools very carefully and made excellent copies of Stradivari.
His wood and workmanship are of the finest quality, and his varnish
too, which is usually red-brown. The color has often turned much
darker in the course of years. Many of his instruments have been
sold as original Italians. Prices: $200.00 to $500.00.

Label: Fait par Fent / Maître Lutier rue Montmartre / Cul-
de-pas Saint Pierre à Paris.

FENDT, BERNHARD — *1775-1832. Born in the Tyrol.*

He learned his trade in Paris under his uncle. In 1798, he went
to England and worked for Thomas Dodd and Betts in London. He
made excellent instruments, some of which are copies of Stradivari
and Amati bearing Betts' name. He had four sons all of whom became
violin makers. Prices: $400.00 to $650.00.

FETIQUE, VICTOR — *Mirecourt, France. B. 1872, d. 1939.*

A first class bow maker, one of the best of that period. He was
apprentice under Fourrier-Maline, also worked for Bazin. About

1900, he was employed by Caressa & Français, later established himself in Paris, where he worked until his death. His bows brought high prizes in many exhibitions and received honors everywhere. He was a cousin of Leon Delunet. Prices: $35.00 to $100.00. His bows are branded.

FICHTL, MARTIN — *Vienna, Austria. B. 1682, d. 1768.*

A member of a large family of violin makers. He followed a large Stainer pattern with high arching. The wood is of good quality, the varnish generally rich red with a yellow ground. His instruments are well liked for their excellent tone and workmanship. Prices: $200.00 to $350.00.

Label: Martinus Mathias Fichtl / fec: Viennae 17.... (manuscript)

FICKER, JOHANN CHRISTIAN — *Worked in (Mark) Neukirchen, Germany, about 1700-22.*

Oldest member of this very large family of violin makers. Ficker violins are well made and many are still in existence.

Other important members of the family were: Johann Gottlob, Johann Georg, Carl Friedrich and Johann Christian II. Most of these makers branded their initials inside the instruments. Prices: $150.00 to $300.00.

FILLION, GEORGES CHARLES — *B. 1869 in Selencourt, France.*

Served his apprenticeship under Arnould in Mirecourt. Worked in Berne and Paris and a few years for W. E. Hill & Sons in London. About 1896, he established himself in Strasbourg. He followed mainly a Stradivari pattern. Neat workmanship; generally orange-yellow varnish. Prices up to $350.00.

FINOLLI, GIUSEPPE ANTONIO — *Worked in Milan, Italy, about 1750-55.*

He was not an important maker and few of his instruments exist today, although his label is found in instruments which are not his make. Genuine examples are priced at $250.00 to $400.00.

Label: Joseph Antoni Finolli in / Milano 17....

FIORINI, RAFFAELE — *Bologna, Italy. B. 1828, d. 1898.*

A very skillful and earnest worker. Learned his trade in Modena. He made beautiful violins and cellos. Prices: $250.00 to $500.00.

FIORINI, GIUSEPPE — *B. 1861 in Bazzano, Italy.*

Son and pupil of Raffaele. He worked for Andreas Rieger in Munich, with whom he became associated as a violin maker and dealer. His instruments are well made, after the Italian school. The varnish is generally red-brown or orange. Prices $200.00 to $450.00.

FISCHER — *A large family of violin makers in the 18th and early 19th centuries, working in different German cities.*

Among the most important are: Johann Adam, Christian Gotthilf, Johann Gottfried, Johann Ulrich, Zacharias, and Joseph. They all worked in the same general style. They made many instruments, mainly following the Italian school and copying Stradivari, Stainer and other old masters. Prices: $150.00 to $300.00.

FISCHER, ANTON — *Vienna, Austria. B. 1794, d. 1879.*

He copied the style of the old Italian school, but was not particularly successful. He used good wood and generally a brown-yellow varnish. Prices $200.00 to $350.00

FLEURY, BENOÎT — *Worked in Paris, France, about 1751-91.*

A very fine craftsman. He generally used a light red-brown oil varnish with a slight tint of orange. The wood is very carefully selected, the maple backs usually having a very narrow flame. The arching is high. Not many of his instruments are in this country, but those seen have sweet pleasing tone. He also made fine cellos. Prices: $250.00 to $500.00.

FLORIANI, PIETRO — *Worked in Riva, Italy, about 1856-75.*

Little is known of this maker. His label was used in many Italian instruments which, however, were not his work.

FORSTER, WILLIAM, SR. — *London, England. B. 1739, d. 1808.*

Many violin makers were in his family of whom he was the most prominent and he enjoyed a great reputation. In his later years, he devoted much time to making reproductions of the old masters. His violas and cellos are very well liked. The varnish, which is of excellent quality, is usually a rich red color with a tint of light brown. Violins, $400.00 to $600.00; Cellos, $500.00 to $1200.00 and higher.

> *Label:* William Forster / Violin Maker / in St. Martin's
> Lane London / 17....

FOURRIER, FRANÇOIS NICOLAS — *Paris, France, 1758-1816.*

He probably learned his trade in Mirecourt and became a very able maker. The wood he selected is not the best but rather of fair quality. He used a fine varnish, generally red. Prices: $300.00 to $600.00.

FRANCAIS, HENRI — *B. 1861, in Mirecourt, France.*

About 1900, he became the partner of Albert Caressa as a successor of Gand & Bernardel, whose pupil he had been. The company is known today as Caressa & Français. The shop is carried on by Emile Français in Paris and a selection of his instruments were exhibited in 1939 at the New York World's Fair. They are very well made, but the prices are high. For his best instruments he is asking $1000.00.

FRANK, MEINRAD — *B. about 1770 and worked until 1832 in Linz, Austria.*

He was most likely a pupil of Havelka, to whose business he succeeded. The model he followed is his own, high-arched, and with narrow, well rounded center bouts. The scrolls are thin and sharp in outline. The work is nicely done and the varnish is yellowish red to dark brown. Prices $150.00 to $250.00.

> *Label:* Meinradus Frank / Fecit Linz anno 18....

FREDI, RODOLFO — *B. 1861 in Todi, Italy.*

He went to Rome, first as a violin teacher, and established himself there as a maker in 1885. He copied successfully the old masters, but followed mostly the models of Stradivari. He used both oil and spirit varnish; the color is usually a beautiful yellow-brown. His instruments possess good tone and are well liked for orchestra. Prices: $150.00 to $300.00.

FURBER — *Family of violin makers in London in the 18th and 19th centuries.*

The better makers were John and Matthew. They followed mostly the Italian style and used a yellow or red-brown varnish. Violin makers of the name of Furber are still working in London today. Prices $200.00 to $400.00.

GABRIELLI, GIOVANNI BAPTISTA — *Worked in Florence, Italy, about 1739-70.*

He was the most important of this family of violin makers, and was a well-known, skillful artist whose instruments are liked for their remarkable tone quality. His workmanship is superior to that of many of his Italian contemporaries. He used only the choicest wood. The varnish is light yellow to orange, a little hard in texture. He is especially known for his violas and cellos. Many of his instruments are branded with his initials. Violins, violas and cellos, $1000.00 to $2500.00, some superb specimens have sold as high as $4000.00.

Label: (manuscript) Gio Batista Gabbrielli / fece in Firenze
17.... (and others)

GAFFINO, JOSEPH — Paris, France. B. early 18th century, d. about 1785.

Of Italian descent and since 1748 associated with Castagneri. His violins are characteristic of the early French school, well made, with light red or yellow varnish. A maker whose name will often be found in instruments not made by him. Originals are priced at $500.00 to $750.00.

Label: Gaffino, Cto di Castagnery / rue des Provinces /
Pariggi 17.... (and others)

GAGLIANO, ALEXANDER — Naples, Italy. B. about 1660, d. 1725.

He was the first of the Neapolitan School and a member of a large family of violin makers. He is supposed to have worked for Stradivari, which is not authentic, although on some of his labels, he calls himself a pupil of Stradivari. The earliest date seen in his instruments is 1695. He used handsomely figured wood of choice quality and turned out beautiful work. The stop is slightly long. The scroll is small and generally not as well cut as the rest of his instruments. The varnish is typical of the Cremonese school, generally dark red to orange. Violins are valued at $1000.00 to $3500.00, violas $1500.00 to $3500.00, cellos as high as $4500.00.

Label: Alexander Gaglianus / me fecit Neapoli 17.... (and others)

GAGLIANO, NICOLO — Naples, Italy. B. about 1695, d. about 1780, though instruments have been seen dated 1793.

Eldest son of Alexander whom he surpassed in quality and accurateness of workmanship. Most of his instruments are built after Stradivari's models of the earlier period. The wood is of finest selection, the varnish generally yellow, sometimes light red-brown. A few of his instruments have ornamental inlay, very skillfully done. The tone is very brilliant. Many of his instruments are used by professional musicians with great success. Violins and violas: $2000.00 to $4000.00; superior specimens of his cellos have been sold as high as $8500.00.

Label: Nicolaus Gagliano Filius / Alexandri fecit Neap. 17.... (and others)

GAGLIANO, GENNARO (JANUARIUS) — *Naples, Italy. B. about 1700, d. about 1770.*

Second son and pupil of Alexander. He generally copied Stradivari's models but sometimes had a higher arching and sound-holes of wider and deeper cut. His best period was between 1730 and 1750. He rarely placed labels in his instruments and hardly ever inserted the date so that it is very difficult to determine the exact date of his work. The wood is of choicest selection, the varnish orange-yellow to red. Tonally, his instruments are probably the best of the Gaglianos. Prices: $2000.00 to $5000.00.

Label: Januarius Gagliano filius / Alexandri fecit Neap. 17.... (and others)

GAGLIANO, FERDINANDO — *Naples, Italy. B. 1724, d. 1781.*

Eldest son of Nicolo. Many disagree as to the perfection of his instruments, but he was fully as fine a maker as his father. He generally followed the Stradivari patterns of the later period. Red-brown or yellowish varnish of excellent quality. He also made cellos, which are probably the best of his work. Violins and violas, $1000.00 to $3000.00; cellos up to $4000.00.

Label: Ferdinandus Gagliano Filius / Nicolai fecit Neap. 17.... (and others)

GAGLIANO, GIUSEPPE (JOSEPH) — *Naples, Italy. B. 1725, d. 1793.*

Second son of Nicolo. He followed his father's models, but the workmanship is not as fine. However, his violins have exceptional quality. He generally used a red-brown varnish. For some time he shared a workshop with his brother, Antonio. Prices: $1000.00 to $2500.00.

Label: Giuseppe Gagliano di Nicola / fece Napoli 17.... (and others)

GAGLIANO, ANTONIO — *Naples, Italy. B. about 1728, d. 1795.*

Third son of Nicolo. He is not as well-known as the other makers of the Gagliano family and not as good in his workmanship and tone. The color of his varnish is red, sometimes yellow. Prices: $750.00 to $1500.00.

Label: Antonius Gagliano Filius / Nicolai fecit Neap. 17....

GAGLIANO, GIOVANNI (JOANNES) — *Naples, Italy. B. 1740, d. 1806.*

Fourth son of Nicolo. He learned his trade under the supervision of his uncle, Gennaro. He is known to have worked also in Venice. Very few of his instruments are seen today. They are fairly well made. Violins: $500.00 to $1000.00; violas $750.00, cellos up to $2500.00 (some superb pieces).

> *Label:* Joannes Gagliano fecit sub Disciplina / Januaris
> Gagliani Neapoli 17.... (and others)

GAGLIANO, RAFFAELE — *B. 1790, d. 1857.*

Worked with his brother, Antonio. (Members of the next generation.) Their instruments are priced from $300.00 to $750.00; some exceptionally fine cellos as high as $1500.00.

> *Label:* Raffaele ed Antonio Gagliano / Quondam Giovanni
> Neapoli 18.... (and others)

There were other less important members of the Gagliano family and their descendants who are still working in Italy today.

GAILLARD, CHARLES — *Worked in Paris, France, about 1850-81. Member of a Mirecourt family of violin makers.*

He was one of C. A. Gand's workmen and followed his style. He was a good imitator and made many copies of the old masters. They are not exceptional. Prices: $150.00 to $200.00.

GALBUSERA, CARLO ANTONIO — *Worked in Milan, Italy, about 1813 to 1832.*

Very little is known about this maker. He usually followed a flat Guarneri model, large pattern. Varnish deep red-brown. Many instruments bearing his label are not genuine. Prices up to $750.00.

GAND, CHARLES FRANÇOIS — *B. 1787 in Versailles, d. 1845 in Paris.*

The oldest member of a large violin making family in Paris. Successor of Nicolas Lupot under whom he had worked from 1802 to 1810. He was one of the most important French makers after Lupot and ranks next to Vuillaume and Pique. Professional musicians find the tone of his instruments magnificent. The varnish is abundant and generally a handsome red-brown. He also made bows which are noted for their light weight and perfect balance. Violins and cellos: $500.00 to $1000.00. Bows up to $75.00.

Label: Gand, Luthier Brevetté / Rue Croix des Petits
Champs 24 / Paris

GAND, GUILLAUME CHARLES — *Versailles, Paris. B. 1792, d. 1858.*

GAND, CHARLES ADOLPHE — *Paris. B. 1812, d. 1866.*

GAND, CHARLES NICOLAS EUGÈNE — *Paris. B. 1825, d. 1892.*

All sons and pupils of Charles François. The youngest combined with Bernardel Bros. in 1866 and the shop was then known as Gand & Bernardel. They made first class instruments and went into commercial production. The varnish used is generally dark red-brown. Commercial prices: $150.00 to $450.00, individually made instruments up to $800.00.

GASPARO DA SALO, see BERTOLOTTI.

GAVINIÈS, FRANÇOIS — *Bordeaux and Paris, France. B. about 1700, d. about 1770.*

He made inferior as well as some very good instruments and they are usually branded. The varnish is yellowish brown and of good texture. He worked on the Italian style. Prices: $250.00 to $500.00.

Label: Gaviniés, Rue / S. Thomas Du Lou- / vre à Paris, 17....

GEDLER, JOHANN ANTON — *Worked in Füssen, South Germany, about 1752-96.*

Probably a pupil of Niggell. His work is fairly good but not exceptional. He used brown varnish. His instruments possess good tone. Many have wave-shaped sides; this was a style all his own. Prices: $85.00 to $150.00.

Label: Joannes Antonius Gedler / F. de Füssen Anno 17....
(and others)

GEDLER, JOSEPH BENEDIKT — *Worked in Füssen between 1780 and 1812.*

He adopted the style of his father, Johann Anton, but his varnish is golden yellow, quite brittle, and the tone very responsive. Prices: $150.00 to $300.00.

GEIPEL — *Markneukirchen, Germany.*

A family of violin makers still in existence. The most important was Hermann, b. 1862. Their instruments are mostly commercially made and not very valuable. Prices: $50.00 to $100.00.

GEISSENHOF, FRANZ — *Vienna, Austria, B. 1754, d. 1821.*

He succeeded to his master Johann Georg Thir. An excellent maker and probably the best of that school. He generally followed the style and patterns of Stradivari. During the first part of his career he worked after the style of Thir and varnished his instruments in a very dark red-brown color. In the second period he changed to a flatter pattern and applied a clearer varnish. The instruments of the last period of his life are of broader model and higher arching and the color is more brownish yellow or still lighter color. His work is beautiful, very conscientiously done, and none of his instruments show careless workmanship. He made violas and cellos as well as violins. Prices: $400.00 to $850.00.

Label: Franciscus Geissenhof fecit / Viennae Anno 18....

GEMUNDER, AUGUST MARTIN LUDWIG — *B. 1814, d. 1895.*

He learned his trade in Germany, and in 1846, came to America and established himself in Springfield, Mass., and about 1860, in New York. He copied old Italian masters, such as Stradivari, Guarneri and Maggini. His wood was well selected, the varnish golden yellow to dark red. His instruments sold from $150.00 to $350.00.

GEMUNDER, GEORGE — *B. 1816 in Ingelfingen, Germany. Came to New York 1849, died there 1899.*

He learned his trade from his father Johann. Later he went to Paris and worked under Vuillaume. He followed his brother August to America and settled first in Boston, later in New York, and finally in Astoria, Long Island. He was considered the best American maker at that time. He was a very clever imitator and the tone quality of his instruments is first class. He used red-brown and dark red varnish. Prices: $250.00 to $500.00.

GERMAIN, JOSEPH LOUIS — *Mirecourt, France. B. 1822, d. 1870.*

He worked for Charles F. Gand, afterwards for J. B. Vuillaume, and then established his own business. He was a very talented maker and is known for his well made basses. The varnish is generally yellow with a slight tint of orange. Violins, $350.00 to $500.00; basses, $300.00 to $500.00.

He had a son, Emile, b. in Paris 1853, who was his pupil and successor. He made many violins and was quite a skilled artist.

GIBERTINI, ANTONIO — *Worked in Parma and Genoa, Italy, about 1797-1850.*

He was a fine maker and was said to be favored by Paganini. As an imitator he was quite skillful. The varnish he used is generally dark red and of fine quality. Prices: $900.00 to $1200.00.

GIGLI, GIULIO CESARE — *Worked in Rome, Italy, about 1721-1762.*

His work is excellently done and probably many of his instruments have been sold under other famous makers' names. He generally followed the patterns of Amati and used a golden yellow varnish with a reddish or brownish tint. Prices: $500.00 to $1200.00.

Label: Julius Caesar Gigli Romanus / Fecit Romae Anno 17....

GILKES, SAMUEL — *London, England. B. 1787, d. 1827.*

A pupil of Charles Harris, Sr., afterwards worked for William Forster. Opened his own shop in 1810. His work is clean and well done, and it is possible that he was in the employ of Betts. He generally followed the Amati style and used a yellow or orange-brown varnish. His cellos are well liked and command a good price today. Prices range from $350.00 to $600.00 on violins and much higher on cellos.

He had a son, William, b. in London 1811, d. 1875.

GLAESEL — *A large family of violin makers in Markneukirchen, Germany.*

Ludwig Gläsel (b. 1842) is the most important maker of this name. He learned his trade in Berlin before he established himself in Markneukirchen. Both his son, Carl, and his grandson, Oscar, became violin makers and others of his descendants are still working today. Oscar, b. 1850, is known for his basses, and there still is a Glaésel in New York who is known for his excellent bass repairing. Prices: $150.00 to $250.00.

GLASS — A family of violin makers in Klingenthal, Germany.

Christian Friedrich worked about 1815 as a bow maker. Johann Traugott, 1819-1895, was probably the most gifted of the Glass family. He worked in the style of Hopf but his instruments are all cheaply made and mostly covered with rosin varnish. Friedrich August Glass worked between 1840 and 1855. Their instruments are not well liked because of the inferior varnish and the rather hard quality of tone. Prices: $50.00 to $150.00.

> *Label:* Fried. Aug. Glass / Verfertigt nach / Antonius
> Straduarius / fecit Cremona An. 17__ (and similar)

GLIER — *Violin makers in Markneukirchen, Germany.*

The oldest one known was Johann Adam Glier, 1693-1777. Others are Johann Gottlieb, 1732-1799, and his son Johann Georg 1762-1845. Their work is fairly good but they never enjoyed a big reputation. Prices: $50.00 to $150.00.

GLIER, ROBERT — *B. 1855. d. about 1924.*

A member of the above family. He established himself in Cincinnati, Ohio, succeeded by his son Robert. He experimented with various kinds of wood, especially that for the tops. He made a number of instruments for the Rudolph Wurlitzer Co. of that city which sold from $75.00 to $150.00.

GOBETTI, FRANCESCO — *Worked in Venice, Italy about 1690 to 1732.*

His work shows Cremonese influence and he ranks almost as high as Sanctus Seraphin and Montagnana. His cellos are generally a broad, flat pattern, the soundholes in the Amati style. He used beautiful wood of fine selection and his workmanship is beyond criticism. His varnish is generally a handsome reddish orange. Prices: $2000.00 to $3500.00.

> *Label:* Franciscus Gobetti / in Venetia 17__ (and others)

GOETZ, JOHANN MICHAEL — *Markneukirchen, Germany, B. 1735, d. 1813.*

A carpenter and violin maker. He used good wood, the belly and bass bar are usually cut from one piece. His instruments, though well made, are not very popular. Prices: $100.00 to $250.00. Descendants of this family are still working in the violin business in Saxony.

GOFFRILLER, MATTEO — *Worked in Venice, Italy, about 1690-1742.*

It is generally believed that he was of Tyrolean origin. He adopted a style very much like that of Carlo Bergonzi, and he may have been one of his or possibly Stradivari's pupils. His workmanship is of the best, the wood carefully selected though usually plain. He is especially famous for his cellos. Scrolls are deeply cut, of perfect design. The varnish is usually a beautiful red and is always applied thickly. The tone quality is excellent, especially that of his cellos and violas. These are first class in every respect and command very big prices today. Violins, $2000.00 to $5000.00; violas, $4500.00; cellos, $7000.00, some superb examples as high as $12,000.00.

Label: Matteo Gofriller fecit / Venetijis Anno 17___ (and others)

GOFFRILLER, FRANCESCO — *Venice and Udine Italy, about 1690-1740.*

Brother of Matteo. Worked chiefly for his brother and only a few instruments bear his own name. He was a very fine workman and certainly lived up to the now famous name of Goffriller. His varnish is yellowish red-brown. Prices: $1500.00 to $3500.00.

GOSSELIN, JEAN — *Worked in Paris, France, about 1814-1830.*

He was an amateur luthier and made violins and cellos after Stradivarius which are quite desirable. His workmanship is clean, the varnish generally red or yellow. Some fine specimens have been sold as high as $600.00.

Label: Fait par Gosselin Amateur / Paris Année 18___

GRAGNANI, ANTONIO — *Livorno (Latin:Liburni), Italy, about 1740-80.*

His instruments are well made but are not classed as high as some of the finer Italian makers. They have a remarkably clear tone. The volute of his scroll is flat on the bottom and top — a striking feature of his work. The varnish is generally yellow-brown, sometimes golden. Some instruments are branded AG over the upper block on the back. Prices: $1000.00 to $2500.00.

Label: Antonius Gragnani fecit / Liburni Anno 17___

GRANCINO, PAOLO — *Worked in Milan, Italy, about 1665-92.*

He probably was a pupil of Nicola Amati and followed this master's style of work. Many of his instruments no doubt have been labelled Amati and sold as such. His scrolls are very long but quite well made. The wood he used is not always the best and often the back and sides are made of poplar. He used a golden yellow varnish, which is quite good. His violas are probably better than his violins. Prices: $1000.00 to $3000.00

GRANCINO, GIOVANNI BAPTISTA — *Worked in Milan and Ferrara, Italy, about 1680-1710.*

A son of Paolo. His selections of wood are better, the varnish is dark yellow or orange red. His instruments are very responsive and powerful in tone. Prices: $1500.00 to $3500.00.

Francesco, son of Giovanni Baptista, worked in Milan about 1690 to 1746, together with his brother Giovanni Baptista, Jr..

> *Label:* Gio.Bapt. Grancino in Contrada / Largha di Milano anno 16.... (and others)

GRAND, GÉRARD — *Worked in Mirecourt, France, from 1771 until about 1819.*

He made numerous instruments, which are, however, inferior in workmanship and varnish. The color is generally a dull yellow-brown. His violins are branded. Prices: $200.00 to $400.00.

GRANDJON — *A family of violin makers of the 19th century in Mirecourt, France.*

Jules Grandjon is the founder of a factory and started violin making commercially. He also had a branch in Paris. Their instruments are rather large and generally light red to red-brown. They are quite well made and many are in existence today. Prices: $100.00 to $150.00.

GRIENBERGER, JOSEPH — *Linz, Austria. B. about 1800, d. 1865.*

His instruments, after the model of Stradivari, are quite well made and possess good tone. The varnish is usually dark brown. Prices: $250.00 to $400.00.

GRIMM, KARL — *Berlin, Germany. About 1794, d. 1855.*

Known as one of the very best makers in Berlin. He made only a small number of instruments and used the choicest wood. He was a clever imitator and some of his instruments were probably sold as old masters. At his death his shop was taken over by his son-in-law, Hellmig.

GUADAGNINI, LORENZO — *B. about 1695 in Piacenza, Italy, d. about 1750.*

He presumably was a pupil of Stradivari in Cremona and his work shows some similarity to that of that master. After 1730, he returned to his home town. His workmanship is excellent, wood and varnish are beautiful, the color usually a golden red. The genuine examples seen of this maker are superb. Prices: $2000.00 to $7500.00.

Label: Lavrentius Guadagnini Pater, / & alumnus Antonj Straduarj / fecit Placentiae Anno 17__ (and others)

GUADAGNINI, GIOVANNI BAPTISTA — B. about 1715 in Piacenza, Italy, d. 1786 in Turin.

The best maker of the Guadagnini family. He started his career in Piacenza, then stayed in Cremona, Milan, Parma, and last in Turin. He did not follow any particular model. Some of Guadagnini's instruments were just good, others super fine. His varnish is varied from a beautiful golden orange to a plain brown. Violins: $4000.00 to $8000.00; violas up to $6000.00; cellos, the finest, $15,000.00.

Label: Joannes Baptista filius / Laurentii Guadagnini fecit / Placentiae 17__ G.B.G. (and others)

Whether there was another maker by this same name, native of Cremona, who has been mentioned in previous dictionaries of violin makers, is questionable.

GUADAGNINI, GIUSEPPE (JOSEPH) — B. 1736, d. 1805.

Eldest son of Giovanni Baptista and probably his father's pupil. He followed the flat Stradivari and Guarneri models. His work is well done but not as fine as his father's. He worked in different cities in Northern Italy, Milan, Como, Parma and last in Pavia. Prices: $1000.00 to $3000.00

Label: Joseph Guadagnini Cremonensis / Fecit Mediolani Anno 17__

GUADAGNINI, GAETANO I — Turin Italy, about 1775-1831.

Son of Giovanni Baptista. His work is very good, though it does not come up to the standards of his father. He used a yellow-brown varnish. There are many guitars in existence made by him. Violins are priced from $1000.00 to $1500.00.

Later members of the Guadagnini family are Gaetano (Turin), Giuseppe II (Rome), Felice (Turin), Antonio (Turin 1831-81) and his two sons, Francesco and Giuseppe. Antonio's violins are priced from $600.00 to $1000.00.

GUARNERIUS, ANDREAS — Cremona, Italy. B. about 1626, d. 1698.

Founder of this famous family of violin makers in Cremona. He was one of the first pupils of Nicolò Amati, and there is a record of his living in Amati's house in 1641, at the age of fifteen. He followed his master's style and patterns, but later on changed to a larger model with flatter arching and gave soundholes and scroll a different shape. He used varnish of various colors, usually a rich orange-brown. He made some very nice cellos, in different sizes: Instruments made by the apprentices he employed were labelled: (*Sub disciplina Andree Guarnerij in eius / officina sub titulo S. Teresie, Cremona* 16____) Violins, violas and cellos: $3500.00 to $9000.00.

> Label: Andreas Guarnerius fecit Cremonae sub / titulo Sanctae Teresiae 16____ (and others)

GUARNERIUS, PETRUS — *Worked in Cremona and Mantua, Italy. B. 1655, d. 1720.*

Eldest son of Andrea. He served his apprenticeship under his father. Then moved to Mantua but returned to Cremona the year his father died, during which time he worked for his brother Joseph. He was a professional musician and as a craftsman he was skillful and had his own style of work. Some of his violins are on a large handsome pattern, others on a smaller Amati pattern. Some are quite highly arched. The soundholes are broader and the scrolls heavier than Amati's. The varnish varies in color but is mostly golden yellow or reddish brown-yellow. He is not known to have made violas or cellos. Prices: $4000.00 to $10,000.00.

> Label: Petrus Guarnerius Cremonensis fecit / Mantua sub tit. Sancta Teresia 17____ (and others)

GUARNERIUS, GIUSEPPE (JOSEPH) — *Cremona, Italy. B. 1666, d. after 1738.*

Youngest son of Andrea. He is a much greater maker than his father, under whom he learned and to whom he succeeded. He had his own model which is narrow in the upper portion while the middle bouts are quite long, which gives his violins a similar appearance to Stradivari's "long pattern." For the backs he often used the beautiful tiger-striped maple. He must have experimented with the soundholes, for some are a little short and others long. He did not always put his finest work into his instruments, as he probably had orders which did not require his best. His varnish is a beautiful golden yellow, sometimes a light brown or dark, rich red. It is of the most exquisite quality. His cellos are exceedingly rare and he used poplar wood for the backs. Prices: $3500.00 to $12,000.00.

Label: Joseph Guarnerius filius Andreae fecit / Cremone, sub titulo
S. Teresie, 17....

GUARNERIUS, JOSEPH (DEL GESU) — *Cremona, Italy. B. 1698, d. 1744.*

(The date of his birth is recorded in the registers of the parish of San Donato in Cremona.)

Next to Stradivari, he was the greatest violin maker of Cremona. He was a genius and worked entirely independently of all his predecessors. Tonally his instruments are equal to Stradivari's and artists sometimes prefer them for their dark quality. He did not always work on the same model and some violins are quite crudely made, especially the scrolls. He used handsomely flamed maple of the choicest selection. Instruments of the period 1730-36 seem to be the finest, while examples of his later years do not show the same excellent workmanship. The varnish is magnificent, the color generally golden orange, at times lighter. A violin of 1743, owned at one time by Paganini, is exhibited in the Museum at Genoa. A very famous example is the one known as the "Plowden." The average prices are between $12,000.00 and $35,000.00, some rare specimens have sold much higher.

Label: Joseph Guarnerius fecit (+) / Cremonae anno 17.... IHS

GUARNERIUS, PETRUS II — *Venice, Italy. B. in Cremona 1695, d. in Venice after 1760.*

Son and pupil of Joseph. His work is much in the style of Petrus I and very nicely done. He used finely selected wood and a varnish of golden brown color. Prices: $3500.00 to $7500.00.

GUARINI — *A trade name used by MENESSON (see this)*

GUERRA, EVASIO EMILIANO — *Turin, Italy. A twentieth century maker.*

Very few of his instruments have been seen in this country. A very beautiful Stradivari model has come to the author's attention, with soft oil varnish of orange color, exceedingly well made and with absolute correct measurements. The soundholes and scroll are excellently cut. His instruments should bring from $350.00 to $500.00.

Label: Evasio Emiliano Guerra / fece in Torino anno 19....

GUERSAN, LOUIS (LUDOVICUS) — *Paris, France. B. about 1713, d. 1781.*

Pupil and successor of Claude Pierray. An excellent, well-known craftsman. He did a lot of experimenting in various woods, arching, thicknesses and dimensions, but none proved very successful. He used a hard spirit varnish which generally is yellow or dull golden orange. He also made violas, cellos and basses. Prices: $300.00 to $600.00. Rare specimens, $750.00.

> *Label:* Ludovicus Guersan prope Co-/ medam Gallicam Lutetiae, anno 17... (and others)

GUETTER — *Markneukirchen, Germany.*

Johann, the earliest of this family of violin makers, was born about 1690, d. 1751. One of the best was Johann Georg (1759-1829). His brother was Georg Adam (1761-1829). Another was Johann Gottlob. A brandmark often used by this family are the initials GAG. Prices: $85.00 to $200.00.

GUIDANTUS, JOANNES FLORENUS — *Bologna, Italy. Late 17th century, died 1728.*

Member of a family of violin makers about whom very little is known. He was an excellent workman and possibly a pupil of one of the Amatis. A few very fine instruments have been seen. Violins, $1000.00 to $1500.00; cellos, as high as $2500.00.

> *Label:* Joannes Florenus Guidantus Fecit / Bononiae Anno 17...

GUILLAMI, JOANNES — *Barcelona, Spain. B. 1725, d. 1767.*

The Italian influence in his work would indicate that he learned under some Italian master. His instruments are exceedingly well made, on a medium arched model. The varnish is generally golden red. Style somewhat after Stradivari. He also made a few cellos. Prices: $1000.00 to $2500.00.

GUSETTO, NICOLAS — *Worked in Cremona, Italy, about 1785-1818.*

A maker of Florentine origin. He is closer to the German than to the Italian style. His instruments, generally built on a broad pattern, are not too well done. His scrolls, however, are very handsomely cut. He used mostly a brown spirit varnish. Prices: $200.00 to $350.00.

GUTERMANN, WILHELM THEODOR — *Munich, Germany. B. 1828, d. 1900.*

Served his apprenticeship under Engleder, and worked for Tieffenbrunner and Anton Hofmann. His work is very accurate, the varnish a rich clear red color. Prices: $100.00 to $250.00.

HAMM, JOHANN GOTTFRIED — *(Mark) Neukirchen, Germany. B. 1744, d. 1817.*

One of the best Saxon makers of that period. He generally used a broad model with very narrow purfling, sometimes ivory edges. Most of his instruments are branded *I*G*H*. He had a son, Christian, who worked in the same style. There were other members of that family: Carl Friedrich Hamm, 1733-1761, and Johann Gottfried, a cello maker. Prices: $150.00 to $300.00.

HAMMA & CO. — *A firm in Stuttgart, Germany, founded by Fridolin Hamma in 1864.*

Known as commercial makers and experts on old violins.

HAMMIG, JOHANN GEORG — *Markneukirchen, Germany. B. 1702, d. 1754.*

The oldest member of this family of violin makers. A good worker. His violins are branded *I*C*H*. He had a son Johann Christian, 1732-1816. Prices: $150.00 to $300.00.

HAMMIG, WILHELM HERMANN — *Markneukirchen, Germany. B. 1838, d. 1925.*

Son and scholar of Wilhelm August, 1837, 1865. Worked for Grimm in Berlin. In 1863, he started business for himself in Markneukirchen and later moved to Leipzig. He was the best maker of the family; his work is very clean and well done. He usually used a brown varnish. Also made cellos. Prices: $400.00 to $500.00.

HAMMIG, GUSTAV ADOLPH — *Worked in Dresden about 1890-1901.*

He was a good bow maker and later made violins and cellos, but is not well known. His bows are priced from $35.00 to $75.00.

HARDIE, MATTHEW — *Edinburgh, Scotland. B. 1755, d. 1826.*

One of the most important Scotch makers. He generally followed the models of Stradivari, although others have been seen. His violins are well made, the selections of wood fine, and the tone quality is often excellent. His varnish, usually of a yellow-brown color. Prices $350.00 to $750.00.

HARDIE, JAMES — *Worked in Edinburgh, Scotland, about 1830-55.*

He was a skilled workman, probably trained under Matthew Hardie, but very few of his instruments have been seen. Prices about $400.00.

HARE, JOSEPH — *Worked in London, England, 1720-1726.*

One of the first English violin makers. A very talented crafts-man, working on a flat pattern and using a red, and nut-brown varnish. Prices: $175.00 to $400.00.

> *Label:* Joseph Hare at ye Viole E Flute / near Royal Exchange / in Cornhill, London / 17....

HARRIS, CHARLES I — *Worked in Oxford and London, England, about 1780-1800.*

A fine maker of violins and cellos, following the models of Amati and Stradivari. The varnish is usually reddish.

His son and pupil was Charles II, also in Oxford and London, from about 1818 to 1830. He worked for John Hart and was a fairly good maker. The instruments of both are priced from $250.00 to $350.00.

HARRIS, GRIFFITH — *An English maker at Swansea, worked about 1819-1840.*

His work is interesting. Prices: $250.00 to $500.00.

HART, JOHN THOMAS — *B. 1805, d. 1874.*

Member of a family of violin makers in London, England, still in existence.

George Hart I (1839-1891) is the author of the books: "The Violin, its famous Makers and their Imitators" and "The Violin and its Music." They are good books and are widely read.

George Hart II, b. 1860. Served as apprentice in Paris, then took over his father's business, now known as Hart & Son. He him-self did not make many instruments, but excellent copies of old Italian masters were made in his shops, priced up to $500.00.

HAVELKA, JOHANN BAPTIST — *Linz, Austria. B. 1741, d.*
about 1800.

His workmanship is good and shows the influence of the Viennese
school. The varnish is generally dark chocolate brown. Made some
very fine cellos. Prices: $250.00 to $400.00.

Label: Joannes Baptista Havelka / Fecit Anno 17.... (manuscript)

HAVEMANN, DAVID CHRISTIAN — *Worked in Klingenthal,*
Germany, about 1722-1730.

He is not a well-known maker and his instruments are only
mediocre. He generally used a light yellow-brown varnish. Prices:
$100.00 to $150.00.

HEBERLEIN — *Markneukirchen, Germany.*

A large family of violin makers to which belong: Johann
Gottlob, the oldest, Ernst Heinrich, Carl August, Richard, a pupil
of Adolph Hammig, and the youngest of the family, Heinrich
Theodor Jr., who was the best maker in the family. The company
still exists. They are commercial makers and have made many
thousand instruments and hundreds of copies of Stradivarius and
Guarnerius, all very well done. Their labels are inscribed with the
names of different copies, such as "Wilhelmj," etc. They had a
regular catalog, listing instruments by numbers, the Stradivari
models from 1 to 8, and the Joseph Guarneri models from 1A to
8A. Their own prices ranged from $50.00 to $250.00 They also
made special models that sold as high as $350.00 Many of these
are in the United States and their selling price today is between
$50.00 and $250.00.

HEINICKE, MATHIAS — *Wildstein, Bohemia. B. 1871.*

He learned his trade in Markneukirchen, Germany, also worked
in Berlin and Budapest and under Degani in Italy. He made many
copies of Italian masters, using both spirit and oil varnish, generally
a golden yellow amber. Not many of his instruments are in this
country and the prices of $150.00 to $300.00 at which they are
valued, are quite high.

HEL, PIERRE JOSEPH — *Lille, France. B. 1842 in Mazirot*
near Mirecourt, d. 1902.

He learned his trade in Mirecourt under Salzard, then went to
Paris to work for Sébastien Vuillaume, and one year for N. Darche.

In 1865, he started his own business in Lille. He was a well-trained, first-class maker. He copied many of the Italian masters and the appearance of his varnish is very much like that of the Cremonese school. The wood is well selected, the color of the varnish generally a handsome red-brown. The tone is excellent. Prices: $200.00 to $350.00. Superb specimens up to $500.00.

At his death, his son Pierre Jean Henri took over the shop.

HELLMER, JOHANN GEORG — B. 1687, d. 1770.

A pupil of Thomas Edlinger, Prague. His instruments are generally quite arched, very well made. He used the finest quality wood and oil varnish, usually red-brown with a yellow ground. Prices: $150.00 to $400.00.

Label: Joannes Georgius Hellmer / Pragensis me fecit 17....

HELLMER, CARL JOSEPH — Prague, Czechoslovakia. B. 1739, d. 1811.

Son of Johann Georg and a pupil of Johann U. Eberle. His violins are very much like his father's but not quite as well made. He generally used a chocolate brown varnish. Prices: $100.00 to $150.00.

HENRY, J. — B. 1823 in Mirecourt, France, d. in Paris 1870.

An excellent bow maker. He worked for George Chanot and for Dominique Peccatte until 1848. He was then associated with Simon and later opened his own shop. The bows he made for his own account are all stamped "Henry Paris." His better bows range in price from $75.00 to $200.00 and are much in demand. There are some exceptional ones which have brought as much as $750.00. Generally the color is a chocolate to medium brown. There are ebony as well as tortoiseshell frogs, some gold mounted.

HENTSCHEL, JOHANN JOSEPH — Worked in Brünn, Czechoslovakia, about 1737-1782.

A good maker whose work is similar partly to the Prague and partly to the Viennese schools. Prices: $100.00 to $150.00.

HEROLD, CONRAD GUSTAV — Klingenthal, Germany.

Worked mostly commercially. The firm is still in existence, but is not very well known. Varnish generally yellow to yellow-brown. Prices: $50.00 to $150.00.

HERON-ALLEN, EDWARD — *Working as a violin maker in London between 1882 and 1895.*

He is the author of the well-known book, "Violin Making As It Was And Is." He studied under George Chanot and was himself a very good workman. Very few instruments having his own name are in existence.

HERZLIEB, FRANCISCUS — *Graz, Austria. B. about 1797, d. 1861.*

He followed the patterns of Amati and Guarneri, though his arching is a little flatter. He was a fair maker, using well selected wood and a yellow-brown or sometimes slightly reddish varnish. Also made some very nice cellos. Prices: $100.00 to $300.00.

Label: Franciscus Herzlieb / fecit graecii anno 18....

HESKETH, THOMAS EARLE — *Manchester, England. B. 1866 and still operating his own shop.*

He served his apprenticeship with George Chanot and, in 1891, went into business for himself. Many of his instruments, among which are fine copies of old masters, are in the British Isles, but very few in the United States.

HILL, JOSEPH — *London, England. B. 1715, d. 1784.*

He was probably a pupil of Banks and Wamsley. An excellent workman of very high rank. Made especially fine cellos. He changed the location of his shop quite frequently and had different signs, the last one being "At the Harp and Flute" in the Haymarket. He had four sons and all became violin makers and his assistants. Violins are priced from $200.00 to $400.00; some of his cellos as high as $1000.00.

HILL, WILLIAM — *London, England. B. 1745, d. 1790.*

Eldest son of Joseph. He learned his trade under his father's supervision, then opened his own shop, but never acquired the skill of his father. Very few of his instruments have been seen.

HILL, HENRY LOCKEY — *London, England. B. 1774, d. 1835.*

Joseph Hill's grandson. He worked for John Betts and was the first of his family to follow the Stradivari patterns. His work is excellent and probably in his time he obtained better prices for his instruments than for Joseph's. He made violas and cellos as well as violins. The varnish varies from red to golden orange. Prices: $500.00 to $750.00.

HILL, WILLIAM EBSWORTH — *London, England. B. 1817, d. 1895.*

Son of Henry Lockey. He worked for Chas. Harris in Oxford and about 1830 returned to London where he opened his own shop. It was first located in Southwark, later in Wardour Street. For his new instruments, he used only the finest materials, but he concentrated on the restoration of and dealing in old instruments. He became one of the greatest experts and was recognized throughout the world as an authority whose word was accepted by dealers and other experts as the final judgment on any instrument. He finally transferred his business to New Bond Street, where it is still conducted under the name of W. E. Hill and Sons.

He started bow-making about 1860. In this he was assisted especially by his son, Alfred E. (1862-1940), and workshops were established in Hanwell in 1890. Alfred's brothers, William Henry, (b. 1857), Arthur F. (b. 1860) and Walter E. (b. 1871) have also been identified with this firm, which is now carried on by Albert Phillips Hill, a brother-in-law, and Paul Hill. This house is known the world over for their fine products. Their bows, which are made in many different grades and styles ranging in price from $30.00 to $150.00 are in the hands of almost all the leading professional musicians. New Hill violins have been sold from $350.00 to $600.00, cellos $450.00 and up.

HJORTH, EMIL — *Copenhagen, Denmark. B. 1840.*

He most likely learned his trade from his father Johannes, b. 1809, d. 1900, whose business he took over in 1865, after having worked in London, Vienna and Paris. Generally followed the models of Amati and Guarneri. His workmanship is fine, especially his oil varnish. He also made some cellos. He had two sons, Othon and Knud, who worked for him. Prices up to $400.00.

HOFFMANN, MARTIN — *Leipzig, Germany. B. 1653, d. 1719.*

Many of his instruments are still in existence. He was an excellent workman and used his own models, with characteristic sharp corners. The varnish is usually yellow-brown, of beautiful luster. Prices: $250.00 to $500.00.

HOFMANN, ANTON — *Vienna, Austria. B. 1814, d. 1871.*

Apprentice in the shop of Martin Stoss and later his successor. He made violins and especially fine cellos, after the model of his master, which is flat and has high sides. Probably many of his instruments have been sold as original Martin Stoss'. He is one of the few makers who used linden wood for the back, and beech for the sides and scroll. He used a dark red or brown oil varnish. Prices: $300.00 to $500.00.

HOMOLKA — *Bohemian family of violin makers.*

To it belong: Emanuel Adam (1796-1849), Ferdinand Josef (1810-62), Johann Stephan (1800-83) and others. The greatest was Ferdinand August, b. 1828, d. 1890. He learned his trade in his father's shop. For a number of years he worked for Viennese and Prague makers, and he carried on in the same style of work when he opened his own shop in 1847. He was a very clever workman and copied the old masters with extreme accuracy. The thicknesses of wood are carefully observed, the arching is medium and the varnish generally dark chocolate brown. The tone is excellent. He had a son, Edward Emanuel, b. in Prague 1860, who took over the business after his father's death. Prices: $150.00 to $350.00.

> *Label:* Ferdinandus Aug. Homolka / Fecit Pragae 18__ (initials in circle)

HOPF — *A very large family of violin makers in Klingenthal, Germany.*

CASPAR — *date of birth not known, died 1711.*

DAVID CHRISTIAN, *Quittenbach* — *About 1760.*

GEORG — *about 1783.*

DAVID AUGUST — *Worked between 1762 and 1786.*

JOHANN CHRISTIAN — *Worked between 1747 and 1776.*

CHRISTIAN AUGUST — *About 1782.*

Made many cheap commercial violins, with rosin varnish, poorly made. However, at other times, he made quite decent instruments worth $100.00 to $150.00.

CARL FRIEDRICH — *b. 1811, d. 1892.*

This maker preferred a model of his own, with flat edges.

DAVID — *about 1830.*

One of the last of this family. His instruments are not well made and are covered with a dull brown rosin varnish. They are priced from $60.00 to $100.00.

Many of their instruments are branded on the back over the top block or inside on the back opposite the sound-post. Some exceptional examples of this family have sold up to $250.00.

HORIL, JAKOB — *Worked in Vienna, Austria, about 1720-1740, after that in Rome, Italy, where he must have died about 1760.*

His work is very well done, more on the German than the Italian style. The varnish is yellow to red-brown. Prices: $250.00 to $500.00.

> *Label:* Jacobus Horil fecit / Viennae Ao 17.... (manuscript) or
> Jacobus Horil fecit / Romae an 17.....

HORNSTEINER — *Large family of violin makers in Mittenwald, Germany, in the 18th and 19th centuries.*

They were mostly commercial makers. The more famous ones were Georg, Joseph, Martin and Mathias. They all worked on about the same style, using a flat Stradivari model and a light yellow-brown varnish of good quality. The wood is plain, but the workmanship accurate, the outlines sharply cut, and their instruments are known for their fine quality of tone. They are priced today at $100.00 to $350.00.

There are still some members of this family conducting business under the name of Hornsteiner, but on a commercial basis. They keep up the same clean workmanship of the older ones and their instruments are being sold from $35.00 to $100.00.

> *Label:* Mathias Hornsteiner, Geigenmacher, / Hofschmid in Mittenwald an der Iser / Anno 18.... (and others)

HOYER — *A family of violin makers in Klingenthal, Quittenbach, and Schönbach, Germany.*

Best represented by Andreas Hoyer, who died in 1788. He was a contemporary and competitor of Caspar Hopf. There were also

Carl Friedrich and Christian Gottfried Hoyer. They usually followed a high arched model and used brown varnish. Prices range from $100.00 to $200.00, for instruments by Friedrich Hoyer of the period 1785-1815, as high as $300.00.

Label: Andreas Hoyer, / Musicus instrumentalis / in Quittenbach 17.... (and others)

HUBER, JOHANN GEORG — *Vienna, Austria. B. about 1741, d. 1772.*

He did not make a large number of instruments, but those seen are very neatly done and possess excellent tone quality. The varnish is generally red-brown which in the course of years became almost black, as the varnish of Viennese makers often did. Prices: $150.00 to $300.00.

HUNGER, CHRISTOPH FRIEDRICH — *B. 1718, d. 1787.*

Worked for J. C. Hoffmann in Leipzig, Germany, established himself there and became quite well known. He made good violas and cellos as well as violins after the Italian style. Prices: $150.00 to $200.00.

JACOBS, (JACOBSZ) HENDRICK — *Worked in Amsterdam, Holland, about 1690-1712.*

The most famous of all Dutch makers. He usually copied the grand pattern of Nicola Amati, with great accuracy. According to tradition he was related to Amati by marriage. He used an abundant reddish brown varnish and whalebone for his purfling. His instruments are well liked and much in demand. Violins: $750.00 to $1500.00; his large size violas have sold as high as $3000.00.

Label: HENDRIK JACOBS ME FECIT / IN AMSTERDAM 16....

JACQUOT, CHARLES — *B. 1804 in Mirecourt, France, d. 1880.*

Pupil of D. Nicolas. About 1819, he went to work for Breton, moved to Nancy in 1823 and there started his own business in 1827. This shop was later run by his son, Pierre Charles (1828-1895), while he went to Paris. He was one of the talented French makers of the 19th century and usually worked after Stradivari and Guarneri, sometimes after Maggini. His selections of wood are fine. He often used one piece backs. The varnish is usually light brown with a yellow base. The scrolls are exceptionally well cut. Prices: $350.00 to $500.00.

There were many other violin makers by the name of Jacquot, too numerous to mention, and most of them were unimportant.

JACQUOT, CHARLES ALBERT — B. 1853 in Nancy, France.

Eldest son of Pierre Charles. He learned his trade under his father, then went to Germany, Brussels and Paris for further instruction. He and his brother, Jules Victor, b. 1855, became partners in his father's business. He is one of the best of the later French makers. He had his own conception of the correct thicknesses of wood, the outlines and patterns. His workmanship is very fine, the tone quality big and responsive. He used a fine oil varnish, generally yellow brown. Prices: $250.00 to $500.00.

JAEGER — A violin making family in Markneukirchen, Germany.

The first was Johann Adam, b. 1688, d. 1765. Their instruments are not exceptional in any way and are valued not higher than $85.00 to $150.00.

JAIS, ANDREAS — Worked in Mittenwald and Tölz, South Germany. B. about 1685, d. about 1750.

He was a first class workman and made violas and viol d'amours as well as violins and cellos. His model is usually high-arched, the varnish yellow-brown or red-brown, and the scroll is sometimes replaced by a finely cut lion's head. Prices: $200.00 to $300.00. His son, Johannes (1715-65) worked on the same style.

Label: Andreas Jaiss Lautten-/ macher in Tölz Ao 17....

JAIS, ANTON — Mittenwald, Germany. B. 1748, d. after 1836.

One of the four sons of Franz Jais (1720, 1757) of Mittenwald, of whom he is the best. The arching is medium high, the varnish yellow or brown. He also made very fine cellos. Prices: $200.00 to $350.00.

JOHNSON, JOHN — Worked in London, England between 1750 and 1760.

A fine craftsman. His instruments are usually built on a high arched model and covered with yellow or golden brown varnish, not too thickly applied. Prices: $250.00 to $400.00.

JORIO, VINCENT — *Worked in Naples, Italy, about 1780-1849.*

His main occupation was the restoration of old instruments. He has made some very fine violins and violas, although many bearing his label and even some branded on the back were probably not made by him. Some originals seen are excellent in workmanship and quality of tone. He used a yellow to orange-brown varnish. Prices: $400.00 to $750.00.

> *Label:* Vincenzo Jorio / Fabbricante / di Strumenti Armonici / Strada S.M. la Nuova N.21 Napoli 18....

KAEMBL, JOHANN ANDREAS — *Munich, Germany. B. 1699, d. 1781.*

One of the better makers of that town. A son-in-law of Paul Alletsee and his successor to the business. He is not an important maker and his instruments are priced at $150.00 to $250.00.

KARNER, BARTHOLOMAEUS — *Mittenwald, Germany, 18th century (exact dates not known).*

His work is good and the selections of wood excellent. The varnish is usually brown. He made some violas which are generally considered to be better than his violins. Prices: $150.00 to $300.00.

Other less important makers by that name were Georg, Johann Georg and Stephan.

KEFFER, JOHANN — *Worked in Goysern and Ischl, Austria, about 1790-1810.*

He was a first-class maker, working on a large pattern, using well selected wood and reddish yellow varnish. The tone is very large and suitable for orchestra. His initials are branded on the back over the top block. He made some large size violas of exceptional merit, which have sold for as much as $400.00. Violins are priced at $125.00 to $300.00.

KEMPTER, ANDREAS — *Dillingen, Germany. B. about 1700, d. 1786.*

He followed the Stainer models, though others of broader pattern have been seen. His arching varies but is generally high. The color of the varnish is usually rich yellow, shading to brown. He was a good workman and his instruments possess a very pleasing tone quality. Prices: $100.00 to $250.00.

KENNEDY, THOMAS — *London, England. B. 1784, d. 1870.*

Son of John Kennedy, a violin maker of little renown. He worked for Wm. Forster and possibly other English makers before he had his own shop. He was especially known for his cellos, built on the Amati style, which probably are as finely made as any in England. Violins are priced about $350.00 to $500.00, some of his cellos much higher.

KESSLER — *A family originating from Markneukirchen, Germany.*

The later Kesslers have been engaged mostly in the commercial field. Prices: $35.00 to $100.00.

KHOEGL, HANNS — *Vienna, Austria. B. about 1630.*

Little is known of this maker. Examples seen were of the Brescian type, built on a small narrow pattern with high arching and brown or reddish yellow varnish. Prices: $150.00 to $250.00.

KITTEL, NIKOLAUS — *Worked in St. Petersburg, Russia, about 1839 to 1870.*

Most likely of German descent. He was the greatest Russian bow-maker and is often referred to as the "Russian Tourte." His bows are rare and very few are to be had. They are much sought by musicians. The balance is perfect, the weight not too heavy. The sticks are stamped "Kittel" and are usually medium brown-red. He ranks with the greatest French bow-makers. He also made some violins, but the author has never seen one. Prices on bows: $250.00 to $1000.00.

KLIER — *A violin making family in Schönbach, Bohemia, from the 19th century on.*

KLOTZ, EGIDI — *Worked in Mittenwald, Germany, about 1675-1725.*

The oldest maker of the Mittenwald school. He was probably a pupil of Stainer, but very little is known of him today.

KLOTZ (KLOZ), MATHIAS — *Mittenwald, Germany. B. 1656, d. 1743.*

The founder of the violin making industry in Mittenwald. Possibly a pupil of Stainer, for style and workmanship of his instruments closely resemble that of Stainer. For six years he worked for

Giovanni Railich in Padua. His workmanship is faultless, the tone beautiful, the wood of fine selection. The varnish is usually yellow-brown, sometimes red-brown. His cellos today command a very good price. His instruments sell from $350.00 to $750.00.

Label: Mathias Kloz, Lautenmacher / in Mittenwald, Anno 17....

KLOTZ, SEBASTIAN — *Mittenwald, Germany. B. 1696, d. about 1770.*

Son of Mathias. He followed the Stainer model, less highly arched. His work is superior to that of any of the Klotz family, the varnish heavier and of finer quality. It varies as to color, but he preferred a rich brown with a yellow ground. Prices: $400.00 to $750.00.

He had an elder brother, Georg (1687-1737), whose instruments are of fine quality but not equal to Sebastian's. They are priced at $250.00 to $500.00.

KLOTZ, AEGIDIUS — *Mittenwald, Germany. B. 1733, d. 1805.*

Son of Sebastian. He followed the workmanship and style of his father in every way and probably many of his instruments have been sold under his father's name. He used a yellow to yellow-brown varnish. Prices: $350.00 to $600.00.

Label: AEgidius Kloz in Mitten / wald an der Iser 17....

KLOTZ, JOHANN CAROL — *Mittenwald, Germany. B. 1709, d. about 1790.*

Son of Mathias. He, too, is a good representative of his family, but favored smaller models. His varnish is generally dark brown. He made some excellent cellos which have reached prices up to $1000.00. Violins are priced from $250.00 to $600.00.

Label: Joan Carol Kloz, in / Mittenwald, an 17....

KLOTZ, JOSEPH — *Mittenwald, Germany. B. 1743, d. about 1810.*

Son of Sebastian. A talented maker, though he was not as well known as the earlier Klotz. His workmanship and the selections of wood are fine. He followed the style of the Mittenwald school and generally used a yellow or reddish varnish. Prices: $200.00 to $350.00, cellos up to $600.00.

Many other members of the Klotz family were violin makers, but not of great importance.

KNILLING — *Family of violin makers in Mittenwald, Germany, in the 18th and 19th centuries.*

Among the more important ones were Johann, Johann Joseph, Joseph Mathias and Johann Joseph II and others of later date. Their instruments are of the usual Mittenwald style, flat model, generally covered with a light yellow-brown varnish. They followed the Stradivari patterns and used wood without figure. Prices: $125.00 to $250.00.

KNITL, FRANZ — *B. 1744 in Mittenwald, Germany, d. 1791 in Freising.*

Good Klotz school, usually yellow-brown varnish. His brother, Joseph, who worked between 1756 and 1790, followed practically the same style. Prices: $100.00 to $400.00.

KNOPF, HENRY RICHARD — *See American section.*

KNORR, ARTHUR — *B. 1886 in Markneukirchen, Germany. Member of a family of violin makers, son of Ernst Robert.*

Though a violin maker, he specialized in the commercial manufacture of bows. His instruments bring from $100.00 to $150.00; the bows seen were priced at $15.00 to $35.00.

KOLDITZ, MATTHIAS JOHANN — *Worked in Munich, Germany, about 1733 to 1760.*

The pattern is generally small, the arching medium, the varnish, red-brown. He used wood of excellent selection and his workmanship is fine. Prices: $150.00 to $300.00.

KÖLLMER — *A German family of violin makers in the late 18th and 19th centuries.*

Johann Nikolaus (1794-1845) was the most important. His instruments, including some cellos, are well made, built generally after the Italian style. They have large tone. He used a yellow-brown varnish, also other colors. Prices: $150.00 to $250.00.

KRAUSCH, GEORG ADAM — *Worked in Vienna, Austria, between 1800 and 1825.*

Very few of his violins have been seen. They are very well made. The selections of wood are excellent, the varnish yellow and usually of good quality. Medium arching. Prices: $150.00 to $300.00.

KRELL, ALBERT — *Cincinnati, Ohio. B. 1832 in Kelbra, d. 1900.*

He had received a good musical training and at the age of 16 he came to America where he worked for different houses before establishing his own business. Though he became quite famous as an early American maker, his work is in no way exceptional. His varnish is hard and thick, usually red. Prices: $200.00 to $350.00.

KRETZSCHMANN — *Markneukirchen, Germany, 18th and early 19th centuries.*

Some violins by members of this family are branded in the back *C*G*K*. Their work is fair but not exceptional. They preferred the smaller patterns. Prices: $100.00 to $200.00.

KRINER, SIMON — *Mittenwald, Germany. B. about 1780, d. 1821.*

A pupil of Anton Jais and at one time one of Hornsteiner's workmen. His work is very clean cut. He made good copies of Italian violins. His shop was taken over by his son, Lorenz, who passed it on to his son, Joseph, b. in Landshut 1836. Prices: $100.00 to $200.00.

KRINER, MATTHAEUS — *B. 1843 in Mittenwald, Germany.*

A follower of the Mittenwald school and a fine workman, employed by Neuner, later by August Riechers in Berlin. In 1892, he opened his own shop in Stuttgart. He did mostly repairs but also made some new violins, on the Stradivari and Guarneri patterns. He used a spirit varnish, generally reddish yellow. He invented a special vibrating bar, which supposedly increased the volume of tone. Prices: $200.00 to $300.00.

KULIK, JOHANNES — *Prague, Austria. B. 1800, d. 1872.*

A pupil of Schembera. Also worked for Martin Stoss in Vienna before he established himself in Prague. He was an excellent craftsman and copied the old Italian masters, mostly Guarnerius. He used fine wood and a spirit varnish which generally is red or golden brown. Prices: $200.00 to $350.00.

LABERTE & MAGNIÉ — *Mirecourt, France.*

One of the most important houses in this center of violin making, founded 1780. Fourier Magnié Co. (founded 1776) joined the firm of Laberte in 1919. They are also the successors of D. Nicolas, Honoré Derazey and others. They employed a large number of highly skilled workmen and the fine old instruments of Marc Laberte's collection served as models for their new instruments and for comparison of tone. Their better commercial instruments are priced at about $300.00.

LAFLEUR, JACQUES — B. 1757 in Nancy, France, d. 1833 in Paris, France.

Learned his trade in Mirecourt, went to Paris in 1783. He was not important as a violin maker, though he made some nice violins and cellos. He is well known, however, for his excellent bows, made after the style of François Tourte. They are perfect in balance and camber, light in weight, either round or octagon. Prices: $65.00 to $250.00.

LAGETTO, LOUIS — Worked in Mirecourt and Paris, France, about 1725-53.

He was of Italian descent, but little is known of his life or work. Instruments seen were covered with a yellow brown varnish and were priced at $350.00 to $800.00.

LAMY, ALFRED JOSEPH — B. 1850 in Mirecourt, France, d. about 1920.

He was established in Paris and was one of the best French bow makers. He had worked for many firms in Mirecourt, also for F. N. Voirin. His bows brought many silver and gold medals on account of their exceptionally fine workmanship. They are stamped: "A. Lamy à Paris." Prices: $75.00 to $150.00.

LANDOLFI, CARLO FERDINANDO—Worked in Milan, Italy, about 1734 to 1788.

His work is excellent. He used fine selections of wood; some backs are bird's eye maple. The arching is medium high, edges deeply fluted, the varnish red-brown or yellow-brown. The cellos he made are usually built on a small pattern. Also made violas. The tone of his instruments is very rich and beautiful. Prices: $1000.00 to $3500.00.

> Label: Carlo Ferdinando Landolfi / nella Contrada di Santa Margarita / al Segno della Sirena, Milano 17.... (and others, also spelled Landolphus)

LANDOLFI, PIETRO ANTONIO — *Worked in Milan, Italy, about 1750-1780.*

He served his apprenticeship under his father Carlo Ferdinando, but was not his equal. He worked on a narrow pattern with high arching, and usually used a very fine reddish yellow varnish. Prices: $750.00 to $1500.00.

> *Label:* Pietro Antonio figlio di / Carlo Ferdinando Landolfi / in Milano al Segno della / Sirena l'anno 17___

LA PRÉVOTTE, ETIENNE — *B. toward the end of the 18th century in Mirecourt, France, d. 1856 in Paris.*

Before he came to Paris, from 1833 to 1837, he had his shop in Marseille. His instruments are not always very carefully made, but the varnish is of fine soft texture.

LASKE (LASCHKE), JOSEPH ANTON — *Prague, Czechoslovakia. B. 1738, d. 1805.*

Served his apprenticeship in Czechoslovakia, Germany and Austria. About 1760, he established himself in Prague. He made excellent instruments, generally medium arched. The varnish is usually yellow-brown. Prices: $200.00 to $300.00.

LAURENT, EMILE — *B. 1854 in Mirecourt, France, d. 1914 in Brussels.*

A pupil of Didelot and A. Darte. Up to 1901, he worked for J. Hel in Lille, then had his own shop in Brussels, Belgium. He followed the style of Stradivari, Guarneri and Guadagnini and used a red-brown or golden yellow oil varnish. Fine workmanship. Prices: $350.00 to $500.00.

Emile II, b. 1875, and Albert, b. 1884, his two sons, learned violin making in his shop. Emile worked for leading French houses, among them Caressa & Français, and between 1908 and 1912 he was in charge of the violin shop of Lyon & Healy in Chicago. On his return to France he opened a shop in Bordeaux, which he transferred to Paris in 1925.

LAVAZZA, ANTONIO MARIA — *Worked in Milan, Italy, about 1703-1732.*

Followed the Stradivari pattern, but must have made only few instruments. The arching is medium, the varnish reddish, the workmanship excellent. Prices: $1000.00 to $1500.00.

Sanctus Lavazza, of whom we have seen some violins and cellos in the price range of $500.00 to $1000.00 was probably the son of Antonio. He also worked in Milan.

LECCHI, GIUSEPPE — *Genoa, Italy. B. 1895 in Felizzano (Alessandria).*

Pupil of Cesare Candi. He follows Stradivari and Guarneri del Gesu models. Also made some good violas on the large pattern (16 11/16" body length). Very few of his instruments have been seen in this country. Prices: $200.00 to $400.00.

LEEB, JOHANN GEORG I — *Pressburg, Slovakia. B. about 1740, d. after 1810.*

A fine workman. Followed the patterns of Amati and Stainer, high arching. The varnish is usually red-brown. The tone is large and of very good quality. Prices: $150.00 to $300.00.

LEEB, JOHANN GEORG II — *Pressburg, Slovakia. B. 1779, d. 1817.*

Son and successor of Johann I. Was considered a better maker than his father. He followed the Amati pattern and used a brown, sometimes yellow-brown varnish. Prices: $200.00 to $350.00.

LEEB, ANDREAS CARL — *Worked in Vienna, Austria, about 1784-1813.*

One of the most gifted makers of the Leeb family. His style is the same as that of the Pressburg branch of the family, but his archings are flatter. The varnish is dark brown; most likely it was lighter when new, as many Viennese violins have turned darker with age. Prices: $150.00 to $600.00.

Label: Andreas Carolus Leeb / Viennae 17___ (and others)

LEFEBVRE, JACQUES B. — *Worked in Amsterdam, Holland, about 1720-1780.*

A French maker who probably learned his trade in Italy, because his work is far better than that produced in France or Holland at that time. He used a flat model, after Stradivari or Amati. Good yellow or light red varnish. Prices: $250.00 to $300.00.

LEFEVRE (LEFEBVRE), TOUSSAINT NICOLAS GERMAIN. — *Worked in Paris, France, about 1762-1789.*

He made violins but is chiefly known as a bow maker. Most of his bows are heavy, but well balanced. They are branded "Lefèvre à

Paris," and are rather rare. They range in price from $75.00 to $200.00.

LEIDOLFF, NICOLAS — *Worked in Vienna, Austria, 1673, d. about 1710.*

He probably served part of his apprenticeship in Italy, for his style of work shows Italian traits. He is one of the better Viennese makers. The model used is medium high arched, the varnish, reddish brown. Prices: $250.00 to $400.00.

LEIDOLFF, JOHANN CHRISTOPH — *Vienna, Austria. B. 1690, d. 1758.*

Son of Nicolas. He followed his father's style, used a high arched model, somewhat after Stainer. The linings are usually hard wood and sometimes he used pear wood for the scrolls. He treated the wood and this makes the varnish of some of his violins look greyish today. Those not treated have a rich dark red varnish. He had many helpers and therefore turned out a large number of instruments. Prices: $250.00 to $350.00.

> *Label:* Johann Christoph Leidolff, / Lauten—und Geigenmacher / in Wienn 17....

LEIDOLFF, JOSEPH FERDINAND — *Worked in Vienna, Austria, about 1756 to 1780.*

He is the best of the Leidolff family. Followed chiefly the Amati pattern. His wood is well selected. Some of his violins have a deep red-brown varnish, almost black, others are dark reddish yellow. Prices $250.00 to $500.00.

> *Label:* Josephus Ferdinandus Leidolff / fecit Viennae 17....

LE JEUNE, FRANÇOIS — *Worked in Paris, France between 1755 and 1789.*

Was the only important maker in this family. His instruments have sold up to $150.00.

LEMBOECK, GABRIEL — *B. 1814 in Budapest, Hungary, d. 1892.*

A pupil of Anton Fischer and later his son-in-law and successor. In 1840, he established himself in Vienna. He was an excellent craftsman, copied many of the old masters and is supposed to have made exact copies of Paganini's Guarnerius violin, brought in by the great violinist himself for repair. Some of his instruments are made after Maggini and branded with his initials. He generally used a yellow or red-brown transparent varnish. Prices: $100.00 to $250.00; superb copies much higher.

LENOBLE, AUGUSTE—*B. 1828 in Mirecourt, France, d. 1895.*

He learned bow making under the famous master François Peccatte. He served his military period between 1848 and 1862, then established himself in Paris. He made excellent bows, following the style of his master. Not all are stamped, but the better bows are branded "Lenoble." Prices up to $100.00.

LEPRI, LUIGI — *Gubbio, Italy, about 1880.*

Little known. Prices: $300.00 to $400.00.

LEWIS, EDWARD — *Worked in London, England, from 1687 to 1700, possibly later.*

His work is accurate and well done and he enjoyed a high reputation in his time. His selections of wood are very fine. The varnish is generally yellow, sometimes golden. Very few of his instruments have been seen. Prices: $150.00 to $250.00.

LIEBICH, JOHANN GOTTFRIED — *Breslau, Germany. B. about 1755, d. 1824.*

He is the most important member of a large family of violin makers. He founded the business which today is still carried on by his descendants. His instruments are well made but never commanded very high prices. They are of the Saxon type. He was succeeded by his nephew Ernst Liebich (1796-1876). Prices: $75.00 to $150.00.

LIPPOLD, JOHANN GEORG — *Markneukirchen, Germany. B. 1739, d. 1824.*

The most important member of the Lippold family. He used fair selections of wood and followed the Saxon school. The color is usually yellow-brown, sometimes red-brown. Prices: $75.00 to $200.00.

Carl Friedrich (1772-1854) and Johann Gottlob Lippold (1777-1808), sons of Johann Georg, are less important, though nice examples of their work have been seen, especially cellos which have sold up to $250.00.

LOLIO, GIOVANNI BATTISTA — *Worked in Valtezze near Bergamo, Italy, between 1740 and 1750.*

His model is similar to Grancino, generally well arched. The varnish is yellow to yellow-brown, the workmanship fair, the wood not exceptionally good. Prices up to $350.00.

LORANGE, PAUL VICTOR — *Mirecourt, France. B. 1873, d. 1920.*

Served his apprenticeship under Delunet, also worked for Blanchard in Lyon and later for Georges Mougenot in Brussels. In 1900, he established himself in Lyon. His work is well done, following the Mirecourt school, always on the flat pattern and generally after the model of Stradivari. Reddish orange varnish. He was also known as an artistic restorer. His business was taken over by his son Paul. Prices: $100.00 to $250.00.

LOTT, JOHN FREDERICK — *London, England. B. about 1775, d. 1853.*

Was an apprentice in the shop of Thomas Dodd. He became an excellent maker and was known for his cellos and basses. His work is exceptionally well done, the scrolls beautifully carved. He used well selected wood and usually a dull yellow varnish having a tint of brown. He had two sons, George F., b. 1800, d. 1868, and John F. Jr., b. 1804, d. 1871, who both followed their father's trade. Prices: $300.00 to $800.00.

> *Label:* J. F. Lott / Maker / London

LOUVET, JEAN — *Worked in Paris, France, about 1750-89.*

He was a brother of Pierre Louvet who made harps, violas and guitars. He is not well known, but some of his instruments are well made and bring fair prices. He also made cellos. Prices: $150.00 to $400.00.

LOWENDALL STAR WORKS — *A commercial concern in Berlin, Germany.*

Founded 1866 in Dresden by L. Löwenthal. The purely commercial violins, of which they exported great quantities, brought from $10.00 to $75.00, the better ones bearing Lowendall labels, from $100.00 to $150.00.

LUPOT, FRANÇOIS I — *B. 1725 in Plombières, France, d. 1804.*

About 1758 he was called to the Court at Stuttgart as a lute maker to the Duke of Wurttemberg. There he stayed until about

1770, when he established himself in Orléans. Later, in 1794, he went to Paris to join his son. He was an excellent maker, but his instruments do not, by far, command the high prices of those by his son Nicolas. He followed the Stradivari patterns. His selections of wood are good, the varnish generally a yellow brown, sometimes golden orange. In his time, he was considered one of the finest French luthiers. Prices: $200.00 to $500.00.

LUPOT, NICOLAS — *B. 1758 in Stuttgart, Germany, d. 1824.*

The eldest son and pupil of François. His first violins are dated about 1776 (Orléans). He was further trained under François Pique in Paris, and in 1798, he opened his own shop there. He is without question the greatest French violin maker and has been called the "French Stradivari." He followed Stradivari's patterns closely and adopted his style of work in every detail. His workmanship is very beautiful and unsurpassed and the varnish excellent. Many of his instruments were given yearly to the winners of prizes at the Paris Conservatoire and are inscribed on back and sides. Spohr used one. His finer instruments are varnished in a beautiful reddish orange, others are dull red, almost chocolate brown. He also made cellos. Prices: $900.00 to $3500.00.

> *Label:* Nicolas Lupot, Luthier rue croix / des petits-champs à Paris
> l'an 18 ... (and many others)

LUPOT, FRANÇOIS II — *B. 1774 in Orléans, France, d. 1837 in Paris.*

Brother of Nicolas. He made violins but is better known for his bows. There are many excellent ones in existence, not all of them stamped with his name. Many are branded under the wrapping. The color is generally a dark reddish brown. Prices: $100.00 to $400.00.

MAGGINI, GIOVANNI PAOLO — *Brescia, Italy. B. 1580 in Botticino-Sero, about five miles from Brescia, d. 1632.*

He was an apprentice in the workshop of Gasparo da Salo (Bertolotti). He began by closely following his master's work but his instruments of that period are not well made and the selections of wood generally ordinary, inlaid in pearl or ivory. Later he changed his style and developed a model more like that used today. The instruments of this period have a higher arching. The workmanship is accurate, the wood finely selected. The typical Maggini model, however, is that of the last period, with its double row of purfling and the low sides. The thicknesses of wood are correct and there is a great improvement in the quality of tone. The varnish is excellent and usually red-brown to reddish orange. The soundholes are rather long, with quite narrow wings. The volute of the scroll is small and has less turns than the ones of today. He also made some violas and cellos. He and Gasparo da Solo were the most important makers of the Brescian school and had great influence on the development of violin making in Italy. His instruments have been sold from $900.00 to $3500.00.

> *Label:* Gio: Paolo Maggini, in Brecia

MAIRE, NICOLAS — *Paris, France. B. 1800 in Mirecourt, d. 1878.*

A pupil of Jacques Lafleur and in 1832 became his successor. He was an excellent bow-maker and his work is well liked by professional musicians but is not frequently seen. Prices: $75.00 to $200.00.

MALINE, GUILLAUME — *B. 1793 in Mirecourt, France, d. after 1850.*

An excellent bow-maker, though not in the class of the finest French makers. Prices: $65.00 to $100.00.

MALINE, FRANÇOIS ALEXIS — *B. about 1822 in Mirecourt, France, date of death not known.*

He should not be confused with the bow-maker, Guillaume Maline. His instruments are well made, built on a large flat pattern. The wood is good, the varnish usually chocolate brown. Prices: $150.00 to $250.00.

MALVOLTI, PIETRO ANTONIO — *Worked in Florence, Italy about 1700-1733.*

He probably made very few instruments and is little known. His work shows some of the characteristics of Gabrielli. The model is small, the arching varying from medium to high. The selections of wood are excellent, the varnish usually yellow-brown. Instruments of superb workmanship have been seen. Prices: $700.00 to $1200.00.

MANN, JOHN ALEXANDER — *Glasgow, Scotland. B. 1810, d. 1889.*

He was one of the few known Scotch makers. It was in 1845 that he first started doing repairs, then more seriously went into violin making proper. He followed the Stradivari models, but it is said that he bought violins in the white and only varnished them. The color is generally a dark yellow, the quality is good. He was an intimate friend of J. B. Vuillaume who is supposed to have offered the "Messie" Strad to him for £160. He declined, stating that this was too much money for a Strad. Prices: $200.00 to $300.00.

MANSUY, PIERRE — *Mirecourt, France, 18th century.*

His instruments are little known, but they are fairly well made, built on a flat model and usually covered with a medium brown varnish. He also made a number of pochettes. Prices: $100.00 to $200.00.

MANTEGAZZA (MANTEGATIA), PIETRO GIOVANNI — *Worked in Milan, Italy, about 1750-90.*

He shared his shop with his brothers Carlo, Francesco and Giovanni, and later established his own business. Little is known of this maker and very few of his instruments still exist. He is one of the many makers whose names have been used promiscuously by violin dealers throughout the world. The spelling of the name varies (Mantegazzia, Montegatia, etc.). Genuine examples have been sold as high as $2000.00.

MARCHETTI, ABBONDIO — *Worked in Milan, Italy, about 1815-40.*

Made only a few instruments. The workmanship is good, the selections of wood fine, the varnish usually red-brown. Prices: $150.00 to $300.00.

MARCHI, GIOVANNI ANTONIO — *Worked in Bologna, Italy, about 1660-1720.*

Generally followed the Gagliano model. The arching is high, the selections of wood excellent. Golden yellow or reddish brown varnish. His instruments have large tone. He also made cellos and some fine, large violas. Genuine examples have been priced up to $850.00, but not infrequently Marchi labels have been inserted in Italian instruments of unknown origin in order to give them a name.

MARCONCINI, GIUSEPPE — *Ferrara, Italy. B. 1760, d. 1841.*

His father Luigi, who supposedly was a pupil of Omobono Stradivari, worked in Bologna and Ferrara about 1760-1791.

Giuseppe was a pupil of Storioni and followed the style of his master. The selections of wood are fine and the workmanship is excellent. The varnish is generally of a reddish color and of very good quality, especially that of his later work. Another maker whose name is often misused. Prices: $400.00 to $750.00.

MARIANI, ANTONIO — *Worked in Pesaro, Italy, about 1636-1680.*

He was inconsistent in his work, some of which is roughly done, and some exceptionally fine. It is mostly modelled after Maggini and Gasparo da Salo. Many of his instruments have the double purfling, some have fine oil varnish, generally deep brown or yellow-brown. He also made violas and cellos. Reproductions of his labels are often found in instruments which are not his work. Prices range from $450.00 to $800.00; exceptional specimens have sold for as much as $1000.00.

Label: Antonio Mariani / Fece in Pesaro / Anno 16.... (Script)

MARTIN — *A large family of violin makers in Saxony during the 18th and 19th centuries.*

Their instruments are fairly well made but not exceptional. Of the many makers of the Martin family Otto Oswald Martin, b. 1870, in Markneukirchen, Germany, deserves special mention. He worked for many dealers in that town, and in 1893, came to America and established himself in Milwaukee. He made copies of Italian masters, but used a spirit varnish of hard texture, usually reddish yellow. His instruments and those of the better makers of his family are priced at $100.00 to $200.00.

MAST, JOSEPH LAURENT — *Worked in Toulouse, France, about 1808-30.*

His home town was Mirecourt and he was the son of the violin maker Jean Laurent. He served his apprenticeship under D. Nicolas and his work is characteristic of that school. Some of his finer examples are beautifully made, of well selected wood. He worked on a large flat Stradivari pattern. His varnish is yellow or reddish yellow. He branded his instruments "Mast fils Toulouse." Prices: $300.00 to $450.00.

MAUCOTEL — *A family of violin makers in Mirecourt, France, to which belong:*

Charles, b. 1807, d. 1860. In 1834, he entered the employ of

Gand in Paris, and in 1844, went to London to work first for Davis, and then to establish his own shop in 1850.

Charles Adolphe, brother of Charles. B. 1820. Worked for J. B. Vuillaume in Paris, but died at the early age of 38.

Ernest, b. 1867, in Mirecourt. A pupil of Paul Bailly and of his uncle Salzard in Moscow with whom he stayed for some time. When he returned to France, he became Silvestre's first workman and, in 1900, his partner. In 1903 he took in Deschamp as a partner who was not a violin maker but a fine connoisseur. His instruments are well made and generally built on the models of Italian masters, such as Seraphin, Montagnana and Goffriller. Prices: $350.00 to $700.00.

MAUSSIELL, LEONHARD — *Nürnberg, Germany. B. 1685, d. after 1760.*

He generally followed the model of Stainer, using a medium arching. Wood and workmanship are good. He also made violas and carved beautiful scrolls, sometimes in the form of a woman's or lion's head. Prices: $250.00 to $750.00.

> *Label:* Leonhard Maussiell Lautten- und / Geigenmacher in Nurnberg 17....

MAYR — *A family of violin makers in Munich, Germany.*

Its most important member was Andreas Ferdinand, born in Vienna, where he, no doubt, served his apprenticeship. He worked in Salzburg, Austria, about 1721-50. Generally followed the Stainer model and did fine, accurate work. The varnish is dark red or brown. He used well selected wood and his instruments are excellent in tone. Also made cellos. Prices: $150.00 to $450.00.

> *Label:* Andreas Ferdinandus Mayr / Hof-Lauten und Geigenmacher / in Salzburg 17....

MAYSON, WALTER H. — *Manchester, England. B. 1835, d. 1905.*

Made his first violin in 1873 and two years later abandoned his career as a merchant to devote himself entirely to violin making. He had a model of his own which he varied according to the quality of the wood used. The varnish is soft and usually a rich red-brown on orange ground. The edges are very rounded and the lower lobes of the soundholes have a peculiar curve. He made violins, violas and cellos. Prices: $75.00 to $250.00.

MÉDARD — *A large family of violin makers in Nancy, France, during the 17th century.*

Their instruments are not often seen, except those by François Médard who worked in Paris between 1690 and 1710. Prices: $200.00 to $300.00.

MEINEL — *A family of violin makers in Klingenthal, Germany, during the 18th and 19th centuries.*

Their instruments, not exceptionally well made, are built in the style of the Saxon school. The selections of wood are only fair, the varnish is hard. There is a similarity to the work of Hopf and Ficker. Some of the better makers of this family were: August, Johann Friedrich, Johann Christian and Friedrich Wilhelm (1737-1802). Instruments seen have sold from $100.00 to $150.00.

MEISEL — *A large family of violin makers in Klingenthal, Germany.*

Their instruments are very much like those by the Meinel family.

Georg, worked 1729-1735.

Friedrich Wilhelm, worked 1769-1799.

Carl Christian, worked 1761-1768.

Johann Georg, worked 1745-1784.

The latter named is one of the best of this family and his instruments are more desirable than the others. Prices of his instruments range from $75.00 to $150.00.

Christian Friedrich Meisel, who worked about 1791-1850, is another more important maker of this family. He followed the Italian patterns and used good woods, but on the whole his work is not very satisfactory.

MELEGARI, ENRICO CLODOVEO — *Worked in Turin, Italy, about 1860-88.*

He was a fine maker of violins, violas and cellos. His work is good, the selections of wood fine, the varnish usually reddish yellow. This maker's name apparently has been used to name violins whose real origin was not known. His brother, Peter, succeeded him. Genuine examples are priced at $500.00 to $1000.00.

MENNÉGAND, CHARLES — *B. 1822, in Nancy, France, d. 1885.*

He served his apprenticeship in Mirecourt, then went to Paris to work for Rambaux, later for Maucotel. Around 1855, he opened his own shop in Amsterdam, but evidently was not successful and returned to Paris. He made exceptionally fine cellos which are well liked by professional musicians. Prices: $200.00 to $350.00.

MENNESSON, JEAN EMILE — *B. 1842, in Reims, France, d. 1920.*

He worked for Mennégand and Deroux. Later, he went to Mirecourt and from there established himself in Reims as a dealer and manufacturer of musical instruments. He made a great number of cheap violins, violas, cellos and basses. These are labelled "Joseph Guarini à Ste-Cécile" and on account of this name many have been sold for Italian instruments. Others are labelled Mennesson & Fils.

MERIGHI, PIETRO — *Worked in Parma, Italy, about 1769-1794.*

An excellent maker whose violins seem to be very rare. He had his own model, which is large, on the style of Guadagnini, with large square shoulders and medium arching. The soundholes resemble Peter Guarneri's. The varnish, chestnut brown to dark red, is of excellent texture. The scroll, large and massive, the volute in his own style. Prices: $750.00 to $1000.00.

MEYER, MAGNUS ANDREAS — *Worked in Hamburg, Germany, 1732-1753.*

Little is known of the background of this maker and his instruments (violins and cellos) are not very popular. His model is short but broad, with medium arching. The wood is ordinary, the varnish usually yellow-brown or golden brown. Some of his instruments have a woman's head in place of the regular scroll. Prices: $50.00 to $150.00.

MEZZADRI, ALLESANDRO — *Worked in Ferrara, Italy, about 1690 to 1732.*

A fine craftsman whose instruments are very rare. Not all are first class specimens, but exceptional ones have been seen. The selections of wood are good. The oil varnish is excellent, generally of a reddish yellow or red-brown color. A Mezzadri label is often found in instruments which are not genuine, but authentic examples are priced between $1000.00 to $2000.00.

Label: Alessandro Mezzadri / Fece in Ferrara l'anno 17___ (and others)

MICHELOT, JACQUES PIERRE — *Worked in Paris, France, about 1760 to 1800.*

He was known chiefly for his excellent guitars but also made fine violins, violas and cellos. Prices: $250.00 to $350.00.

MILTON, LOUIS FRANK — *B. 1898 at Marston, Bedfordshire, England.*

A descendant of an English family of skilled woodworkers. He took up violin making in 1918 and has made over 200 instruments. The varnish is a rich golden amber or beautiful red color. Fine workmanship, big responsive tone. There are not many of his instruments in this country. They sell from $100.00 to $150.00.

Label: Louis F. Milton / Bedford England

MIREMONT, CLAUDE AUGUSTIN — *B. 1827, in Mirecourt, France, d. 1887.*

Son of Sebastian Miremont and apprentice under Collin-Mézin. He worked in Paris up to about 1852, then came to America and established himself in New York. In 1861, however, he returned to Paris. He was a great copyist and made many instruments after the patterns of Guarneri, Stradivari, Gagliano and others, also bows. He used exceptionally good wood and his varnish, generally red-orange, is excellent. His better instruments sell from $300.00 to $500.00.

MOECKEL, OSWALD — *B. 1843, d. 1912.*

Member of a family of violin makers in Berlin, Germany. He was a pupil of Karl Grimm and Christian Adam and was known as one of the best Berlin makers. He copied the old Italian masters quite well, but his instruments are not worth very much in this country. He had two sons, Otto and Max, whose instruments are little known in America. Prices: $100.00 to $150.00.

MOITESSIER, LOUIS — *Worked in Mirecourt, France, about 1781-1824.*

Not very well known. He tried to make violins with all parts in maple but had no favorable results. Though he was a good teacher in violin making, his workmanship is not especially fine, his varnish poor, usually brown. His label often mentions Paris as his residence, but as far as records show, he never left Mirecourt. Prices: $100.00 to $200.00.

MONGEL, A. — *Violin maker in Paris, France, early 19th century.*

Little known. His instruments are fair. Priced at $150.00.

MONTAGNANA, DOMINICUS — *Venice, Italy. B. about 1690, d. about 1750.*

Records show very little of this man's life, though he was one of the greatest masters. Possibly he was a pupil of Nicola Amati at the same time as Stradivari, as his work shows many of the characteristics of Amati's and Stradivari's instruments. He generally used a large pattern, with sharp long corners and medium arching. It is similar to Stradivari's early work. The wood he selected is of exceptional quality and his workmanship unsurpassable. The varnish is usually a beautiful golden orange-red. The tone is very large and robust. He was probably the greatest maker of the Venetian school and ranks with Carlo Bergonzi. He also made beautiful cellos which command very high prices. His instruments are priced from $3000.00 to $12,000.00.

Label: Dominicus Montagnana Sub Si-/ gnum Cremonae Venetiis 17....

MORELLI — *A trade name used by a wholesale house in New York.*

Instruments so marked are not Italian but were made in Germany by a commercial concern and exported, like those of Roth and Heberlein. Prices: $50.00 to $250.00.

MORI COSTA, *see Costa.*

MORRISON, ARCHIBALD — *Glasgow, Scotland. B. 1820, d. 1895.*

He was a violinist and later took up violin making. He worked for Alexander Mann, and in 1865, opened his own shop. He copied the old masters, mostly Amati and Stradivari, occasionally also Guarneri. He may be considered one of the finest Scotch makers. Used excellent selections of wood and a varnish of fine texture, generally golden orange. Prices: $400.00 to $600.00.

MOUGENOT, GEORGES — *B. 1843 in Mirecourt, France, d. after 1910.*

A pupil of Deroux, Sr.; he also worked for Darche and started his own business in Liège, Belgium, in 1868. In 1875, he took over the shop of N. F. Vuillaume in Brussels. He followed the Stradivari, Guarneri and Bergonzi models. His work is excellent, his varnish a beautiful golden red or orange-brown. His instruments are very well liked, but few are seen in this country. Prices: $200.00 to $400.00.

MOUGENOT, LEON — *B. in Mirecourt, France, 1874.*

Son of Joseph and pupil of his uncle Georges Mougenot of Brussels. He worked for Blanchard in Lyon, for Lombard in Paris, and for Hill & Sons in London. He established himself in 1899 in Mirecourt. He had many apprentices working for him. He followed Stradivari and Guarneri patterns and also copied Lupot and Vuillaume. His workmanship is excellent. His varnish is not exceptionally good, as it is hard and chips very easily. The color is generally yellow with a slight tint of brown. His factory instruments sold from $50.00 to $150.00; some made by his own hands have been priced as high as $200.00.

MUNCHER, ROMEDIO — *B. 1874, working in Cremona, Italy.*

He copies the old masters, and, for a modern maker, his instruments are quite nice. Yellow or orange varnish. Prices: $200.00 to $300.00.

NADOTTI, GIUSEPPE — *Worked in Piacenza, Italy, about 1757-89.*

Little is known of his training, which, judged from his instruments, must have been a good one. His workmanship is remarkable. He generally followed the Amati patterns and used a yellowish brown varnish. Prices: $400.00 to $500.00.

Label: Joseph Nadotti Fecit / Placentiae 17....

NEMESSÁNYI, SAMUEL FELIX — *Budapest, Hungary. B. 1837, d. 1881.*

Pupil of Schweitzer and Zach. The best Hungarian maker of his time. He especially copied Guarneri del Gesu, and Lütgendorff says that his instruments are so well made and their tone quality is so good that they could hardly be distinguished from the originals after which they were modeled; but the author has seen four of these copies which, while they are excellent reproductions of Guarneri, differ widely in tone as well as in appearance when actual comparison is made. Many of his instruments, however, have been sold as Italians. The selections of wood are excellent. The varnish is usually very beautiful and of a golden orange color. Nemessányi's instruments are quite rare today and fetch exceptionally high prices: $600.00 to $800.00.

NEUNER, MATHIAS — *Worked in Mittenwald, Germany, between 1795 and 1830.*

Member of a large family of violin makers and dealers in that town. He was influential in the development of the firm Neuner & Hornsteiner. His own instruments are finely made and superior to those made in the shop. They are built on a flat Stradivari model and are usually covered with a yellow brown varnish. Prices: $150.00 to $350.00.

NEUNER, LUDWIG — *B. 1840, d. 1897.*

Worked in Munich, Berlin and Paris and for a number of years with J. B. Vuillaume. After his return to Mittenwald, he became a partner of the firm of Neuner & Hornsteiner.

NEUNER & HORNSTEINER — *Mittenwald, Germany.*

One of the largest business houses for commercial violins, violas and cellos. They employ a large staff of workers and make many thousands of instruments yearly. They come in different grades and, though of mass production, the workmanship is good. Where cheap violins with excellent tone are required, none better could be found than those by Neuner & Hornsteiner. The model is always flat, usually patterned after Stradivari or Guarneri. The varnish is almost invariably yellow with a tint of brown. Prices range from $35.00 to $150.00, cellos up to $250.00.

Label: Neuner & Hornsteiner / Mittenwald in Baiern 18....

NICOLAS, DIDIER — *Mirecourt, France. B. 1757, d. 1833.*

He and his son Joseph (1796-1864) are the only important makers in this large family of violin makers. He called his shop "A la Ville de Cremonne" and so branded his instruments. He made many violins, of which some are fair and others exceptionally good, all built on a large, broad, flat pattern. The distance between the soundholes often seems too great. The varnish is red-brown or yellow-brown. In later years, Nicolas employed a large number of workmen who made instruments on a commercial basis, which are also well made and possess good tone. His brand was purchased by Derazey and later by Mougenot, and for this reason so many violins are seen branded D. Nicolas which properly belong to a later period. The commercial instruments are priced from $100.00 to $250.00; those made by Didier personally, as high as $450.00.

NIGGELL, SYMPERTUS — *Füssen, South Germany. B. 1710, d. 1785.*

The author has seen some exceptionally fine examples of this maker's work and thinks that he was one of the greatest German makers. He usually followed the Stainer pattern and his instruments are often similar to Albani. The selections of wood are excellent and the craftsmanship superb. The color of his varnish is light red, yellow-brown or red-brown. Prices: $500.00 to $1200.00.

> *Label:* Sympertus Niggell / Lauten- und Geigen-macher in Fussen / 17—

NOVELLO, PIETRO VALENTINO — *Worked in Venice, Italy, about 1790-1800.*

A pupil of Anselmo Bellosio of that city. His work is fair, following the Venetian school. Very few of his instruments have been seen. Prices: $300.00 to $500.00.

NÜRNBERGER — *Family of bow and violin makers in Mark-neukirchen, Germany.*

The most important representative is Franz Albert, son of Robert, b. 1854. He is considered one of the best German bow makers of his time. He followed the patterns of the finest French bow makers and his work is well liked and much in demand. His business was taken over by his sons, but their bows, of the commercial type, are not as well made nor as valuable as their father's. The old bows have sold from $40.00 to $100.00; the new commercial bows, though they are not as fine, command about the same prices in the better grades, namely $30.00 to $100.00.

OBICI, BARTOLOMEO — *Worked in Verona, Italy, about 1665-1685.*

Probably the pupil of some Brescian maker. The tone of his instruments is excellent. They are usually built on a large pattern, some seen are after the style of Maggini. The varnish is light yellow or yellow-brown, the selections of wood fine. Prices: $500.00 to $750.00.

ODDONE, CARLO GIUSEPPE — *B. 1866 in Turin, Italy.*

He learned his trade under the guidance of Gioffredo Rinaldi, with whom he stayed between 1889 and 1899. He then went to London and worked for Chanot. In 1901, he returned to Turin and opened his own shop. He generally followed the patterns of Guarneri and Stradivari. His workmanship is excellent, his varnish good, usually a plum red, sometimes medium yellow. He is considered one of the best modern Italian makers. Prices: $200.00 to $350.00.

ODOARDI, GIUSEPPE — *Ascoli Piceno, Italy. B. 1746, d. about 1786.*

A little known Italian master who possessed great talent. His work shows similarity to Montagnana. He experimented with various woods and some of his instruments, as stated on their labels, are made from the plane tree. He used a yellow brown or dark brown varnish. His instruments are well made and genuine examples are quite rare, selling for as much as $850.00. Reproductions of his label, however, are found in old violins which some dealers so baptized.

The Antonio Odoardi who, according to Joseph's label, must have been his father, made instruments valued today up to $500.00.

> *Label:* Joseph Odoardi fecit in Piceno / prope Asculum An. 17.... / De ligno Platano

OLRY, J. — *Worked in Amiens, France, about 1832-1854.*

A pupil of Georges Chanot. He was quite a skillful maker and his instruments have good tone. He generally followed the flat French patterns, Stradivari model. Varnish usually red brown. Prices: $150.00 to $250.00.

OMOND, JAMES — *Stromness, Scotland. B. 1833, d. in the early 20th century.*

A teacher who, after his retirement, became a violin maker. He learned this trade under Petherik and Hart. He was a skillful workman and made a number of violins and cellos, following the patterns of Stradivari and Guarneri. The wood is handsome, the varnish a light yellow-brown. Prices: $300.00 to $400.00.

ORNATI, GIUSEPPE — *B. 1887 in Albairate, Italy.*

Son of the Italian violin maker Carlo. He served his apprenticeship under Leandro Bisiach, worked under Luigi Montanari, and
in 1902, established his business in Milan. His instruments have received high honors in Italy. They are very well made and he is one
of the finest of the modern school. Varnish golden yellow. Prices:
$300.00 to $450.00.

OTTO — *A large family of violin makers in Germany.*

PACHEREL(E), PIERRE — *B. 1803 in Mirecourt, France, d.
1871 in Nice.*

A friend of J. B. Vuillaume with whom he had worked as a
fellow apprentice in Paris. He established himself in Nice after working for some time in Genoa and in Turin under Pressenda. His instruments are well made and show his good training. He generally followed the Stradivari model. The varnish is very thick and usually of
a medium red color. Also made some very fine cellos. Prices: $200.00
to $400.00.

PADEWET, JOHANN — *Karlsruhe, Germany. B. 1850, d. 1902.*

An apprentice to his father, whose business he took over in 1873.
He made many violins, mostly on the Stradivari patterns, and used
both spirit and oil varnish. His instruments are not very popular and
never brought very good prices, usually about $100.00.

His son, J. Karl Padewet (b. 1887) became his successor in
1907. He received his training in Markneukirchen and worked for
Fiorini in Munich and Winterling in Hamburg. His instruments are
priced up to $125.00.

PAGEOT, LOUIS SIMON — *Worked in Mirecourt, France,
about 1780-1795.*

Originally a violin maker, he turned to making bows exclusively.
More important was his son:

Simon Pajeot, b. 1791, d. 1849. He is supposed to have made
many thousands of bows, including those made for Lafleur. His own
are branded "Pajeot." Some of them are excellent playing sticks.
Prices range from $75.00 to $250.00.

PAILLIOT (PAILLOT) — *Mirecourt, France, early 19th cen-tury.*

A little known maker, although he made some good violins, on a large, flat pattern. His work is handsomely done and the varnish a beautiful, transparent light red. He branded his instruments on the shoulder button and back. Some of his cellos are excellent and are priced as high as $400.00. His violins sell for $150.00 to $300.00.

PALLOTTA, PIETRO — *Worked in Perugia, Italy, about 1788-1821.*

A pupil of Giovanni Rossi, very little known. He made several good violas and cellos. Some of his scrolls show the gouge cuts on both sides of the cheeks. His cellos bring $400.00 to $600.00.

PAMPHILON, EDWARD — *Worked in London, England, be-tween 1680 and 1685.*

Little is known about this early maker. His instruments are small, very highly arched and mostly in the Brescian style, having double purfling. The scrolls are small, the varnish red-brown. Prices: $250.00 to $350.00.

PANDOLFI, ANTONIO — *Worked in Venice, Italy, about 1710-1740.*

The instruments seen are good Venetian work and have very fine tone. He usually followed a broad pattern and used a yellow-brown varnish. Prices as high as $850.00.

PANORMO, VINCENZO — *B. 1734 in Monreale, Sicily, d. 1813 in London, England.*

He worked in Cremona and possibly was a pupil of Bergonzi, because his style of work often resembles Bergonzi's. He stayed in Paris from about 1753 to 1782, then established himself in London. He was a craftsman of exceptional abilities. His selections of wood are excellent and the varnish is either yellow or reddish. The tone is remarkably good and very well liked. The arching often rises grad-ually from the purfling to the center, without the usual fluting. Many of his instruments in earlier years have probably been sold as Stradi-varis and Bergonzis. They are valued from $800.00 to $2000.00.

Label: Vincenzo Trusiano / Panormo fecit / anno 17__ (and others)

PANORMO, JOSEPH — *London, England. B. 1773, d. after 1825.*

Eldest son of Vincenzo. He was not as fine a craftsman as his father but was especially successful with cellos. He followed his father's models which are generally those of Stradivari. He usually used a yellow to golden yellow varnish. His instruments have sold from $650.00 to $1500.00.

PANORMO, GEORGES LOUIS — *London, England. B. about 1774, d. after 1842.*

Second son of Vincenzo. His work is very fine and is classed with the best English makers. He is known as a maker of exceptionally fine guitars and he also made good bows ranging from $35.00 to $100.00. For his violins and cellos, he used the patterns of Stradivari. Orange varnish. Prices from $600.00 to $1200.00.

PANTZER, JOHANN KARL — *Worked in Klingenthal, Germany, about 1737-1741.*

He followed the Saxon style and was known as one of the better makers of Klingenthal. His varnish is good, usually a brown to reddish brown. Prices: $150.00 to $200.00.

PAQUOTTE, JEAN BAPTISTE — *Paris, France. B. 1827, d. 1900.*

He started as a bow maker in Mirecourt. About 1741, he went to Paris as a pupil to his uncle, Sébastien Paquotte. He later worked for Lafleur, and in 1863, took over his uncle's shop. He retired from business in 1888 and left it to his sons, Henri Félix and Placide. His bows are sold from $35.00 to $100.00.

PARKER, DANIEL — *Worked in London, England, about 1700-1740.*

An excellent maker, whose instruments are very rare in this country. His earlier violins are built on Stainer and Amati models, those dated after 1710 are copied after Stradivari. The varnish is of finest quality, the color a beautiful golden brown to orange red. Value up to $1000.00.

PASTA — *A family of violin makers in Milan and Brescia, Italy.*

Bartolomeo (Milan, about 1680-90) and Gaetano (Brescia, about 1710-60) state in their labels that they were pupils of the Amatis, and there is also in their work a slight resemblance to J. B.

Rogeri. A viola seen by Antonio Pasta, with a body length of 16¼",
sold for $1500.00.

PAULI, JOSEPH — *B. 1770, d. 1846. Worked in Linz, Austria.*
The most important of this family of violin makers originating
from Tachau, Bohemia. He followed the Viennese school and copied
Stainer and Amati patterns. He used fine selections of wood and generally a red-brown varnish. Prices: $100.00 to $400.00.

Instruments by the lesser known Johann Gottfried Pauli (1707-
1771) sell for about $100.00.

PAULUS — *A family of violin makers from Markneukirchen,
Germany, 19th century.*
There were Adolf, Reinhold, August, Robert, Albin Ludwig,
Richard and Johann Paul. Their instruments are of the ordinary
type, fairly well made but not exceptional. Prices: $75.00 to $125.00.

PAZZINI, GIOVANNI GAETANO — *Worked in Florence, Italy,
about 1630-1666.*
According to his label, he was a pupil of Maggini. Although he
does not rank with other important makers of his time, his instruments are well made, usually built on a high model, with very good
selections of wood and dark brown varnish. Prices: $600.00 to
$800.00.

PECCATTE (PECCATE), DOMINIQUE — *Paris, France. B.
1810 in Mirecourt, d. 1874.*
A bow maker of great renown. He worked for Vuillaume between 1826 and 1837. He then opened his own shop where François
Lupot had lived. He returned to Mirecourt in 1847. His sticks are
selected with greatest care, his work is superb and probably the equal
of Tourte. Some, but not all of his bows are branded. They have been
sold from $100.00 to $800.00, some exceptional collector's pieces at
much higher prices.

PECCATTE, FRANÇOIS — *B. 1820 in Mirecourt, France, d.
1855 in Paris.*
Younger brother of Dominique, a good bow maker. For three
years he worked for J. B. Vuillaume in Paris, later, on his own.
Very few of his bows have been seen in this country.

PECCATTE, CHARLES — *B. 1850 in Mirecourt, d. about 1930.*

Son of François. Learned his trade in the shop of J. B. Vuillaume, where he was instructed by F. N. Voirin. Later he worked for Lenoble and, about 1870, went into business for himself. He was a fine bow maker, but his work is not as much in demand as that of Dominique. He used an exceptionally fine selection of pernambuco wood and his bows have sold from $75.00 to $350.00, outstanding pieces higher.

PEDRINELLI, ANTONIO — *Crespano, Italy. B. 1781, d. 1854.*

A very good maker who followed the old masters, such as Stradivari, Amati, and others. His selections of wood are of the best. His varnish is usually orange or plum-red. His instruments are well liked and command good prices, between $700.00 and $1000.00; some of his cellos have sold for as much as $1200.00. Many violins seen with his label are not genuine.

> *Label:* Antonio Pedrinelli / Fe in Crespano 18.... (and others)

PELLIZON — *A family of violin makers in Gorizia, Italy, 19th century.*

To it belonged Antonio and his four sons: Giuseppe, Carlo, Antonio and Filippo. Their instruments are fair, generally following the Amati school. Prices: $100.00 to $250.00.

E. PERRIN FILS — *A violin house in Mirecourt, France, about 1840.*

Commercial makers of good quality instruments (violins, usually large pattern). Orange varnish. Prices: $50.00 to $150.00.

PERRY, THOMAS — *Worked in Dublin, Ireland, about 1767-1830.*

He made very many instruments and probably was the best Irish maker. He worked on his own patterns, used fair selections of wood and usually a red-brown or orange-yellow varnish. He was associated with Wm. Wilkinson, his son-in-law, and some of his labels read Thomas Perry & Wm. Wilkinson. Prices: $150.00 to $350.00.

PFRETZSCHNER — *A large family of violin makers in Markneukirchen, Germany.*

Johann Gottlob, b. 1753, d. 1823, was probably the best maker of this family. He copied the Stradivari model, though his pattern is generally longer and narrower. The workmanship is good, the varnish usually yellow-brown. Prices: $100.00 to $150.00.

Hermann Richard, b. 1857, was a good bow maker. He worked for J. B. Vuillaume in Paris and, about 1880, started business for himself. He made numerous bows, copying such makers as Vuillaume, Tourte and Voirin. The sticks are stamped "H. R. Pfretzschner." Prices: $20.00 to $50.00, exhibition pieces higher.

There were also Carl Friedrich, Christian Gottfried, Carl Gottlob and Richard.

PIEGENDORFER, GEORG — *Augsburg, Germany. B. 1849, d. 1906.*

One of the best modern Bavarian makers of his time. He followed the Stradivarius and Guarnerius patterns, used good seasoned wood and generally a yellow varnish. Prices: $150.00 to $200.00.

PIERONI, LUIGI — *Worked in Gubbio, Italy, about 1833-47.*

His work is poor and the varnish not very good. He probably did not make many instruments. Some seen have been valued as high as $200.00.

PIERRAY, CLAUDE — *Worked in Paris, France, about 1698-1726.*

He is probably the best maker of the early Parisian school. Like all the earlier French makers, he followed the Italian style. His selections of wood are excellent, but not all of his instruments show his best capabilities. He generally used a yellow to yellow brown varnish. Some of his cellos are exceptionally fine and have been priced as high as $1200.00, while his violins range from $250.00 to $600.00.

> *Label:* Claude Pierray / proche la Comédie / à Paris 17.... (and others)

PILLEMENT, F. — *Lived in Paris, France, about 1774-1831.*

Most likely he learned his trade in Mirecourt. His instruments are not of one standard quality; some are cheaply made and others quite good. They are generally covered with a red brown or dark brown varnish. Branded "Pillement à Paris." Prices: $150.00 to $200.00.

PIQUE, FRANÇOIS LOUIS — *Paris, France. B. 1758, d. 1822.*

He seems to have stayed in Paris all his life. He was an excellent maker. His work is remarkably well done and the wood always of the finest quality. He generally followed the Stradivari patterns. His oil varnish, very often applied too thick, is a beautiful red or red brown. It is said that Lupot, his pupil, made violins which Pique varnished and sold under his (Pique's) name. Prices range from $650.00 to $1000.00; some masterpieces have sold up to $1600.00.

> *Label:* Pique, rue de Grenelle / St. Honoré, au coin de celle / des 2 Ecus; à Paris, 18.... (also manuscript labels)

PIROT, CLAUDE — *Worked in Paris, France, between 1800 and 1833.*

His work is fair but not outstanding. He used a flat model and generally a thick, dull red varnish. Prices: $100.00 to $200.00.

PIZZURNUS, DAVID — *Worked in Genoa, Italy, about 1760-1780.*

A little known maker. He followed a flat model and used good selections of wood. The varnish is reddish yellow or yellow-brown. This is another maker whose name has been falsely used and is found in many instruments not of his make. Originals have sold from $400.00 to $750.00.

PLACHT — *An old family of violin makers in Schönbach, Czechoslovakia.*

Ferdinand, Franz, Johann Georg and Martin are some of its more important members. They all worked in about the same style. The arching is generally rather high. The color is varied. Their instruments are often seen and sell from $75.00 to $200.00.

PLATNER, MICHAEL — *Worked in Rome, Italy, about 1735-1750.*

He probably learned his trade in the same shop as David Tecchler as their work is quite similar. Some of his instruments are built on a Guarneri pattern and they are generally highly arched. The selections of wood are excellent; the varnish is good and usually golden yellow or yellow-brown. Prices: $400.00 to $1000.00.

> *Label:* Michael Platner fecit / Romae Anno 17....

POGGI, ANSALDO — *B. 1893 near Bologna, Italy.*

He was a violinist and became so interested in the art of violin making that he went to G. Fiorini and served as an apprentice. His instruments have won prizes. He usually followed the Stradivari and

Guarnri models and used a dull yellow varnish. Prices: $200.00 to $400.00.

> *Label:* Ansaldo Poggi / allievo di G. Fiorini / Fece in Bologna anno 19....

PÖHLAND — *A family of violin makers in Klingenthal, Germany, from the 18th century on.*

They are of little importance today. Their measurements are often poor. Prices range from $50.00 to $100.00.

POIRSON, JUSTIN — *B. 1851 in Mirecourt, France, d. 1925.*

A good bow maker who learned his trade under Nicolas Maire of Paris. He also worked for J. B. Vuillaume, and Gand & Bernardel. About 1879, he established himself in Paris. His bows are well made but do not compare with many of the better French makers. They are branded "Poirson à Paris." Prices: $35.00 to $75.00.

POLLASTRI, AUGUSTO — *Bologna, Italy.*

A modern maker, pupil of Raffael Fiorini. He is a very skillful artist and generally follows the Stradivari patterns. The varnish is usually a dark red. His instruments are well liked and sell up to $400.00.

POLLASTRI, GAETANO — *B. 1886 in Bologna, Italy.*

Pupil and brother of Augusto and following his brother's models. Oil varnish, generally red. Good workmanship. Prices $250.00 to $500.00.

POLLER, MICHAEL — *See Boller.*

POSCH (BOSCH) ANTONIO — *Vienna, Austria. B. 1677, d. 1742.*

He was comparatively well known, worked usually on high arched patterns and often treated his instruments with acid before varnishing. His son, Anton Stephan (1701-49), had a similar style of work and his instruments are of about the same quality. Prices: $200.00 to $400.00.

POSTACCHINI, ANDREA — *Fermo, Italy, late 18th and early 19th centuries.*

He generally used a flat model and copied the old Italian masters. His selections of wood are excellent and his workmanship is superb. The varnish is usually reddish yellow or brown.

He had a son, Andrea II, who worked in Fermo up to about 1857. Their style of work is much alike. It is a name which has often been abused to denominate violins of unknown origin. The originals are priced from $450.00 to $1000.00, some exceptionally fine specimens, especially cellos, as high as $2000.00.

Label: Andreas Postacchini Firmanus fecit / sub titulo S. Raphaelis Archang. 18— (and others)

POSTIGLIONE, VINCENZO — *Naples, Italy. B. 1835, d. about 1915.*

At the age of twelve he became an apprentice to Vincenzo Jorio. He later started his own shop and was one of the better modern makers of Naples. He copied the old masters, mostly Stradivari and Guarneri. His varnish is usually brown, sometimes red-brown. Prices: $250.00 to $500.00 Many instruments bearing his label are not genuine.

PRAGER, GUSTAV — *Markneukirchen, Germany. B. 1866.*

A maker of violins and bows. There are still Pragers working in Markneukirchen today who make excellent bows, using a very light pernambuco wood of a yellowish color. They sell for $15.00 to $50.00.

PRESSENDA, JOANNES FRANCISCUS — *B. 1777, d. 1854.*

A pupil of Lorenzo Storioni in Cremona. He was established in Alba, in Carmagnola and later, about 1820, in Turin, Italy. He generally followed the Stradivari models. His work is exceptionally fine in every respect, the wood carefully selected and very beautiful. The tone is excellent. The color of his varnish is generally wine red. His work is absolutely accurate as to dimensions. Many instruments bearing his name are not genuine. Prices range from $1000.00 to $3000.00; some of the choicest examples of his violins and cellos have sold up to $3500.00.

Label: Joannes Franciscus Pressenda, q. Raphael / fecit Taurini anno Domini 18....

PRESTON — *London, England, 1824.*

This maker's work is fair. Some of his cellos are excellent. He usually used a red-brown varnish. Prices up to $400.00.

PRÉVÔT, P. CHARLES — *Worked in Paris, France, about 1775-1788.*

Judging from his work, he was probably schooled in Mirecourt. He used a flat model in the usual French style. The selections of wood are fair, the workmanship very fine. His varnish is yellow-brown or red-brown. Prices: $200.00 to $300.00.

RAILICH, GIOVANNI — *Worked in Padua, Italy, about 1672-1678.*

Little is known of this maker except that he was the teacher of Matthias Klotz. His instruments are well made, the selections of wood fine. Prices: $300.00 to $500.00.

RAMBAUX, CLAUDE VICTOR — *Paris, France. B. 1806, d. 1871.*

He learned his trade in Mirecourt under L. Moitessier, later worked for Gand, Sr., in Paris. About 1838, he opened his own shop, in which he worked until 1857. He was known for his artistic repairing but did not make many new instruments. They are not exceptionally good and do not command big prices. $100.00 to $500.00.

RAUCH, SEBASTIAN — *Worked in Komothau, later in Leitmeritz, Bohemia. B. 1711, d. 1801.*

He used a high-arched model on the style of Stainer. His work is very well done, the selections of wood are good. His instruments are covered with a brown spirit varnish, generally quite dark, others yellow-brown. Prices: $200.00 to $300.00.

There was also a Sebastian Rauch in Prague and another in Breslau.

RAUCH, JOSEPH — *Prague, Czechoslovakia. B. 1701, d. after 1760.*

The pattern he used is similar to that of Stainer. His varnish is dark brown but was probably lighter in earlier years. He did fine and accurate work. Prices: $250.00 to $500.00.

RAUCH, THOMAS — *Prague, Czechoslovakia. B. 1702, d. after 1746.*

Brother of Joseph. His work, very similar to Joseph's, is almost as fine. The wood is well selected, the varnish dark brown. The tone is of exceptional quality. Prices: $150.00 to $350.00.

REICHEL — *A large family of violin makers in Markneu-*
kirchen, Germany, from the 17th century on.

The house, now working on a commercial basis, is still in existence. Among the more important members were: Christian
(worked 1677-97), Johann Caspar (1693-1755), Christian Friedrich
(1729-1814), Johann Gottfried (worked about 1735-1770), Johann
Friedrich (1746-1826) and Johann Adam (1782-1836). They all
worked on about the same style. The best was probably Johann
Adam, who branded his instruments "I.A.R." High arching. Prices:
$100.00 to $150.00.

REITER, JOHANN BAPTIST — *Mittenwald, Germany. B. 1834,*
d. 1899.

A pupil of Jais and later of Jean Vauchel of Würzburg. He
bought the latter's tools and supplies and returned to Mittenwald in
1857. He taught violin making there.

His son, Johann, b. 1879, succeeded his father and became a
very fine maker. Their instruments sell from $75.00 to $150.00.

REMY, MATHURIN FRANÇOIS — *Worked in Paris, France,*
about 1760-1800.

A member of a well-known French family of violin makers. For
his better instruments he used finely selected wood and yellow or red
varnish. The arching is medium. The less expensive instruments range
from $150.00 to $350.00; fine copies as high as $600.00.

> Label: Remy, / Luthier & Facteur de Harpe / A Paris.

His son, Jean Mathurin, b. 1770, d. 1854, was probably as fine
a maker as his father. He again had two sons, Hippolyte and Jules,
who carried on the business after his death.

RENAUDIN, LEOPOLD — *Ghent and Paris. B. 1749 in Mire-*
court, France, died a victim to the French Revolution
in 1795.

He was a fair maker, worked on the higher arched models, but
his instruments are not well liked, although they have sold up to
$350.00.

RIECHERS, AUGUST — *Hannover and Berlin, Germany, B.*
1836, d. 1893.

Learned his trade under Carl Friedrich Ficker in Markneukirchen, also worked for L. Bausch. In 1862 he opened a large

shop in Hannover, which was later transferred to Berlin. He was an important dealer employing many workmen and was well known for his repairing as well as for his new instruments. They are quite well made but more on the commercial style. He usually followed the Stradivari pattern. Prices: $150.00 to $350.00.

RIEF, ANTON — *Vils, Tyrol. B. 1694, d. 1766.*

His work is excellent, the selections of wood fine and the varnish usually brown. Prices: $250.00 to $350.00.

Of his many descendants should be mentioned: Matthäus (1728-1794), Dominicus (1759-1814) and Johann Georg (1765-1848). Dominicus was a fine workman. The wood he selected is of good quality and the varnish usually yellow-brown. His instruments are priced from $150.00 to $200.00.

RIEGER, JOHANN — *Mittenwald, Germany. B. about 1735, d. 1768.*

His instruments are fairly well made, but only a few have been seen. It is the usual Mittenwald work. Some fine copies have sold from $200.00 to $300.00.

RIEGER, GEORG — *Worked in Mittenwald, Germany, about 1760-1791.*

His style of work is different from that usually adopted in Mittenwald. The selections of wood are good, the workmanship is excellent, the varnish generally a dull yellow or dark brown. Prices: $200.00 to $300.00; fine examples as high as $400.00.

Among the later makers of this family are Anton and Joseph Rieger, who are quite well known.

RINALDI, GIOFFREDO BENEDETTO — *Lived in Turin, Italy, about 1850, d. 1888.*

A pupil of Pressenda, a very skillful worker, especially on cellos. Superb examples of his cellos have sold for as much as $2500.00.

RIVOLTA, GIACOMO — *Worked in Milan, Italy, in the early 19th century.*

He usually used a yellow-brown or light red-brown varnish. Very few of his violins have been seen, though many instruments have been sold under his name which are not genuine. His cellos are exceptionally fine and are well liked. The workmanship is of the finest. Violins, $500.00 to $1000.00; superb copies of his cellos up to $1800.00.

> *Label:* Giacomo Rivolta / Nella Contrada di *Sta* Margherita / all'Insegna del *Sto* Re Davide / Milano 18....

ROCCA, GIUSEPPE ANTONIO — *B. 1807 in Alba, Italy, d. about 1868.*

He studied violin making under Pressenda in Turin and his work shows many of his master's characteristics. He left Turin only toward the end of his life and died in Genoa. His instruments are exceedingly well made, though not as fine as his master's. His varnish is usually orange-red, but some seen are of a light yellow-brown color. He selected his woods with great care, usually using one piece backs. He copied the old masters with great accuracy, mostly Stainer and Guarneri. He often changed the wording of his label and also branded his instruments with his initials "G. R.". Prices range from $850.00 to $1800.00; some exceptionally fine cellos have sold as high as $3500.00.

> *Label:* Joseph Antonius Rocca / fecit Taurini / anno Domini 18....
> (and others)

ROCCA, ENRICO — *Genoa, Italy.*

Son and successor of Joseph. He made fine instruments in his father's style which, however, are not nearly as valuable. He preferred one piece backs and generally used a light brown varnish. His instruments are priced from $400.00 to $650.00. He also made some good violas which have sold up to $450.00.

RODIANI, GIOVITA — *Brescia and Bologna, Italy. B. about 1545, d. about 1625.*

He possibly worked in the shop of Gasparo da Salo of Brescia, as his work shows much of this master's style. The varnish is the typical yellow-brown of that school. His instruments are very rare and a few are found in museums. They command a good price and have sold for as much as $1000.00.

> *Label:* Giovita Rodiani. In Brescia

ROGERI, GIOVANNI BATTISTA — *Brescia, Italy. B. about 1650, latest date recorded 1730.*

The Rogeri family should be clearly distinguished from the Ruggeri family of Cremona. Rogeri was born in Bologna and this is indicated on his label by the abbreviation "Bon." He worked as a pupil under Nicola Amati in Cremona simultaneously with Stradivari. His work shows the characteristics of his master, especially his "grand pattern." In 1670 he left Cremona and settled in Brescia. His varnish is generally a beautiful golden orange-red and he used only the finest selections of wood. He ranks very high among the old Cremonese makers and too much cannot be said of his excellent craftsmanship. His violins have sold from $1000.00 to $6000.00, his cellos up to $8000.00. He also made some basses which are now very rare and have brought as much as $1000.00.

Label: Io: Bapt. Rogerius Bon: Nicolai Amati de Cremona alumnus Brixiae fecit Anno Domini 17....

ROGERI, PIETRO GIACOMO — *Brescia, Italy. B. about 1680, d. after 1730.*

Son of Giovanni Battista, pupil of Nicola Amati. He followed his father's style but never equalled him in workmanship. His models are narrower. The selections of wood are fine, the varnish rich orange-yellow tinted with red. He also made violas and cellos. Prices: $1500.00 to $3000.00.

Label: Pietro Giacomo Rogerius filius Jo. Bapt. Brixiae 17....

ROMBOUTS, PIETER — *Amsterdam, Holland. B. 1677, d. about 1740.*

A very able maker, schooled under Hendrick Jacobs. His patterns are very similar to Nicola Amati and Nicolo Gagliano. The workmanship is excellent, the varnish thick and generally a golden red. He used whalebone purfling. He made violas and cellos as well as violins. Prices: up to $1000.00.

Label: Pieter Rombouts / Amsterdam 17....

RONCHETTI, DOMENICO — *Worked in Italy about 1760-1770.*

A little known maker who made few instruments. His violas are well liked, however, and sell for as much as $500.00.

RÖSCHER, CHRISTIAN HEINRICH WILHELM — *Lived in Bremen, Germany, about 1865, d. about 1880.*

His work is fairly good, following the Saxon school. The varnish is usually brown on a yellow ground. Prices: $150.00 to $250.00.

ROSSI, ENRICO — *Pavia, Italy. B. 1848, d. after 1920.*

He followed the model of the old masters. His workmanship is very good, the selections of wood are excellent. Varnish golden red. His instruments, which include violas, have sold from $250.00 to $500.00.

ROTH — *A family of violin makers in Markneukirchen, Germany, still in existence.*

They made hundreds of instruments, in many different qualities, selling from $50.00 to $350.00 They are known for their reproductions of Guarneri and Stradivari. Ernst Heinrich Roth, b. 1877, is now the most important. The others worked more or less commercially.

RUGGERI, FRANCISCUS — *B. 1620 in Cremona, Italy, where he lived until about 1694.*

The oldest and most important member of this famous family. He was Nicolò Amati's first pupil, yet his work differs from that of his master in many points. The arching is higher, the soundholes shorter and more open and his pattern broader. His varnish is usually golden orange, sometimes orange-red. He generally selected beautifully flamed maple. He also made violas and cellos. The tone is large and of excellent quality and his instruments rank very high. They are considered on the par with Rogeri, some of them even superior. Prices: $3500.00 to $8500.00.

Label: Francesco Ruggieri detto / il per Cremona 16....

RUGGERI, GIACINTO GIOVANNI BATTISTA — *Worked in Cremona about 1665-1696.*

Son of Francesco from whom he learned his trade. He used a broad model and followed his father's patterns. Varnish mostly dark brown. His instruments have excellent tone quality, though the workmanship is not equal to Francesco's. His violins have sold from $2000.00 to $3000.00; his cellos up to $5000.00.

RUGGERI, VINCENZO — *Worked in Cremona about 1690-1735.*

Son and pupil of Francesco. However, his work does not equal his father's. He made some fine violins, but chiefly cellos which are of superb quality. The selections of wood are the best. The varnish is usually yellow-brown. Prices: $2500.00 to $5000.00.

RUPRECHT, WILHELM — *Lived in Vienna, Austria, in 1839, d. 1862.*

A very skillful workman. He generally followed the Guarneri del Gesu and Brescian models. Many instruments have double purfling and some are ornamented on the back with a five pointed star, inlaid. Prices: $400.00 to $500.00.

SACQUIN — *Established in Paris about 1830, d. after 1860.*

Supposed to have been a pupil of Aldric. His instruments are of good quality, covered with a red or yellow varnish, and branded inside. He generally worked after the style of Stradivari. Prices range from $150.00 to $400.00.

SAINT PAUL, PIERRE — *Worked in Paris, France, about 1740-1757.*

His instruments, built on a small pattern, have quite good tone, although his work is rough. The varnish is a dull yellow color. Prices: $150.00 to $250.00.

SALO, GASPARO DA — *See Bertolotti.*

SAJOT — *Worked in Paris about 1720-1735.*

Little-known. Some of his instruments seen here are built on a large pattern, with dark yellow varnish. Prices: $100.00 to $200.00.

SALOMON, JEAN BAPTISTE — *Started his career in Paris, France, about 1740, d. after 1772.*

The business was carried on after his death by his widow until about 1789. He followed the style of Chappuy and specially Guersan as to varnish, which, in his finer instruments, is a beautiful golden yellow. His work is inconsistent and it is valued accordingly. Prices are between $250.00 and $450.00; the author has seen two fine examples which sold for $600.00. He also made violas and cellos.

> *Label:* Salomon Luthier à St. Cécille / Place de l'école à Paris 17.... (script)

SALZARD — *Mirecourt, France.*

François, b. 1808, d. 1874, and Dominique, about same period, were the more important representatives of this violin making family. They may have worked temporarily in Paris but made their home in Mirecourt. Flat broad pattern, dark cherry-red varnish. Prices: $100.00 to $250.00.

SANTAGIULIANA, GAETANO — *Worked in Vicenza, Italy, early 18th century.*

Little is known of this maker, but his work is exceptionally well done. Dark red and golden orange varnish. Medium arching. Prices: $650.00 to $900.00.

SANTAGIULIANA, GIACINTO — *Worked between 1770 and 1830 in Vicenza, and temporarily in Venice, Italy.*

He was a fine craftsman and followed the patterns of Amati, using fine selections of wood and a golden yellow varnish. Prices: $600.00 to $900.00.

Label: Jazintus Santagiuliana fecit / Vicetiae 18....

SANTUCCI, SEBASTIAN — *B. 1873 in Corsica, established in St. Raphael.*

His work is fair but not exceptional. He followed the Amati and Stradivari models. The varnish is usually yellow-brown. Prices: $150.00 to $250.00.

SARTORY, EUGENE — *B. 1871 in Mirecourt, France.*

Served his apprenticeship as a bow maker under Charles Peccatte in Paris, later worked for Alfred Lamy. In 1889, he established himself in Paris and is still carrying on the business there. He made only bows of the finest quality and his work shows the excellent training he enjoyed. There are many bows on the market stamped Sartory that are not genuine and do not come up to the standards of this fine artist. The originals sell from $50.00 to $125.00, some exceptional pieces even higher. He sent bows to the 1939 World's Fair in New York, which formed a remarkable and interesting display.

SAWICKI, CARL NIKOLAUS — *Vienna, Austria. B. 1792, d. 1850.*

One of the better Viennese makers who very quickly became known. He generally worked on the Stradivari patterns, but also on that of Guarnerius del Gesu. His wood is of finest quality, his varnish usually a yellowish brown, sometimes reddish yellow. His instruments have a large, powerful tone. The author has seen some very fine copies in this country and cannot praise his work too highly. Prices: $400.00 to $800.00.

SCARAMPELLA, PAOLO — *B. 1803 in Brescia, Italy, d. 1870.*
Originally a carpenter, he changed his trade to violin making and also made guitars and mandolins. His instruments are very well made. Prices: $450.00 to $600.00.

SCARAMPELLA, GIUSEPPE — *Son of Paolo, b. about 1838, d. after 1885.*
He studied under Nicolo Bianchi of Genoa, later went to Paris. In 1866, he returned to Italy and worked for Luigi Castellani in Florence. He established himself in that town and became violin maker to the Conservatory of Music. So far, his work has been mentioned as fair but of no great value. However, in America, his instruments are well liked and in demand. His selections of wood are good; the varnish is generally red with a slight tint of brown. Prices: $250.00 to $700.00.

SCARAMPELLA, STEFANO — *Mantua, Italy. B. 1843 in Brescia.*
Brother and pupil of Giuseppe, considered the better maker of the family. He usually followed a model with rather high, well rounded arching, but also copied the famous old makers. The soundholes are very similar to Stradivari's. The scrolls are wide and large. The color of his varnish is deep orange or red orange-brown. Prices: $300.00 to $600.00, some exceptional examples $750.00.

SCHALLER — *A large family of violin makers, originating from Schönbach and Markneukirchen, Germany.*
To it belong: Oswald, Reinhold, Ignaz, Johann, Joseph, Christian, Friedrich Wilhelm and others. Most of them worked for dealers and for the commercial trade.

Oswald Schaller, b. 1857 in Markneukirchen, established his business in Frankfurt-on-Oder in 1881. He followed the models of the old Italian school. His workmanship is good but of the ordinary Saxon type, the wood of fair quality, the varnish usually reddish yellow. He also applied some sort of a coating inside which was supposed to give the instrument more tone. Prices: $100.00 to $200.00.

Reinhold Schaller, brother of Oswald, b. 1859, had his own business in Löbtau in 1898. His models are those of Stradivari, Amati and Stainer. He generally used a yellow-brown spirit varnish.

SCHÄNDL, ANTON — *Worked in Mittenwald, Germany, about 1750-1800.*

The most prominent member of a very old family of violin makers in that town, son of Michael. His instruments are well made, the selections of wood excellent. He generally followed the Stainer model but stayed within the tradition of his family. His violins and cellos are priced at $150.00 to $400.00.

SCHEVERLE, JOHANN — *Worked in Prague, Czechoslovakia, about 1730-1770.*

Very little is known of this maker, but a few good instruments have been seen which sold as high as $250.00.

SCHLOSSER — *An old family of violin makers native of Klingenthal, Germany.*

To them may be attributed instruments branded *I*G*S*. They are generally varnished in a dull yellow-brown color. The most important maker of the family was Johann Christian, who worked about 1738-1773. He followed the type of Pfretzschner. His instruments are nicely made and sell from $75.00 to $150.00.

SCHMIDT — *A family of violin makers in Markneukirchen, Germany.*

Ernst Reinhold, b. 1857, son of Ernst Cornelius, was the founder of the firm, E. R. Schmidt & Co. and its president. They had many employees and their commercial products were sold all over the world. Their line comprises a large variety of models and styles in different prices, ranging from $25.00 to $125.00.

SCHNEIDER — *An old family of violin makers of Klingenthal, Germany.*

Its best representative is Christoph Carl. He made a number of cheap instruments in the usual Klingenthal style, covered with a rather poor varnish. However, there are also finer examples and the author has seen some that sold up to $250.00 and others as low as $75.00.

SCHÖNFELDER — *A large family of violin makers in Markneukirchen, Germany.*

Its most important members are Johann Adam, (1707-1763) and Johann Christian (1775-1821). Their instruments are well made, with good selections of wood, following the Tyrolean school. The varnish is usually yellow-brown or red-brown. Prices: $125.00 to $350.00.

SCHONGER, FRANZ — *Erfurt, Germany, late 18th century.*

He followed the Italian models, type of Maggini, with high arching. His work is well done. He usually used a yellow-brown varnish. At his death in 1776 his son, Carl, took over the shop. Prices: $100.00 to $200.00.

SCHORN, JOHANN PAUL — *Worked in Innsbruck, Austria, about 1680-1719.*

He followed the Tyrolean school and used medium high arched models. His varnish is very good and usually reddish brown. Prices: $150.00 to $225.00.

SCHUSTER — *A very large family of violin and bow makers in Markneukirchen and Schönbach, Germany.*

Georg I(1685-1759) and his son Georg II (1718-1807); Johann Christian (1753-1820); Joseph (Schönbach, 1766, 1790); Joseph Anton (Schönbach, about 1780); Carl Friedrich (1788-1864 and his son Carl August (1818-51); Matthias (about 1820); Hermann (b. 1830, d. about 1890) and his younger brother Heinrich Moritz; Joseph Ignaz, bow maker, b. 1865; Kurt, b. 1878, worked in Leipzig; Adolph Kurt, b. 1890, a very skillful bow maker, pupil of W. A. Pfretzschner and August Rau. His bows are stamped with his name and sell from $15.00 to $60.00.

Johann Christian and Kurt were the best makers of the family. Kurt was a pupil of Gläsel and of August Fiorini in Munich. He worked in various German towns and also travelled in Holland, England and France. He finally established himself in Leipzig about 1908. His work is excellent, the varnish usually a golden yellow (oil). Prices: $100.00 to $250.00.

SCHWEITZER, JOHANN BAPTIST — *Budapest, Hungary. B. about 1790, d. 1865.*

A pupil of Franciscus Geissenhof, established himself in 1825. He was a great copyist of the Italian masters and did very fine work, especially after the style of Stradivari and Amati. He also made many cellos which are excellent and have sold from $400.00 to $1000.00. Wood and workmanship are beautiful, the varnish is usually yellow-brown. He must have tried out different compositions for his varnish, as the quality is sometimes rather poor. Hundreds of instruments are found today bearing his label which are nothing more than cheap German commercial products of very little value. Original violins sell from $300.00 to $500.00.

Label: Joh. Bapt. Schweitzer fecit ad Formam / Antonii Stradivarii
Pestini 18....

SEIDEL — A family of violin makers of Klingenthal and Mark-neukirchen, Germany, best represented by Christian Wilhelm, b. 1815, d. after 1889.

He made many copies of German and Italian models which are of good quality and good tone. They are usually varnished in a yellow or yellow-brown color and are branded *Seidel*. Prices: $75.00 to $125.00.

SERAPHIN, SANCTUS (SANTO SERAFIN) — B. 1699 in Udine, Italy, went to Venice in 1717 and died there about 1748.

According to his label, he was a pupil of Nicola Amati. His model is often the "grand pattern" of Amati and not infrequently shows influences of Francesco Ruggeri. He was undoubtedly one of the very finest Venetian makers. His workmanship is perfect and ranks with the great old masters. His soundholes are cut after the Amati pattern, the archings medium high. The selections of wood are superb. The varnish used is usually reddish or yellow-brown and of an excellent quality. His instruments are much sought among artists. He made cellos with the same great skill. Prices range from $2500.00 to $5000.00, some masterpieces as high as $8000.00.

Label: Sanctus Seraphin. Utinensis / Fecit Venetijs anno 17....
(and others)

SGARABOTTO, GAETANO — B. 1878 in Vicenza, Italy.

He was a self-made maker, started his career in Milan, then established himself in Vicenza. He followed the Amati and Stradivari patterns, and other Italian models. The color of his varnish is usually yellow to golden orange. He operated a branch shop in Brescia. Prices: $250.00 to $350.00.

SGARBI, ANTONIO — B. 1866 in Finale Emilia, Italy, son of the violin maker Giuseppe Sgarbi (1818-1905).

In 1890, he took over his father's business in Rome and, in

1905, established himself in Palermo as a violin maker to the Conservatory "Vincenzo Bellini." An excellent craftsman, following the old Italian models, mostly Stradivari. His instruments have received many medals on exhibitions. The varnish is usually a golden yellow brown. Prices: $250.00 to $400.00.

SILVESTRE, PIERRE — *Lyon, France. B. 1801, d. 1859.*

Pupil of Blaise in Mirecourt. He also studied under Lupot and Gand Sr. and in 1829, he established himself in Lyon, France. His brother, Hippolyte, was taken into the business about 1831 and stayed with him until 1848 when he retired. Pierre continued alone until his death. His work is perfect. He followed the Stradivari pattern but gave his instruments a flatter arching. His varnish is varied — a golden yellow to a rich, rose red. He made many violins, also cellos. They are considered exceptional values and sell from $400.00 to $800.00.

SILVESTRE & MAUCOTEL.

This firm was first organized by a nephew of Pierre, whose original name was Hippolyte Chrétien, but who adopted the name of H. C. Silvestre. He began his apprenticeship in Mirecourt in 1845, and later, went to Lyon to complete it under his two uncles, Pierre and Hippolyte. With one of their best workmen, Ernest Maucotel, he formed the company which is now known as Maucotel & Deschamp, in Paris. They produced instruments commercially and brought out a variety of models. Prices today range from $50.00 to $150.00.

SIMON, P. — *B. 1808 in Mirecourt, France, d. 1882 in Paris.*

Learned his trade in Mirecourt, then worked for Peccatte in Paris, later for J. B. Vuillaume. In 1846, he established his own business and bought out the shop of his former master, Peccatte. From 1848 to 1851, he had J. Henry as his partner, after which he worked alone until his death. He was an excellent bow maker, only used the finest materials and branded his sticks "Simon, Paris." Prices: $75.00 to $200.00.

SIMOUTRE, NICOLAS — *B. 1788, d. 1870, worked in Mirecourt and Metz.*

A pupil of Nicolas Lupot in Paris. About 1817, he established his own business. He copied Guarneri, Stradivari and other old Italian masters. For his cellos he used the larger patterns. His work and wood selections are quite good. He had a son, Nicolas Eugène, who was less important. Prices: $150.00 to $350.00.

SITT, ANTON — *A Hungarian maker. B. 1819, d. 1878.*

He learned his trade under the guidance of J. B. Schweitzer of Budapest. After 1843 he went to Vienna and, in 1848, to Prague. He followed the Stradivari, Guarneri and Amati models. Not very many of his instruments are seen in this country. Prices: $200.00 to $350.00.

SKOMAL, NIKOLAUS GEORG — *Worked in Graz, Austria, about 1790-1820.*

He very likely learned his trade in Prague, for his instruments show the style of this school. He followed a flat model and used a yellow-brown to dark red-brown varnish. The wood selected is of fine quality and his instruments possess good tone. Prices: $200.00 to $500.00.

SMITH, THOMAS — *Worked in London, England, about 1750-1799.*

Pupil of Peter Wamsley. He made only few violins but many cellos. He followed the style of his master and also copied Italian models. The workmanship is very good, the varnish a yellowish brown. His cellos have sold from $250.00 to $350.00.

SOCQUET, LOUIS — *Paris, France. About 1750.*

A fair maker, probably trained in Mirecourt. His models are those of the old Parisian school; the varnish is usually a greyish yellow color. He also made cellos. Prices: $150.00 to $200.00.

> *Label:* Socquet / Au Génie de l'Harmonie / Place du Vieux Louvre, à Paris 17....

SOFFRITTI, ETTORE — *B. 1877 in Ferrara, Italy.*

Learned his trade in the shop of his father, Luigi, whose business he is still carrying on. He follows the models of the Cremonese school. His workmanship is good, the color of his varnish golden yellow to golden red. Prices: $150.00 to $250.00.

SOLIANI, ANGELO — *Modena, Italy. B. 1752, d. after 1810.*

His models resemble very much Guadagnini's, but are flatter, and his scrolls are smaller and more deeply cut. Wood and workmanship are excellent, the varnish yellow to red-orange. The author has seen two of his instruments which were outstanding. The tone is exceedingly good. Prices: $400.00 to $1000.00; some exceptional copies have been sold at higher prices.

Label: Angelus Soliani Fecit Mutinae 17.... (image of sun)

SORIOT, D.

A trade name given to instruments manufactured by the house of Laberte in France. These have sold up to $350.00.

SPIDLEN, FRANZ — *B. 1867 in Bohemia.*

He started his career in Russia about 1894, after an apprenticeship under Metelka and Vitaček. At the death of Salzard, he took over this maker's business in Moscow. He returned to Prague in 1909. He generally copied Guarneri and Stradivari models, using brown oil varnish and branding his instruments in the back. Prices: $75.00 to $150.00.

STADLMANN, JOHANN JOSEPH — *Vienna, Austria. B. 1720, d. 1781.*

Son and successor of Daniel Stadlmann (about 1680-1744) who was one of the better Viennese makers of his time. Johann Joseph was a great artist and, like his father, always worked from a form. He copied Stainer and generally used the high arching. The varnish is golden brown, but in some instances, has through oxidization turned almost black. The tone is very fine, wood and workmanship are excellent. Prices: $250.00 to $500.00.

His son, Michael Ignaz (1756-1813) was considered an equally good maker. He followed a Stradivari model with flat arching and generally used a red-brown varnish.

Label: Joann Joseph / Stadlmann / Kayserl. Konigl. / Hof Lauten und Geigenmacher in Wienn 17....

STAINER, JACOBUS — *Absam, Tyrol. B. 1621, d. 1683.*

The greatest violin maker of the German school. He ranks exceptionally high and is only surpassed by the greatest Italian makers. It is not definitely known that he was a pupil of Amati, but from all indications, he must have learned his trade from the Amati school. He worked with the greatest care, used very selected wood. His varnish is usually yellow-brown and decidedly of Italian character. His instruments are all built on a high arched model, probably better suited for players at that time. In 1669, he was bestowed the title of Musician to the Court by Kaiser Leopold. He was then already famous. Later, however, he was put in prison due to religious conflicts, and he was released a sick and poor man, unable to readjust his life. He continued to make violins, but with his large family to support it was very difficult for him. He suffered a nervous breakdown and died, insane.

A characteristic feature of his instruments is that the arching of the table is higher than that of the back. The soundholes are short, cut after the German style. The quality of tone is very sweet, yet with good carrying power. His name, after his death, became very famous and his instruments were in great demand. Violin makers all over Europe began to imitate his work and inserted reproductions of Stainer labels in their own instruments. Today genuine Stainer violins are comparatively rare. Prices range from $1500.00 to $2500.00.

> *Label:* (manuscript) Jacobus Stainer in Absam / prope Oenipontum fecit 16....

STAINER, MARCUS — *Absam, Kufstein and Laufen, Tyrol. B. about 1619, d. after 1680.*

He was the elder brother of Jacobus and worked in Kufstein about 1647-1659. He was not as skillful as Jacobus but made excellent instruments. The author has seen one made by Marcus with his brother's label which had been sold as a Jacobus. He generally used a large pattern and his varnish was a reddish yellow-brown. Prices: $600.00 to $1200.00.

STAININGER, JACOB — *Probably a native of Fuessen, Tyrol.*

He worked in Mainz and other German towns. He was a fine maker and his instruments are quite well liked, but there are not very many in this country. He followed the models of the Italian school and usually used a dark orange varnish. Prices: $150.00 to $350.00.

STAUFFER, JOHANN GEORG — *Vienna, Austria. B. 1778, d. 1853.*

He was one of the best Viennese guitar makers and made other string instruments as well. He followed the Stainer outline for his violins but used a flat pattern. The varnish is yellow and red-brown of hard glossy texture. Very few of his instruments have been seen in this country. Prices: $250.00 to $400.00.

He had a son, Johann Anton, who worked with him but was of no great importance.

STORCK, JOHANNES FRIEDRICH — *Worked in Augsburg, Germany, about 1750-1780.*

Followed the Stainer pattern. His selections of wood are very good and some of his violas turned out better than his violins. Prices: $150.00 to $300.00.

STORIONI, LORENZO — *Cremona, Italy. B. 1751, d. after 1801.*

He probably was the last great Cremonese maker, although the instruments of his contemporary, Giovanni Baptista Ceruti, are also very fine. His work does not come up to the high standard of some of his famous predecessors. The quality of his varnish is more like that of the good Milanese school and the color red-brown or yellow-brown. He generally followed a large pattern, with medium arching, somewhat on the style of Guarneri. He also made violins and cellos. Prices: $1200.00 to $3000.00. Exceptional specimens higher.

Label: Laurentius Storioni fecit / Cremonae 17...

STOSS, MARTIN — *Vienna, Austria. B. 1778, d. 1838.*

He was an exceptionally fine maker and followed a flat Stradivari model. His work is extremely neat and carefully done. His varnish was originally yellow or red with a yellow ground, but on most instruments seen today, due to the treatment of the wood before varnishing, it has turned very dark and is now a deep red-brown. His cellos are much sought. Prices: $400.00 to $800.00.

There were other makers by the name of Stoss who, however, are not of great importance.

Label: Martin Stoss / fecit Viennae / 18 ... (initials in circle)

STRADIVARI, ANTONIO — *Cremona, Italy. B. about 1644, d. 1737.*

He was Nicola Amati's pupil and the greatest of all violin makers, a craftsman who has never been surpassed and probably never will be. There is not much information as to his personal history that can be reliably passed on. To learn as much of his life as is possible, the author would suggest reading the "Life of Antonio Stradivari" by Hill of London, England. It is a magnificent book, giving much valuable data, not only pertaining to Stradivari but to the old masters in general.

The date Stradivari actually started making violins on his own is not known. The first violin seen bearing his label is dated 1666. The influence of the Amati school is evident in these early instruments, which already show exceptional skill, though the selections of wood are not quite as fine as those of later years. In the period between 1685 and 1694 he changed his models, the arching becomes much flatter and the pattern slightly larger, the middle bouts more pronounced and the soundholes placed in a more slanting position. This is known as the Amatisé type. In the second period, up to about 1700, he used handsomer wood of finer selection, and the varnish is often reddish brown. After 1690, he introduced his "long pattern," which is somewhat flatter, has slightly narrower bouts and a body length ¼" over normal. The third period begins with the year 1700 and includes his best work dating between 1714 and 1720. This is the so-called "golden period," and most of the famous instruments belong to it. But there is really no decline noticeable even until his death, except for a slightly rougher cut of scroll and soundholes and a less perfect arching, due to his aging hand and eye.

Stradivari probably made about 1500 instruments, including some 25 violas and 100 cellos. About 600 violins, 13 violas and 60 cellos are known to exist today. Instruments made in his shop and not by him were marked "sub disciplina" or "sotto la disciplina di Antonio Stradivari." His own instruments have sold from $8,500.00 to $40,000.00 and some exceptionally noted ones much higher.

Label: Antonius Stradivarius Cremonensis / Faciebat anno 17...
(Initials in double circle under cross) (and others)

The violin making industry has produced thousands of commercial copies bearing facsimili of Stradivari's label, and this has been going on for over 150 years. These instruments are worth very little and only occasionally a more valuable copy is seen.

STRADIVARI, FRANCESCO — *Cremona, Italy. B. 1671, d. 1743.*

He was a son and pupil of Antonio. After the death of his father, he continued to work with his brother, Omobono. He never signed his instruments until after his father's death. His patterns are the same, but the workmanship is inferior to that of Antonio, although he was considered a great violin maker. The tone of his instruments is excellent, the selections of wood superb. The varnish is usually a golden orange with a slight tint of brown. Prices range from $5,000.00 to $8,000.00.

> *Label:* Franciscus Stradivarius Cremonensis / Filius Antonii Faciebat Anno 17....

STRADIVARI, OMOBONO — *Cremona. B. 1679, d. 1742.*

The youngest son of Antonio by his first wife. He learned in his father's shop and continued to work there with his brother, Francesco, after Antonio's death. He was the last member of the family to become a violin maker. He did not, of course, have the outstanding talent of Antonio, but there are some examples of his work that are magnificent and certainly worth more praise than some biographers grant him. His selections of wood are excellent. The varnish is usually brown. He followed the models of his father and his instruments command a good price today: $5,000.00 to $10,000.00.

> *Label:* Omobonus Stradivarius filius Antonij / Cremone Fecit Anno 17.... (manuscript)

STRNAD, CASPAR — *Prague, Czechoslovakia. B. 1752, d. 1823.*

He followed the large Stradivari pattern but used no form. The top has quite a flat arching. The wood is of good selection and generally quite heavy. He usually used a red oil varnish of good quality. He was one of the first Prague makers to change over to the flatter archings. He finished his instruments in different grades, some are fair, others excellent. Prices: $150.00 to $300.00.

STROBL, JOHANN — *Worked in Hallein, Tyrol, about 1700, d. 1717.*

A well-known maker in his time. He followed the Amati high arched patterns. His instruments, made of finely selected wood, are often without purfling. His varnish is not too good, usually yellow-brown. He had a son, Johann, who was less important as a maker. His instruments are priced from $100.00 to $250.00.

SÜSS, JOHANN CHRISTIAN — *Markneukirchen, Germany. B. 1829, d. 1900.*

Worked for Christian Knopf in Dresden, where he had received his training. He developed considerable skill and his bows are quite well liked. He generally followed the Tourte type and is probably one of the best German bow makers. Prices: $25.00 to $60.00.

SZEPESSY, BELA — *B. 1856, in Budapest, Hungary.*

A pupil of Nemessányi until 1874. He was then employed by Zach of Vienna and also worked in Munich. He later went to London and opened his own shop there. He followed Stradivari, Guarneri, and Amati models. His oil varnish is of a golden yellow or red-brown color. His instruments are well made, the wood carefully selected, but very few are seen in the United States. He also made fine violas and cellos. Prices: $300.00 to $500.00.

TANEGIA, CARLO ANTONIO — *Worked in Milan, Italy, about 1725-1737.*

He followed the style of the old masters, especially Grancino. He is a little known but exceptionally fine craftsman who deserves more credit than he is usually given. Prices: $800.00 to $1000.00.

TASSINI, BARTOLOMEO — *Worked in Venice, Italy, about 1740-1756.*

Possibly a pupil of the Testore school. His selections of wood are excellent. The varnish is a golden yellow or orange-red. His cellos are considered better than his violins. His instruments have sold from $1000.00 to $1200.00.

Label: Opus Battholomaei / Tassini Veneti / 17....

TECCHLER, DAVID — *B. 1666, worked in Rome, Italy, about 1705 to 1743.*

The spelling of the name varies. His early work seems to be of the Stainer type, but later, he followed the Italian school and became the most important Roman maker. His instruments possess large tone. The pattern is generally quite arched. The selections of wood are excellent, the workmanship perfect, the varnish usually a rich reddish yellow. The corners are long and the soundholes wide. He also made cellos, on a broad pattern. He is supposed to have worked in Venice before going to Rome but did not agree with other violin makers of that city and therefore moved. His violins are priced from $2500.00 to $4000.00, his cellos about $6000.00 and some exquisite pieces as high as $10,000.00. Tecchler and Goffriller cellos rank next to Stradivari.

Label: David Tecchler Liutaro / Fecit Romae Anno 17.... (and others)

TEDESCO, LEOPOLDO IL — *Rome, Italy. B. around 1625.*

From about 1652 to 1654, he worked in Cremona under Nicolo Amati. He then established himself in Rome. He followed the Amati models, but his work is not as fine as his master's. The varnish is good.

TESTORE, CARLO GIUSEPPE — *B. about 1660, in Novara, Italy, d. about 1717.*

A pupil of Giovanni Grancino. In 1687, he established himself in Milan. He is probably the most important maker of the Testore family. His instruments are rare, the reason possibly being that they have been sold for Grancinos. He carefully selected his wood for its tonal qualities, though it is not always handsome. The varnish is usually yellow-brown. For the backs of his cellos he often used pear wood. He also made basses which are exceptionally fine. Some of his instruments are branded with the sign of an eagle. Characteristic of his style of work is the scroll which is flat at the back, not fluted like that of other makers. His instruments are well liked for their fine carrying power. Prices range from $1000.00 to $2500.00

> *Label:* Carlo Giuseppe Testore in / Contrada Larga di Milano / al segno dell'Aquila 17.... (and others)

TESTORE, CARLO ANTONIO — *Milan, Italy. B. about 1688, d. after 1764.*

Eldest son and pupil of Carlo Giuseppe. He followed the style of the old masters, Amati, Stradivari, and Guarneri. His selections of wood are exceedingly fine, his varnish is of a yellow-brown color, thick and often quite dull. Prices: $650.00 to $1800.00.

> *Label:* Carlo Antonio Testore figlio Maggiore / del fu Carlo Guiseppe in Contrada lar-/ ga al segno dell' Aquila Milano 17....

TESTORE, PAOLO ANTONIO — *Milan, Italy. B. about 1690, d. after 1760.*

Younger son and pupil of Carlo Giuseppe. He worked with his brother until about 1710, after that on his own. He followed Amati and Guarneri models, often omitting the purfling or inserting it only in the table, while the back has an ink lined imitation purfling. His selections of wood are poor and his instruments not too well made. Prices: $500.00 to $1000.00, some violas and cellos much higher.

THIBOUVILLE-LAMY, LOUIS EMILE JEROME — *Mirecourt and Paris, France. B. 1833.*

The owner of one of the most important factories of musical instruments in Mirecourt which dates back to 1790. They worked on mass production purely in a commercial way, manufacturing many thousands of instruments a year which have been sold all over the world. Their violins are not built on any specific model but generally correspond to the Stradivari and Guarneri patterns. Cheaper instruments sold from $15.00 to $50.00, better ones up to $150.00.

THIR, ANTON I — *Worked in Pressburg, Slovakia, about 1750-1790.*

His work is similar to Leidolff, following the high-arched Stainer model. The varnish is usually red-brown and, like that of other Viennese makers, has taken on a very dark shade. Prices: $250.00 to $400.00.

THIR, ANDREAS — *Pressburg. B. 1765, d. after 1798.*

Son of Anton. His work is very good and similar to that of Leeb whose pupil he may have been. He usually followed the Amati model, with medium arching. Yellowish brown varnish. Prices: $200.00 to $350.00.

THIR (THIER), JOHANN GEORG — *Vienna, Austria. Started violin making in 1738, d. after 1781.*

One of the very fine Viennese makers. He followed his own pattern, somewhat like Stainer, long and narrow, with medium high to high arching. His soundholes are placed closer together than is customary with other makers. His cellos are built on the large pattern. His earlier instruments are very dark in color, but later he used clearer varnish, applied on a yellow ground. In 1781, his business was taken over by Franciscus Geissenhof, but his label was still used by Geissenhof until about 1791. Prices: $200.00 to $400.00.

> *Label:* Johann Georg Thier, Lauten- und / Geigenmacher in Wien 17.... (and others)

THIR, MATHIAS — *Worked in Vienna, Austria, about 1770-1795.*

Brother of Johann Georg and fully as fine a maker, if not better. His selections of wood are handsome. He used a medium to high arching. The varnish is dark reddish brown. His workmanship is excellent and his instruments have good tone. Prices: $200.00 to $500.00.

His son, Anton II, worked on the same style as his father. He spelled his name Thier.

THOMASSIN, LOUIS — *B. 1855, in Mirecourt, France.*

An excellent bow maker, pupil of Charles Bazin. About 1882, he worked for F. N. Voirin in Paris and, in 1891, went into business for himself. He branded his bows "L. Thomassin." They are excellent sticks, well balanced, and are liked by the professional musician. Prices: $50.00 to $150.00.

THOUVENEL, HENRY — *Worked in Mirecourt, France, about 1850 to 1869.*

His selections of wood are fair, the work is well done. His model is that of Stradivari, the pattern large, the varnish generally red-brown. Prices: $200.00 to $300.00.

TIEFFENBRUCKER, CASPAR — *B. 1514 in Füssen, Tyrol, d. about 1571 in Lyon, France.*

Better known under the French name of Duiffoprugcar. He was German by birth but became a French citizen in 1558. He was a maker of lutes and guitars and other musical instruments, but he is not known to have made violins. The many so-called Duiffoprugcars originated for the most part from France, others from Germany. They are richly ornamented, carved and inlaid, showing sceneries usually of old castles, the scrolls often in the form of a man's head, the sides bearing Latin inscriptions. These instruments have very little commercial value except as antiques in the hands of collectors. Prices: $75.00 to $150.00. Vuillaume, Bernardel and Chanot made some very fine copies of this maker and the prices of these are much higher.

TIEFFENBRUNNER, GEORG — *Munich, Germany. B. 1812, d. 1880.*

Pupil of Kriner in Landshut. Little is known of this maker's work, of which only few examples exist. Prices: $75.00 to $150.00.

TOBIN, RICHARD — *Worked in London, England, about 1790, d. about 1836.*

A pupil of Perry of Dublin. For many years he worked for John Betts. He was very skillful, selected the finest woods and usually followed the Stradivari and Guarneri patterns. His cellos are exceedingly good and among the best of English make. His scrolls are beautifully cut and as nicely made as many of the old Italian masters. His varnish varies in color. Prices: $350.00 to $500.00.

TONONI, FELICE — *Worked in Bologna, Italy, about 1670-1710.*

Little is known of this maker and few of his instruments have been seen. He followed a high arched model. His work is excellent and the tone beautiful. Yellow to yellow-brown varnish. His cellos are well liked. In the last years he worked together with his son, Joannes. Prices range from $1000.00 to $3000.00.

TONONI, GIOVANNI (JOANNES) — *Worked in Bologna and Venice, Italy, about 1689-1713, the date of his death.*

His work is much better than his father's and is probably the finest in the Tononi family. Of the various models he used, the most frequently met is one after Nicola Amati, except that the pattern is larger. His work is impeccable; the selections of wood are of the finest. The varnish, of very beautiful texture, is golden orange or light red-brown. He made violins as well as violas and cellos, priced from $1500.00 to $3500.00, exceptional examples as high as $6000.00.

> *Label:* Ioannes de Tononis Fecit / Bononiae Anno 17....
> *or*   : Ioannes Tononus fecit Bononiae / in Platea Parraglionis / anno Domini 16....

TONONI, CARLO — *Worked in Bologna and Venice, Italy, about 1689-1717.*

Son of Joannes. His work shows the fine training received from his father. His instruments are beautiful and are much in demand. He followed the larger patterns, with medium, sometimes high arching. The selections of wood are excellent. The varnish is yellow-brown, sometimes golden red-brown. His instruments are known for their large tone. Prices range from $1500.00 to $3000.00, for exceptional pieces up to $5000.00.

> *Label:* Carolus Tononi fecit Bononie in Via / Sancti Mamulis sub Signo Sancte Caecilie Anno Domini 17.... (and others)

TOPPANI, ANGELO (DE) — *Worked in Rome, Italy, about 1735-1750.*

One of the better Roman makers of his time. He followed the high-arched models, robust in appearance. His work is excellent, the varnish usually a golden yellow. He also made fine cellos, but there are very few original instruments of his make in the United States. Prices: $850.00 to $1500.00.

> *Label:* Angelus de Toppanis fecit / Romae Anno Doi 17....

TOURTE, PÈRE — *Worked in Paris, France, between 1740 and 1780.*

He was a lute maker but later chose to make bows, and he is the originator of the bow as it is today, except for some slight changes which were made by his son François. He worked with his eldest son,

Xavier, for many years. His bows have many advantages over the old style and were probably excellent for violin playing at that time, but for our modern artists they are not satisfactory because they are light in weight and quite weak and would not stand the strain of vigorous playing.

TOURTE, XAVIER — *Worked in Paris, France, about 1770-1786.*

Known as "Tourte aîné" (the elder), to distinguish him from his younger brother, François. He contributed to the further improvement of the bow and carried on the work where his father left off. His earlier bows are not very desirable today, but the later ones, being of superior quality of wood, are very well liked by artists. Prices: $150.00 to $300.00.

TOURTE, FRANÇOIS — *Paris, France. B. 1747, d. 1835.*

Often referred to as the "Stradivari of bow making." The greatest of all bow makers and the inventor of the modern bow. No decided improvements have been made since and his bows are still the most valuable of any make, the finest in balance and the most sought after. He knew how important it was to the violinist to have a bow that would execute his technique at his will. Such a bow he was able to create, after much study and experimenting, while working for his father. He cut the wood straight with the grain and never varnished, but only oil polished the sticks. He was still making bows at the age of 77. They are now available only at very high prices: $500.00 to $2000.00, and some exceptional specimens (collector's pieces) have been sold as high as $3500.00.

TRUCCO, GIROLAMO — *Worked in Savona, Italy, around 1840.*

A violin and guitar maker, very little known. His name has been used indiscriminatingly by violin dealers. However, some original instruments have been seen and sold as high as $600.00.

TUBBS, JAMES — *London, England. B. 1835, d. 1919.*

Son of the bow maker Thomas Tubbs, from whom he learned his trade. He was in the employ of W. E. Hill & Sons from 1860 to about 1875, then went into business for himself and had his shop on Wardour Street, London. He had a son, Alfred, who assisted him in his work and who died in 1912. Tubbs was probably the greatest English bow maker and made some 5000 violin, viola and cello bows. His work is accurate and beyond criticism. He selected his wood with great care and his bows are well liked for their perfect balance. They are priced from $65.00 to $150.00, some superb copies, gold trimmed, as high as $250.00.

TUBBS, EDWARD — *A member of this family established in New York.*

VALENZANO (VALENCIANO), GIOVANNI MARIA—*Worked in Valenza, Rome and Trieste, Italy, about 1771-1825.*

He followed the patterns of the old masters but was not consistent in his style of work which sometimes is closer to the Milanese school, at other times to the Neapolitan. His much abused name appears in instruments which are not even copies of his work. He was a fine craftsman, used excellent wood and usually a light red-brown to yellow-brown varnish. Prices: $500.00 to $1000.00.

> *Label:* Joannes Maria Valenzano / Astensis in Roma fecit 18.... (and others)

VANDELLI, GIOVANNI — *Worked in Modena, Italy, about 1796 to 1839.*

His instruments are very well made, but not many have been seen. Amati model, reddish yellow varnish. Prices: $400.00 to $600.00.

VAN DER SLAGHMEULEN, JOHANNES BAPTIST — *Worked in Antwerp, Belgium, about 1660-1679.*

A little known maker although he was an excellent craftsman. His work resembles the Brescian school and has high arching. The varnish is usually yellow-brown to brown. Prices are about $500.00.

> *Label:* Joannes Baptista Vander Slagh / Meulen, tot Antwerpen 16....

VAROTTI, GIOVANNI — *Worked in Bologna, Italy, about 1786-1815.*

His earlier instruments are built on a peculiar pattern, but the later ones, usually higher arched, are much better. The varnish is red-brown. The tone is excellent. Prices: $500.00 to $800.00.

> *Label:* Joannes Varotti Fecit / Bononiae Anno 17....

VATELOT, MARCEL — *B. 1884. Came from a small town near Mirecourt, France.*

A pupil of Poiron. Worked for different houses in Mirecourt, then in Paris for Brugère and Marchand. In 1910, he founded his own shop in Paris. He is a fine luthier and follows the style of Stradivari and other old Italian makers. The varnish is deep red. A quartet of his instruments was exhibited at the 1939 New York World's Fair. Prices are not known.

VAUCHEL, JEAN — *Worked in Mainz, Würzburg and Damm, Germany. B. 1782, d. 1856.*

Spohr and Paganini considered him one of the best makers of his time. His work is artistically done, the tone excellent. Prices: $100.00 to $250.00.

VENTAPANE, VINCENZO — *Worked in Naples, Italy, between 1750 and 1799.*

He usually followed the Stradivari models, with medium arching, and used a yellow-brown varnish. His work is cleanly cut and he was very careful in the selections of his wood. Genuine instruments, of which there are very few, are exceptionally beautiful. The tone is large and pleasing. He also made violas and cellos. Prices: $500.00 to $1000.00.

VENTAPANE, PASQUALE — *Worked in Naples, Italy, in the 18th century.*

He probably was related to Vincenzo, but no record of his past has been found. There are some cellos of his make in the price range of about $500.00.

VENTAPANE, LORENZO — *Worked in Naples, Italy, about 1809-1828.*

A follower of the Gagliano school, using mostly the Stradivari patterns and exceedingly handsome wood. The varnish is golden orange, sometimes dark orange-yellow. He also made violas and cellos. His name, however, appears in many violins which are not genuine. His own instruments are exceptionally fine and have sold from $500.00 to $1000.00. Superb specimens of cellos up to $1500.00.

> *Label:* Lorenzo Ventapane / Fabbricante / di / strumenti da corde abita Calata Borgo di Loreto No. 23.

VERZELLA, FRANCESCO — *Worked in Constantinople, Turkey, toward the end of the 19th century.*

Of Neapolitan origin. He also made guitars and mandolins. Prices: $150.00 to $300.00.

VIEDENHOFER, BERNARD — *Worked in Budapest, Hungary, about 1790 to 1812.*

Pupil of Hueber. A maker of little reputation. He followed the higher arched models and used generally a dark brown varnish of hard texture. His instruments sold from $100.00 to $150.00.

VIGNALI, GIUSEPPE — *B. 1888 in Verucchio, Italy, established in 1910, died very young.*

A good maker of the later Italian school, usually following the Stradivari models. Varnish, orange-red. His instruments have sold up to $350.00.

VIGNERON, JOSEPH ARTHUR — *Paris, France. B. 1851, in Mirecourt.*

An excellent bow maker, following the style of Tourte and Peccatte. He worked for Gand & Bernardel from 1880 to 1888. His bows are stamped "A. Vigneron à Paris." They are often met and are well liked by professional musicians. Prices are from $50.00 to $150.00.

VINACCIA, ANTONIO — *Worked in Naples, Italy, about 1760-1775.*

Member of an Italian family of violin and mandolin makers. Little is known of his life, but his instruments are very beautiful and well made. He followed the Gagliano style. The varnish is golden orange or red-brown. Prices: $700.00 to $1000.00.

> *Label:* Antonius Vinaccia Fecit / Neapoli Anno 17....

VINACCIA, GENNARO — *Worked in Naples, Italy, about 1755-1778.*

Son of Antonio. He made a great number of violins and, like his father, followed the Gagliano type. The arching is medium, the varnish dark yellow or orange-brown. This maker's name also has been substituted when collectors or dealers could not decide on the origin of certain instruments. The originals have sold from $750.00 to $2000.00.

VINCENZI, LUIGI — *B. 1775, d. about 1820 at Carpi, Italy.*

His instruments are graceful in design and usually covered with a beautiful amber varnish. He also made excellent cellos. Very few examples of his work are in existence. Prices: $500.00 to $800.00.

VOGLER, JOHANN GEORG — *Würzburg, Germany. B. 1692, d. 1750.*

He learned his trade in Füssen and made a number of violins, violas and cellos. His work is not particularly well liked. Prices: $150.00 to $250.00.

VOIGT — *A large family of violin makers in Markneukirchen, Germany.*

The most important are the following:

Simeon (Simon), b. 1711, d. 1781. His work is fair but not exceptional.

Johann Georg, b. 1748, d. 1802. One of the best makers of this family, but his instruments are not very popular and do not command high prices: Usually from $100.00 to $200.00.

Carl Hermann, b. 1850 in Markneukirchen. He started his career as a bow maker but later learned violin making under Nemessányi of Budapest. Afterwards, he worked for Gabriel Lemböck. In 1876, he bought the business of Schmidt in Vienna and there opened his own shop. He generally followed the Stradivari pattern and used a golden red varnish. He was also a fine repairer. He retired in 1910 and sold his business to Georg Rauer. His instruments, including cellos, are priced from $100.00 to $500.00.

Arnold, b. 1864 in Markneukirchen. After serving his apprenticeship under Heinrich Theodor Heberlein, he worked for Schünemann in Hamburg and Schwerin. In 1888, he went to London and made violins which were sold by the firm of his brother Albin Voigt. In 1890, he returned to Markneukirchen and worked under his own name. He copied the Italian masters and his work is considered very good. Prices: $75.00 to $200.00.

VOIRIN, JOSEPH — *B. 1830 in Mirecourt, France.*

He learned bow making in Mirecourt and established himself in Paris in 1855. He was later manager for Gautrot in Château Thierry. He seldom branded his bows and this is probably the reason why he is not so well known, though he was a skillful maker. Prices: $50.00 to $150.00.

VOIRIN, FRANÇOIS NICOLAS — *B. 1833, d. 1885.*

Brother of Joseph. He learned his trade in Mirecourt, France. In 1855, he entered the employ of J. B. Vuillaume in Paris, with whom he stayed for a number of years. He established his own business in 1870. He is considered the best French bow maker with the exception of François Tourte and D. Peccatte. His bows are stamped "F. N. Voirin." They are noted for their perfect balance. Prices are from $75.00 to $600.00 and some exceptionally fine collector's pieces are valued up to $750.00.

VOLLER, WILLIAM — *London, England. B. 1860.*

Associated with his brother Charles. Made extremely clever copies of the old masters seldom bearing their own label.

VUILLAUME, JEAN BAPTISTE — *Paris, France. B. 1798, d. 1875.*

Son of Claude (Mirecourt, 1772-1834). He was the best maker of his family. At the age of 19, he went to work for Lété in Paris. About 1828, he opened his own shop and started copying old masters, chiefly Stradivari. He is an unsurpassed master in the art of copying and many of his instruments are so well made that they have passed for originals. Especially many of the so-called Duiffoprugcars seen today were made by Vuillaume. His work is accurate and above reproach and so cleverly done that if it were not for the varnish, they could stand comparison with the old Italian masters. The varnish, however, is of harder texture. He made approximately 3000 instruments, violins, cellos and violas. He was also an excellent bow maker and followed the style of Tourte, but used an oval underlay for his frogs. He was the originator also of the metal bow, but it met with no success. Many of his pupils became very well known bow makers. He was a connoisseur and collector and bought the entire collection of Tarisio. Among these famous instruments were the "Messie" and the "Alard" Stradivaris. His violins, violas and cellos sell from $800.00 to $2500.00, his bows from $75.00 to $750.00.

> *Label:* J. B. Vuillaume No. .... / Rue Croix des Petits Champs No. 30 Paris 18.... (manuscript) (and many others)

VUILLAUME, NICOLAS FRANÇOIS — *B. 1807, d. 1876.*

Up to 1828, he worked with his brother Jean Baptiste, then established himself in Brussels, Belgium. He followed his brother's models very closely, but his instruments are not as well made. His copies of old masters are fine. Prices: $300.00 to $500.00.

VUILLAUME, SEBASTIEN — *Paris, France. B. about 1835, d. 1875.*

A nephew of Jean Baptiste. Made quite a number of instruments, but very few are in this country. He copied the old masters, mostly Stradivari. His business was taken over by Audinot. Prices: $300.00 to $400.00.

WAGNER, BENEDICT — *Worked in Ellwangen, Germany, in the 18th century.*

He followed different patterns, but the best are those with flat arching. He used varnish of different shades of brown. His instruments are usually branded. He also made very fine cellos. Prices: $150.00 to $350.00.

WAMSLEY, PETER — *Worked in London, England, about 1727-1751.*

He was a well-known maker of his time and was considered a master craftsman. He usually followed the Stainer pattern but also imitated other old masters. Many of his instruments are unpurfled and are usually covered with a red-brown or dark red varnish. He employed several apprentices and workmen in his shop. His instruments sold from $100.00 to $250.00.

> *Label:* Made by Peter Wamsley / at ye Golden Harp in Pickadilly / London

WEICHOLD, AUGUST — *Dresden, Germany. B. 1800, d. 1862.*

He was not a very skillful workman, but he started a business which flourished under the direction of his son Richard, 1823-1902. Richard was a pupil of Pfretzschner in Markneukirchen. He made many commercial violins, violas and cellos and was a manufacturer of strings which were known the world over for their fine quality. In 1881, he retired because of deafness. His commercial instruments sold from $30.00 to $100.00.

WEIGERT, JOHANN BLASIUS — *Worked in Linz, Austria, about 1717 to 1755.*

Little is known of this maker in the United States, but he made excellent instruments, especially violas. He usually followed Stradivari models. Violins sold from $50.00 to $100.00, violas as high as $350.00.

WEIS, JACOB — *Worked in Salzburg, Austria, about 1714-1740.*

His violins are quite rare. He also made violas and lutes. His workmanship is good, the varnish usually yellow to yellow-brown. He often carved the head in form of an angel's head instead of the scroll. Prices: $125.00 to $200.00.

> *Label:* Jacob Weis Lauten- und Gei / 17 genmacher in Salzburg 77 (hand printed)

WERNER, FRANZ — *Worked in Vienna, Austria, about 1813-1825.*

Pupil of Franciscus Geissenhof. He usually followed the Stradivari model. The selections of wood are excellent and the workmanship is good, but the tops are rather thin. The varnish is of beautiful quality and usually yellow-brown. Prices: $200.00 to $300.00.

WIDHALM, LEOPOLD — *Nürnberg, Germany. B. 1722, d. 1776.*

One of the very finest German makers of his time. He used a high arched Stainer model but of his own style and character, usually quite broad in pattern. The purfling is broad and the scrolls are exceptionally well cut. The wood is of excellent selection, the varnish a very lustrous color, usually red-brown, and quite thick. Many of his instruments are still in existence and they are well liked for their fine tone quality. Prices: $200.00 to $350.00.

> *Label:* Leopold Widhalm, Lauten- und / Geigenmacher in Nürnberg fecit. A. 17....

WIDHALM, (MARTIN) LEOPOLD — *Nürnberg, Germany, B. 1747, d. 1806.*

Son of Leopold. He learned his trade in his father's shop and took over the business at his death. He followed the same style and many of his instruments bear his father's label and dates. Only the varnish is not as good. Prices: $150.00 to $300.00.

WILLEMS, HENDRICK — *Worked in Ghent, Belgium, about 1651-1698.*

A fine maker, following the Brescian school and Stainer model with high arching and sharp, protruding corners. His selections of wood are excellent; for his backs, he used maple, beech, nut or linden wood. The varnish is usually yellow-brown. Prices: $250.00 to $350.00.

WINTERLING, GEORG — *B. 1859 at Watzkenreuth, Bohemia.*

After an apprenticeship under Benedikt Klier, he worked for various German makers and in 1900 established himself in Hamburg. He was a fine craftsman and connoisseur and possessed an important collection of string instruments. When he retired in 1920, his shop and store were turned over to his assistants, Schreiber and Lugert.

WITHERS, GEORGE — *London, England. B. 1847 in London, d. 1931 in Surbiton (Surrey).*

Brother and successor of Edward Withers. Comes from a large

family of violin makers. He was a fine craftsman, worked after Stradivari models, usually used yellow oil varnish. The firm of George Withers & Sons was carried on by his sons, Guarneri, who had worked as an apprentice in Mirecourt, France, and Walter George. The house was originally established by Norris & Barnes in 1765.

WUNDERLICH — *A family of violin and bow makers in Mark-neukirchen and Leipzig, Germany.*

The best known was Friedrich, b. 1876. He went to work for Nürnberger in Markneukirchen. In 1898, he moved to Leipzig and there opened his own shop as a bow maker. He copied the great masters, but favored François Tourte. He made all parts himself and the pernambuco selected is very fine. The sticks are not varnished but oil rubbed and can be easily cleaned with alcohol, which will not spoil the finish. His bows come in different grades and sell from $15.00 to $65.00.

WUTZELHOFER, SEBASTIAN — *Worked in Brünn, Czechoslovakia, about 1782-1825.*

He followed mostly the Stradivari pattern. His work is very clean and well finished. the varnish usually yellow-brown. Very few of his instruments have been brought to this country. Prices: $100.00 to $200.00.

ZACH, THOMAS — *Budapest, Bukarest, and Vienna. B. 1812, d. 1892.*

Pupil of Dvorak and Sitt in Prague. He also worked for J. B. Schweitzer in Budapest and became his successor. He sold this shop, however, but years later started again in Vienna where he became well known. He was one of the better makers of his time. He copied Stradivari and Guarneri and used wood of very fine selection. His varnish is handsome but too soft. Prices: $150.00 to $300.00.

ZACH, CARL — *Worked in Vienna, Austria, and other cities from 1886 to 1897.*

He was the son of Thomas and carried on his father's business after his death, then known as Carl Zach & Co. (brand mark C Z & Co.). Years ago the Boston Symphony Orchestra was equipped with a full set of Zach's instruments. Some of his works are good, especially his violas. They have sold as high as $350.00.

ZACHER, MAXIMILIAN — *Worked in Breslau, Germany, about 1730 to 1770.*

He is little known but was a good maker. He worked on a large pattern, usually with high arching and deep grooved edges. His varnish is generally yellow. Prices: $150.00 to $250.00.

Label: Maximilian Zacher, Lauten- und / Geigenmacher in Breslau / anno 17....

ZANOLI, GIOVANNI BATTISTA — *Worked in Verona, Italy, about 1730-1757.*

A violin maker of little importance. He made a number of cheap instruments, but a few are fair. The varnish is poor and usually red-brown. He had a particular style of his own. The model is flat. Prices: $150.00 to $350.00.

Label: Joannes Baptista Zanoli / Verone fecit Anno 17....

ZANOLI, GIACOMO — *Worked between 1740 and 1757, originally in Venice, later in Padua, Italy.*

After the death of his father Giovanni Battista, he took over the business in Verona. He was an unreliable maker, but when the occasion arose he could make a really fine instrument and used wood of excellent selection for these special pieces. He followed a flat pattern, somewhat like Joseph Guarnerius. His better instruments are covered with a beautiful reddish brown or golden orange varnish, plentifully applied. They are very rare. This is another maker whose name has served to denominate instruments of unknown origin. Genuine examples sell from $500.00 to $2500.00.

Label: Fato in Verona / de Giacomo Zanoli / 17....

ZANOTTI (ZANOTUS), ANTONIO — *B. about 1690-95, worked in Mantua about 1724 to 1750.*

As stated on one of his labels, he was a pupil of Geronimo Amati, son of Nicola. His models are usually medium flat. His work is excellent and some examples seen rank with the better classic masters. The varnish is an orange-brown. Prices: $1000.00 to $3000.00.

ZANTI, ALESSANDRO — *Worked in Mantua, Italy, about 1765-1819.*

He generally followed the models of Stradivari and Guarneri.

ZIANNI, PIETRO — *Worked in Bologna, Italy, about the middle of the 18th century.*

He usually followed the long Stradivari pattern. He used good materials and the work is fair. Prices: $200.00 to $300.00.

American Makers

INTRODUCTION

Violin making, which can be an art as well as a craft, and to some extent, a science, has reached a level of merit among many American makers, which is unfortunately not appreciated by amateur players, although a growing number of professional violinists, violists and cellists are using modern American instruments which exceed in merit, at comparative prices, those of any other country.

If one considers the qualifications necessary for expert violin making, this should not be surprising. With all his genius, Stradivari could hardly have reached his pinnacle of perfection had he not been given the benefit of three generations of experience of the Amati family. Nor do I believe he would have reached it without almost daily encouragement and discouragement freely given by the great musicians of his time — for Italy was then the heart which gave life to the art of music in Europe.

Today, in America, we have makers who brought with them or inherited the accumulated knowledge of the shops of Europe — Italy, France, England, Germany. We have a majority of the best professional musicians of the world. The contact between makers and musicians here has inevitably produced violin making of real quality.

Mr. Fairfield, by making the names of a great many of these makers available, has, I believe, done a real service to them. Unfortunately, the following biographical list cannot be complete. Some makers, through indifference or other reasons, did not care to give the necessary information. Others of possibly real merit have as yet only local reputation and were unknown to the author.

The comparative values of instruments of Stradivari, Guarneri and the many other classical makers are really the composite opinion of thousands of violinists over many generations, and these opinions have created both the relative values and the demand. Since violin making in America is generally a contemporary art, this composite opinion of value has hardly had time to form in any permanent way and Mr. Fairfield has wisely decided to refrain from any attempt to rank the various makers listed.

The greatest handicap to modern violin making is undoubtedly the erroneous impression of many people that a violin must be old to be good — or even worse — that it is good because it is old. Age and use are no doubt of importance, all other factors being equal. The fact that every great violinist since before the days of Paganini has paid his hard-earned money for an old instrument cannot be overlooked. However, thousands of old violins have been and are being purchased in this country which can not stand up, in comparison, to a good modern instrument. Moreover, a good new violin will improve, provided, of course, that it is properly made and of good wood thicknesses and, possibly most important, that it is covered with a varnish which will allow it to improve and which will not become a hard and brittle strait-jacket around the instrument in the course of time.

The great Italian school of violin making of the 17th and 18th centuries has never been equalled. However, a good beginning has been made, and with the support of both amateur and professional musicians, American violin making can become great. It is gratifying to see the emphasis given to American makers for the first time in a book of this scope, and I hope that in due time another edition will be possible including an even greater list of the American makers.

REMBERT WURLITZER

ABERNETHY, J. H. — *Danville, Va. B. near Stanley, N. C., May 19, 1886.*

Came to Virginia in 1912. His father was a craftsman but not a violin maker. He is self-taught, having for over twenty years searched and researched for information from all possible sources,—English, French, Italian and American books. However, he received much help from Mr. W. F. Hammer, a fine maker of Portsmouth and Norfolk, Va. Mr. Abernethy follows the Stradivari model, uses only the best oil varnish and prefers burnt orange, golden brown and reddish orange colors. He has made 18 violins and they sell as high as $300.00.

> I have had the pleasure of inspecting some of Mr. Abernethy's instruments and can praise him highly for his work and fine tone quality. As a self-taught violin maker, he deserves great credit.

ADAM, ERNST F. — *St. Louis, Mo. B. March 24, 1891 in Rolla, Phelps County, Mo.*

He began violin making and repairing at the age of 12 and received instruction from various makers. In 1912, he moved to St. Louis, where he had the opportunity of studying the work of such masters as John Hertenstein, Frank Gray, Louis Albers, Scott Herrington and others. Mr. Adam has to date made 68 violins. He prefers the Stradivari and Guarneri patterns and only uses very old wood. The varnish varies in color from light yellow to red and dark brown. His violins retail from $250.00 to $500.00. He also does fine repair work.

AERTS, RENE — *Compton, Calif. B. March 22, 1883, in Brussels, Belgium.*

Served his apprenticeship in Mirecourt, France, also worked in Markneukirchen, Germany, and London, England. He conducted his own shop in Brussels, Rue de la Régence, until 1932. He then came to the United States and became an American citizen in 1940. His work is very beautiful, copied from the famous old Italian makers, the oil varnish dark red to golden yellow. Members of the Pro Arte Quartet use his instruments exclusively. Mr. Aerts was the violin maker to the Conservatory of Brussels and the Museum of Rare Old Instruments by appointment of the Belgian Government. His violins sell for $400.00, violas $500.00, cellos $600.00. Mr. Aerts and his son, Marcel, specialize in appraisals and reparation of valuable instruments.

AERTS, MARCEL — *Compton, Calif. Son of René. B. in Paris in 1910.*

Served his apprenticeship under his father and with Jeandat of Mirecourt. He was awarded the second prize in the International Competition at Brussels in 1930. Poidras stated at that time that it was a beautiful piece of work and he predicted a fine future for this young violin maker. Marcel became an American citizen in 1939 and is now working with his father.

> Aerts, Father and Son, are both skilled craftsmen and their instruments are excellent. Their workmanship is exact and beautifully done in every detail. They use the most handsome wood, and have been highly praised by some of the greatest artists as Ysaye, Kreisler, Elman, Zimbalist and Thibaud.

ALBERT, CHARLES FRANÇOIS — *See front section.*

ALLISON, IVAN W. — *Charleston, W. Va. B. February 11, 1884, in Kanawha County near Charleston, W. Va., to which town he moved in 1916.*

He is an electrician by trade and of English and Scotch descent. In 1928, he began violin making and has to date made 45 violins and 2 violas and is now working on a cello. He first conceived the idea from Prof. A. W. Asher who taught music and also made some violins. He was greatly helped by Mr. Harrison B. Smith Jr. as he had free access to his music library which included many books on violin construction. His patterns and materials were mostly bought from W. E. Hill & Sons, England. He follows the Stradivari patterns and uses Hill oil varnish. The colors have varied in the past but he is now considering making his own varnish which will be golden and golden brown. Mr. Allison inscribes his name and date on the upper bouts of the table and back and his scrolls bear the initials I A at the foot of the pegbox. His violins sell for $250.00.

> The violin Mr. Allison sent me for inspection, dated 1941, certainly shows excellent craftsmanship. His work is very clean, all measurements correct, the scroll finely carved and the model very attractive. The tone quality is mellow, yet powerful, and I think this is partly due to the varnish he used, which is of a fine, flexible texture.

ANNIS, D. S. — *Beach City, Ohio. B. near Granite Falls, N. C., January 2, 1887.*

His first violin was made under the instructions of Nicholas Maurer of Beach City and he received further help from the experienced violin maker Ezra Gesaman in Massillon, Ohio. Mr. Annis also consulted the instruction books of Voigt & Geiger, Justin Gilbert and other works. He has made about 75 violins, mostly on the "Strad" pattern. He also made five copies of the "Paganini" Joseph Guarneri, one of which was exhibited at the 1941 Ohio State Fair and was awarded first prize in the amateur contest. He has repaired a great many violins. His instruments have sold for an average of $35.00 to $50.00 and up to $100.00.

BALL, FRANK C. — *Springfield, Mass. B. at Abbotsford, Prov. of Quebec, Canada, May 8, 1881.*

His first instructor in violin making was John Bradford in Granby, P. Q., Canada. In 1907, he worked for Walter Goss, later for O. H. Bryant, both of Boston. He has made about 120 violins, 3 cellos and 2 violas, using choicest European woods, and the finest American wood obtainable. His earlier instruments are on models of Joseph Guarneri del Gesu and Nicolo Amati, but for the past ten years he has used Stradivari models only. The oil varnish is red and orange-brown shaded to red. His instruments sell for $75.00 to $300.00 and one was sold for $500.00. Mr. Ball has a fully equipped modern workshop and is well known in his locality.

BARNES, HORATIO M. — *Irvine, Ky. B. in Jefferson, Ohio, May 19, 1913.*

He is strictly an amateur, but has a keen and absorbing interest in violins and violin making. Though he has only made one violin, he has done considerable repairing and restoring of old instruments.

BECKER, CARL — *Chicago, Ill. B. in Chicago, 1887.*

His father, Carl Becker, Sr., was a famous violin soloist and teacher, and his grandfather, Herman Macklett, was a pioneer American violin maker of outstanding ability. His fondness for violin work started during his early youth. His first violin was made at the age of 14. For 22 years, he worked with John Hornsteiner, a descendant of the well known old Mittenwald family of violin makers. Mr. Becker has been with William Lewis & Son for the last 14 years. He is an outstanding violin maker, one of the best in America today, and enjoys an excellent reputation also as an expert restorer and repairer. After many years of experimenting, he has perfected an oil varnish of his own formula. It is beautiful, soft and transparent, golden orange faintly tinted with red. He allows from 15 to 18 months to complete varnishing an instrument. He uses only the finest old European woods, selected for tone quality and beauty. Since his association with Lewis & Son and up to 1937 he has made more than 325 instruments, violins as well as violas and cellos. They are being used by some of the great artists and many of the leading professional musicians. Prices range from $400.00 to $550.00.

BEEMAN, HENRY W. — *New Preston, Conn. B. May 27, 1858.*

He makes violins as a hobby in his leisure time during the winter months. His instruments have not been offered for sale and their actual value has never been set. Mr. Beeman is a descendant of a long line of expert woodworkers in the various branches, and learned violin making through advice from numerous fine violin makers whom he has known. During the past 41 years, he has made 60 violins, 8 cellos and 1 viola. He uses Stradivarius models exclusively and applies the greatest care in the construction of his instruments, which compare very favorably with the best modern makers.

BENNINGTON, JAMES — *Mercer, Pa. B. Nov. 1, 1868, at Waynesburg, Pa., of Scotch descent.*

He learned his trade from his grandfathers, and has made more than 100 violins which he placed mostly in the hands of young people in school club orchestras. His living is not dependent upon the violins he makes and, therefore, he does not set a price on them. He only uses waterstain and oil varnish and follows the Strad patterns. At present, his workshop is crowded with repair jobs and he does not find time to make new instruments.

BERGER, KARL A. — *New York, N. Y. B. in Basel, Switzerland, November 13, 1893.*

His masters were Meinel of Basel and Postiglioni of Naples. He worked for Silvestre & Maucotel in Paris. In 1912, he came to the United States and here worked for Fred Hermann. In 1924, he established his own business. He exhibited a violin which won a silver medal at the Sesquicentennial International Exhibit in Philadelphia in 1926 and at the Exhibition Internationale de Musique in Geneva, Switzerland in 1927.

Mr. Berger has made about 250 instruments,—violins, cellos and violas. He follows the Guarneri and Stradivari patterns, but also has his own models which he has changed at different periods. He uses both oil and spirit varnish, mostly the latter, but he does not stain his wood before varnishing. The base is always yellow, regardless of the color applied for the finish. His instruments sell from $300.00 to $500.00.

BLAIR, GEORGE HARVEY — *Spokane, Wash. B. in Peacham, Vermont, August 21, 1868.*

Started violin making at the age of 14 and has made over 300 violins, 2 cellos and 4 violas. All of his latest instruments have been varnished with amber oil, which takes many years to harden. He believes it to be the same as the old Italian varnish. Mr. Blair learned his trade through intensive study of old master instruments and is otherwise self-taught. His latest instruments have sold for $300.00.

BOURK, LOUIS C. — *Denver, Colo. A French Canadian, born in Arthabaskarville, near Quebec, Canada, 1861.*

He came to Colorado in 1882 and has been in the music business in Denver for forty years. He was taught the art of violin making by Joseph Munger of Waterbury, Conn., in 1896. Mr. Bourk has made 54 violins and a few cellos. He uses a varnish of yellow amber color and most of his wood is old Bohemian, of very fine quality. He uses his own model which shows some similarity to Stradivari. His violins sell from $200.00 to $300.00.

> I have examined two of Mr. Bourk's violins, Nos. 45 and 50. The tone is very much alike in these two instruments and is of a very pleasing quality. The workmanship is fine, the scrolls excellently carved, the measurements quite correct.

BUDINI, GIOVANNI — *Albany, N. Y. B. in Cesenatico (Prov. of Forli), Italy.*

He was an apprentice under Chas. C. Ehricke in Albany. He follows the Strad models and uses oil varnish exclusively. He has made approximately 10 violins. They sell from $300.00 to $500.00.

BUFFIN, MAXWELL E. — *Miami, Fla. B. in Frankfort, Ky. January 1, 1888, of Irish descent.*

His first attempt at making violins was at the age of twelve. While he has not served a formal apprenticeship, Mr. Buffin has studied violins and their construction in San Francisco, Chicago, New York and Cincinnati. As a repairman, he has done work for many music stores. At present he is devoting his full time to making and repairing instruments. He has made 50 violins and over 150 bows and is now also making basses. His instruments are all hand made and no power tool is used. He even makes his own pegs and fingerboards. He has never been a strict copyist but prefers the Amati and Stradivari patterns principally, with his own modifications. He uses only oil varnish, made after his own formula, from reddish-brown to dark brown in color. His instruments sell from $100.00 to $300.00. Many professional players recommend them for their full round tone and great carrying power.

BUTLER, FRANK H. — *Douglass, Texas. B. February 17, 1898, in Ranger, Texas.*

A self-taught amateur violin maker, Mr. Butler started his work in 1936 and has made 1 viola and 17 violins. His knowledge was gathered from books and from actual experience. He copies the "Alard" Stradivari and uses a commercial violin varnish. His instruments have sold as high as $200.00, but some are probably worth more.

> I have examined Mr. Butler's work and find that as an amateur's it is quite good. With a little professional coaching, Mr. Butler could make some very fine instruments.

CARLISLE, JAMES REYNOLD — *Amelia, Ohio. B. April 8, 1886.*

Started violin making in 1910 and has to date made approximately 1500 violins. Up to 1920 he did much experimenting in regard to varnish, arching, graduating, etc. Of his first instruments, some turned out good, others poor, but he has steadily improved and, for a number of years now, he has been making excellent instruments. Mr. Carlisle has his own formula for spirit varnish which has proved very successful; he calls it "Italian Sunshine Varnish," because several weeks of strong sun light are required to make it. He followed the Stradivari models but has lately derived best results from Guarneri del Gesu patterns. None of his ancestors were violin makers. One of the reasons for Mr. Carlisle's success is the help and encouragement given him by Mr. Rudolph Wurlitzer of Cincinnati. Mr. Carlisle has sold many of his instruments to the Cincinnati Symphony Orchestra. His violins are priced at $100.00 and $150.00, and a special grade at $300.00. He only uses fine old seasoned wood, and the colors vary from a golden brown to a cherry red.

> I have inspected, and sold in the past 18 years, many of Mr. Carlisle's instruments, and can say that the later ones are exceptionally fine in workmanship, varnish and tone. His models are fine and his measurements correct. The prices he asks for them are certainly very attractive from the buyer's point of view.

CARLSON, JOHN EMIL — *Chicago, Ill. B. in Grangesberg, Sweden, 1891.*

A student of Carl Becker and now in the employ of William Lewis & Son, Mr. Carlson has made approximately 50 violins on his own variation of a Strad model. For these instruments, he used an oil varnish of his own formula, varying in color from orange to red-brown. Their commercial value has been placed at $200.00.

CARTER, JEROME — *Omaha, Neb. B. in 1878 near North English, Iowa.*

In his early years, he took up violin-making as a hobby and worked at it during dull seasons on the farm. In 1915, he came to Omaha and opened a violin making and repairing establishment. He has recently completed his 105th violin. He follows Stradivari and Guarneri models, also other models of old masters on special order. He has his own formula for an oil varnish which he uses exclusively. His instruments have sold from $150.00 to $200.00.

CARVER, H. W. — *Wewoka, Okla. B. March 17, 1892.*

A manual training teacher and amateur violin maker. Made two instruments on the Guarneri model, covered with oil varnish. They are valued at $250.00 to $500.00.

CATRICALA, VINCENT — *Watervliet, N. Y. B. in Italy, June 8, 1900.*

A graduate of the Troy Conservatory of Music where he majored in violin. Later he went to Boston as a professional violinist and also taught at the Boston Music School Settlement. In 1926 he returned to Troy, studied violin making under Charles Ehricke and established his own business there. So far he has made 9 violins, and 1 viola following the Stradivari and Guarneri patterns and using only oil varnish, of a red color. In 1939 and 1940 his violin No. 6 was exhibited at the New York World's Fair and his No. 7 was dedicated to the Fair in a special program. For this he was presented with a diploma of merit and a bronze medal by the Fair Commission and he was the only American maker to receive such an award. His instruments sell from $300.00 to $500.00.

> I have examined one of Mr. Catricala's violins which I find to be excellent in workmanship and model. His varnish is very nice, and he certainly deserves to be ranked with the better craftsmen in this country.

CHAMBERLAND, ARTHUR — *North Troy, Vermont. B. in 1888 at St. Germaine, P.Q., Canada.*

His father made a few instruments, but not professionally, nor did anyone of his ancestors. In 1919, he moved from Thetford Mines, Canada, to North Troy, Vt. He makes violins only in his spare time, being a farmer, and usually spends his winter days making and repairing them. He is self-taught. He uses both oil and spirit varnish which he makes himself. The first coats are usually spirit and the top, oil. The colors are golden-red, golden-yellow and brown. He has made about 150 violins and repaired possibly 500. His first violins were sold at a very moderate price, but his later ones have been sold from $100.00 to $350.00.

CHAPIN, JOHN OLIVER — *San Francisco, Calif. B. April 29, 1900, at Inkster, N. D.*

He started his violin making career during the years of 1916-17 with Voigt of Chicago, a well-known violin maker. He was in France in 1918 and spent several years touring the world. In 1923, he settled in San Francisco and opened his own shop. He has made 14 violins on the Gilbert model but is still trying out new methods. His instruments have sold as high as $250.00. Mr. Chapin uses only the best imported woods from England, Switzerland and Germany and has for years used the Millington varnish, in ruby red and brown colors. He follows the patterns of the old masters, mostly Stradivari, and is now working on his 79th violin.

> I have not personally inspected one of Mr. Chapin's instruments, but from photographs I have seen, his selections of wood are beautiful and his workmanship is excellent.

CHASE, HOWARD N. — *Bennington, N. H. B. in Nashua, N. H. July 11, 1907.*

His interest in violin-making was roused through the possession of an old European violin which was not very good, but inspired him with the thought that he could do a better job himself. He sought the assistance of Mr. Herrick, a violin maker of Hillsboro, and studied up on the subject through extensive reading. He enjoyed the acquaintance of several violin makers and has found this very helpful in improving his work. Mr. Chase generally follows a Stradivari model and uses old native wood, making all parts himself, including the purfling, and using yellow brown and red brown oil varnish. His earlier instruments sold for $65.00 and up. Mr. Chase leaves his violins heavy in wood, which he believes insures a long life and gives a better tone quality.

> I have examined photographs of Mr. Chase's violins which show that he is a really fine craftsman. The wood selections are beautiful and his work well done in all details. The purfling is accurately set and probably as neatly done as any maker can do it. It is to be hoped that Mr. Chase will make many more instruments and that he will find the recognition he deserves.

CONWAY, GEORGE S. — *Newark, Ohio. B. in Central Ohio in 1872.*

He was first instructed in violin making by Urbin Lyon of New York, and then worked for Leo Rushenberg of Denver, Colo., later establishing his own business in Newark, Ohio, which he still carries on. Besides considerable repair work and tonal reconstruction, he has made at least 150 violins. He uses oil varnish in reddish brown and amber red colors. He copies the "Alard" Strad of 1715, occasionally also Joseph Guarnerius, always endeavoring to bring the tone of his instruments as near to the original as possible. The price of Mr. Conway's violins is $300.00, higher for instruments finished in imitation of old.

COOPER, HARVEY A. — *Quincy, Ill. B. in Ripley, Ill. February 18, 1892.*

His knowledge of violin making has been gained from books and through the acquaintance of different makers in this country. He is an amateur violin maker but is deeply interested in all string instruments. He made a few violins and is now working on a bass.

CORNELL, DR. L. H. — *Fort Jones, California. B. May 8, 1870, in Centralia, Ill.*

A dentist who has been making violins and bows since he was 18 years of age, and in this he is self-taught. For the bows, which are priced between $10.00 and $75.00, he uses the Tourte model, for the violins mostly that of Stradivari, and they have sold from $25.00 to $300.00. His varnish is made as prescribed in an old Latin paper dated 1550, and Dr. Cornell writes that its spectrum, is identical with that of the varnish of old Cremona violins. He has studied it also under ultra-violet rays, by which the composition of the different coats and types of varnish is clearly shown. As a ground coat he uses a fatty golden yellow oil varnish, over which he applies a rose red or a reddish brown copal varnish, and this he claims, is the same procedure Stradivari followed and produces the same effect.

COVELL, JASPER L. — *Morenci, Mich. B. in New York June 21, 1880.*

Learned his trade from an old violin maker in New York. When he moved to Michigan in 1906, he became acquainted with A. C. Saunders who taught him more than he could learn from books or other makers. His violins, of which he has made between 50 and 60, are covered with an amber oil varnish of his own make, usually brown, of soft texture. He also makes his own filler and spirit varnish for repair work. Mr. Covell sells a pure amber varnish and filler, although the amber today is very hard to get. The lowest price he has sold his instruments for is $250.00. He now spends most of his time on repair work rather than making new violins.

CREVOI, EDWARD — *Cleveland, Ohio. B. in Vitebsk, Russia, September 6, 1902.*

A citizen of the United States since 1910. He comes from a family of cabinet-makers. He was a professional violinist and violist, having studied under well known teachers such as Leon Sametini, Maximilian Pilzer and others, and has played under many of the foremost conductors. Due to the strong competition in this field, Mr. Crevoi changed over to violin making five years ago and opened his own shop. He had spent all his spare time in watching violin makers and reading all the books he could find to learn this art. Today he has established a fine reputation as a craftsman, for before an instrument is let out of his shop it must meet with his own rigid requirements as to tone and appearance. He has made a number of violins and violas preferring the models of Stradivari and Amati and at present is working on a cello. He uses oil varnish of a golden brown color, varying in shades, and generally one-piece curly maple backs. He has a fully-equipped shop and has invented many tools to aid him in his work. His instruments sell from $200.00 to $400.00.

DAVIS, SAM — *Homestead, Fla. B. Dec. 20, 1873, at La Guardo near Nashville, Tenn.*

Aided by the late Frank Steadman of New York, V. C. Squier of Battle Creek, Mich. and A. W. Swearengen of Cincinnati and Miami, he began to study violin making in January, 1936. His first five violins were constructed from a form and outline made up according to the directions given in Heron-Allen's book. Later, he followed the "Messie" Strad pattern and acquired from W. E. Hill & Sons, London, a complete set of patterns, neck, outline and archings, copied from this famous instrument. Originally, he used Squier's varnish but has now perfected his own. He has made 33 violins, 4 violas and 2 cellos, using his own design for the violas and cellos (body length 16½" and 30" resp.). He uses both imported and American grown wood. His instruments have been highly recommended by professional players and have sold as high as $200.00, but have been appraised from $500.00 to $800.00.

DEBUSSY, CHRISTIAN F. — *Brooklyn, N. Y. B. in New York City March 30, 1872.*

He apprenticed to a pattern maker and carver and later became a master pattern maker himself, a job which requires great patience and utmost skill. When he was 15, he was presented with a violin and took lessons from Max Grau. He longed to have a violin with greater power and more brilliant quality and, being without means, the idea occurred to him to make his own. He contacted violin makers and gathered all information and advice possible. In 1910, he made his first violin and 3 the following year. He makes his own oil varnish and takes great pains in applying it, caring not whether it takes one or three years to finish an instrument. His sole object is to eventually make a violin that combines all the essential qualities and maximum power of tone. Mr. Debussy has made about 27 violins but has not set any prices on them, as he is not dependent on this income for a living.

> I have had the pleasure of examining and listening to two of Mr. Debussy's finest instruments and find his workmanship to be superb in every respect, very cleanly cut, exact and beautiful to look at. He has a fine varnish of his own and the tone quality of his instruments is sonorous, brilliant and powerful. They compare favorably with any new instruments I have seen by any maker.

DEGANI, GIULIO—*Cincinnati, Ohio. B. in 1875 at Montagnana, Italy.*

He comes from an old family of violin makers, and has made approximately 100 violins, 5 violas, 10 cellos and 5 basses. He follows the Stradivari models and uses oil varnish, mostly of a golden yellow color. His violins sell from $150.00 to $200.00. Mr. Degani was a pupil of his father, Eugenio Degani, a well-known maker of the Venetian school. (See front section.) He is recognized as a fine craftsman among artists and professionals.

DEL PRATO, RAYMOND — *Chicago, Ill. B. in Paris, France, 1905.*

Pupil of his father, François. Served his apprenticeship in Mirecourt, France, and later worked with Charles Enel and F. Billottet in Paris. He came to the United States in 1928, and is now with William Lewis & Son with whom he has been for most of the time that he has resided in this country. He has made between 75 and 100 violins, mostly on the Strad pattern, and varnished with a reddish-orange oil varnish.

DISMUKES, CORBIN — *Shreveport, La. B. in Magnolia, Ark., January 1, 1906.*

Learned violin making through the study of books, such as that by Heron-Allen and the "Encyclopedia of the Violin" by Bachmann. He is presently employed in repairing all types of musical instruments and only makes violins as a hobby in his spare time. The first one was made in 1921 when he was 15 years old, another in 1938, and since then, Mr. Dismukes has made 7 violins and 1 viola. He follows the Stradivari models and uses a light red oil varnish, applied on yellow ground.

> I have examined Mr. Dismukes' work and find him a good craftsman. His instruments are well made and possess good tone.

ELLERSIECK, HELMUTH — *Los Angeles, Calif. B. 1886 in Germany, the son of a Norwegian violin maker.*

He served his apprenticeship from 1900-03 under Ernst Kreul of Markneukirchen, one of the finer makers of that town, and received the highest honors of the graduating class of that year. He subsequently worked for Oswald Moeckel and August Friedel in Berlin, for Hjorth in Copenhagen, and for Rummelhoff-Hanssen in Oslo. He came to the United States in January 1927, and started his own business in Los Angeles, where he has been ever since. He is now an American citizen. Mr. Ellersieck prefers Stradivari and Guarneri models and his patterns are all taken from original instruments which have passed through his hands. He uses his own oil varnish, preferably orange. He has repaired instruments for many of the leading artists of the country and enjoys a fine reputation as a master craftsman. His violins retail from $250.00 to $500.00, his cellos for $600.00.

> I have examined a number of Mr. Ellersieck's instruments and can truthfully say that he is an artist in his work. It is excellently done, very accurate; his models are fine and his instruments have great carrying power as well as tone.

Albert Ellersieck: see front section.

FLAGG, RUSSELL DE GREE — *Rutland, Vt. B. in Hinesburg, Vt., October 29, 1892.*

At the age of 14, he started to study violin making with Chas. A. Estabrook. His grandfather, Henry Lewis Flagg of Essex County, N. Y., was a pioneer and a craftsman who made many violins. His father, Frank Flagg, was a musician, a vocalist and bandsman. Mr. Flagg has made about 100 violins and is now finishing his 4th viola. He follows generally the Stradivari model but has copied Amati, Guarneri and others. He uses only the best oil varnish obtainable and does his own coloring to suit his taste. The colors vary from orange to orange-red and red-brown. He devotes part of his time to the restoration of violins. The price of his instruments is $150.00 and up.

FOSTER, MALCOLM — *Middletown, Conn. B. March 10, 1894 in West Torbrook, N.S., Canada.*

An amateur maker, who, by profession, is a professor of mathematics in Wesleyan University. His interest in violins dates back to early childhood. He is entirely self-taught, has made five violins, the first one in 1929. They are all on a Guarneri pattern, either $13\frac{7}{8}$" or 14" in body length, the scrolls carved in the style of Guarneri's last period. He uses an oil varnish and favors brown and red colors. The wood is entirely of European growth. Two of his instruments have been submitted to bona fide experts and have been appraised at $350.00 and $800.00. He has not sold any as yet. Mr. Foster's second violin was presented to the Acadia School of Music at Wolfville, N.S., to be used by certain deserving students who cannot afford good instruments. He believes that the finest violins are being made today by a few of our modern craftsmen.

FRASER, OLIVER L. — *Saginaw, Mich. B. in Le Roy, N. Y. in 1847.*

A self-taught violin maker. Began making instruments in 1888 at Saginaw, where he resided until his death in 1929. His violins were all hand made, his own models or old master-copies. His "Celtic" model was the most popular brand and was sold in two price grades, at $300.00 and $500.00. His instruments vary in color, but brown, with a golden ground, predominates. He made about 600 violins, all of which found a ready sale.

FRASER, CHELSEA — *Saginaw, Mich. B. 1876 in New Sarum, Ont., Canada.*

Served his apprenticeship under his father, Oliver, after which he became a manual training instructor in the Grand Rapids schools where he remained for 20 years. He was the first practical violin maker ever to supply amateurs with violin making kits and has developed an extensive national business in this line. Each kit includes his own illustrated instruction book and patterns. In 1932, he began violin making in Saginaw under his own name. He faithfully reproduces Stradivari's "Le Messie" and the Guarneri "King Joseph." He makes his own oil varnish. His violins, hand tooled throughout, are sold direct to the user, coming in two price grades, at $150.00 and $300.00. Experts have judged his instruments exceptionally fine in tone and workmanship.

FRIEDRICH, JOHN — *B. 1858. Residing at Peekskill, N. Y.*

Served as apprentice in Kassel, Stuttgart and Berlin, Germany. He then came to America and established the firm known as John Friedrich & Bro. The elder partner, Otto, died in 1884. Friedrich made many instruments in the earlier years, but later on, his business was devoted chiefly to selling and repair work. About 1935, they went out of business and John Friedrich retired. Their instruments are priced from $100.00 to $350.00.

FROSALI, MARIO — *Los Angeles, Calif. B. in Legnano, Italy, in 1886.*

A graduate from the Conservatory of Music at Florence as a professor of violin in 1908. His hobby has always been that of violin making. He made his first violin when he was 9 years old and a family friend, Giuseppe Scarampella (a very well known violin maker), having seen this, encouraged the lad in this direction. As a professional violinist and teacher, he had but little time to devote to violin making and only in the last 5 or 6 years has he turned his hobby into a professional business. He is now chiefly repairing instruments. He has made 17 violins, most of them imitations of Stradivari, Guarneri and Guadagnini. Others are built on his own pattern. He has also made 2 violas, 2 cellos and some violin bows. He generally uses orange and red oil varnish. His instruments have sold for $400.00 and up.

> I have seen at least five of Mr. Frosali's instruments and can say that he is one of the best modern violin makers in this country. His work is exact, the measurements correct and he does a beautiful job of imitating the old masters. The tone of his instruments is superb. He certainly deserves great credit for his artistic work.

GALLAGHER, DARIUS M. — *New York, N. Y. B. in New York City, March 27, 1909.*

Started violin making in 1936. He learned without professional assistance, although from time to time, he visited violin makers and obtained helpful suggestions. His classification as a maker is strictly that of an amateur. He has completed 6 instruments and has several more in the making. He uses both oil and spirit varnish, colors ranging from light brown to brownish red.

> Mr. Gallagher's work is excellent. He takes great pains and his measurements are correct in every detail. He is a fine craftsman.

GARDING, EDGAR — *Paynesville, Minn. B. May 4, 1916, at Paynesville in Central Minnesota.*

A self-made violin maker who learned his trade through experimenting and contacting other makers. During his six years' experience, he has developed his own theories about the production of tone quality and varnishing. He has made 14 violins, following Stradivari, Amati and Guarneri models as to outline, arching them according to the density of the wood. He has also tried out a model of his own. He applies an oil varnish base and spirit varnish for the upper coats, in amber color and transparent brown mahogany. Mr. Garding offered his instruments for sale only recently, because he first wished to see if they matured to his liking, which they did, and they have met with the approval of renowned players. They are priced from $250.00 to $1000.00.

GATES, FRANKLIN H. — *Montclair, N. J. B. in Minneapolis, Minn. July 13, 1888.*

He did not serve an apprenticeship under any master but studied many books on violin making and has always been clever with tools. He has been greatly helped and inspired by some of the leading violin houses and makers of New York. Mr. Gates has made, to date, 5 violins and has 2 under construction on the new Mertzanoff scientific drawings. He uses oil varnish and favors chestnut brown. His present research work on American and tropical woods aims to achieve special tone qualities and he is also testing various forms of construction to produce freer vibration. Balancing the pull of the four strings, Mr. Gates states, improves the tone quality. So far, Mr. Gates has not sold any of his instruments.

GAULT, WILLIS M. — *Washington, D. C. B. June 10, 1908, in Worcester County, Md.*

He has been interested in violin making ever since he was a boy and he made his first violin at the age of 14. Much of his knowledge was gained through D. G. Struble of Washington, D. C. He has made 52 violins, all built on a Guarnerius pattern, and 6 violas. The color of his oil varnish is orange and in some cases brown or red. Many of his instruments were given away, others were sold at a very low price from $40.00 to $100.00, and the owners are all completely satisfied.

AUGUST GEMUNDER & SONS — *New York. This firm was founded in 1846 by August Gemunder (b. in Ingelfingen, Germany, 1814, d. in New York 1895).*

For the history of August and George Gemunder, see Front Section.

GEMUNDER, AUGUST M. — *B. in New York 1862, d. 1928. Son of August Gemunder, Sr.*

He and his brother, Rudolph F. Gemunder (b. 1865, d. 1916), were well known among American artists.

GEMUNDER, OSCAR A. — *B. in New York 1872, brother of Rudolph and August, Jr.*

He learned the art of violin making from his father and has made many instruments on the models of Stradivari, Guarneri, Amati, and Maggini. The "Gemunder" model of 1905 was made and finished in five different styles. Also special copies from original old masters were made. All of these instruments are varnished with the finest oil varnish and shaded in the old masters' style. Violins, violas and cellos retail from $200.00 to $800.00 each. Oscar is the last living member of this famous family of violin makers who, during their time in New York, have made a total of over 1000 instruments.

GEORGE, CARL H. — *Chicago, Ill. B. 1882 in Hamburg, Germany.*

Moved to Toronto, Canada, at the age of four, later to Chicago, and at the age of fourteen he entered the employ of F. Ferron and F. Wagner as an apprentice. He spent several years in London, Paris, and Berlin, studying famous collections of old masters. He has been making instruments continuously since 1899, namely, 350 violins, 12 violas and 22 cellos. Prices range from $500.00 to $700.00. Mr. George uses his own model, which is based on Stradivari and Guarneri patterns. He uses oil varnish exclusively; the color usually a reddish gold. He has received many letters of commendation on his violins from great artists for his fine workmanship and tone quality. (His father was a piano maker.)

GOULD, JOHN ALFRED — *Boston, Mass. B. in Windermere, England, March 11, 1860.*

He began his career as a repairer for Archer in Liverpool. In 1883, he went to Canada and two years later, to Boston where he worked for O. Weemann. In 1889, he opened his own shop, which is now a well established and important house for rare old violins, accessories and general musical merchandise, with workshops in Boston and Winthrop.

GLIER, ROBERT—See Front Section.

GOZZO, MICHAEL — *Hartford, Conn. B. in Bagni Canicattini, Italy, February 19, 1892.*

Served his apprenticeship under his grandfather Michael Gozzo I. He has made about 98 violins, 5 violas and 6 cellos, using Stradivari, Guarneri and his own models, applying an oil varnish of his own make in the Italian style. The colors are reddish brown and brown. His instruments sell from $350.00 to $1500.00.

GRANTHAM, W. A. — *Marshall, Texas. B. at Enondale, Miss.*

A self-taught maker who learned by doing repair work and by studying good books, among them, one published by Chelsea Fraser. He started making violins in 1933 and has made 9 instruments which have sold from $60.00 to $70.00, although some of them have been appraised to be worth more than $100.00. He follows a Stradivari model and uses the Fraser varnish.

GRAY, CHARLES B. — *Philadelphia, Pa.*

Mr. Gray, of Gray Machine Co., Philadelphia—the originator of the First Practical Metal Cutter or Nibbler—does not make or sell violins as a means of livelihood but is highly interested in violin making as a science. He made his first violin about 45 years ago and has a collection of violins, violas and cellos made by him that he regards as high class instruments. On these he has experimented until he found the proper graduations for producing a well rounded and resonant tone. Mr. Gray's opinion is that even the best instrument can be spoiled tonally by the bass bar. (The author fully agrees with him on this point.) He states he has experimented with bass bars until he was able to get the right size and weight and the correct place for the high point without any guess work. Thus he now can make a good instrument at all times, eliminating the element of chance. He has developed some charts useful to violin makers. Mr. Gray has done a great deal of research on varnish and he states there is little doubt that he has secured the same materials that were used in the 16th century when no dyes were used for coloring. The colors he has obtained, from light to dark shades, are brilliant and transparent and positively sun and light proof. In fact the direct sun rays enrich the color instead of fading it.

GREEN, JAMES F. — *Wichita Falls, Texas. B. at Coldwater, Kansas, April 27, 1890.*

He is purely an amateur and has made 25 full size violins, of different, original designs. The first one was made in 1916. They have never been sold and therefore no commercial price has been placed on them. Mr. Green uses oil varnish of different colors and has experimented with different woods, such as pine, mesquite, mahogany, redwood, lin, walnut, spruce and maple. He believes that Stradivari is the greatest master and advises amateurs to copy him. Mr. Green has some very original ideas which are artistic and out of the ordinary, especially in the style of his soundholes and the shape of the middle bouts.

GREEN, WYMAN R. — *Madison, N. J. B. in Moultrie County, Illinois, 1881.*

He began experimenting with violin tone production in 1911. He is a self-taught amateur maker and has made 6 violins, some of them being experimental models. The experiments have involved contour, graduation of back and belly, bass bar and soundpost. His models are original, and he uses the finest hard maple for the backs and selected Sitka spruce for the tops. Mr. Green has experimented with a variety of clear commercial varnishes, coloring them with earth pigments, but he also employs special violin varnishes supplied by the leading violin houses in the United States and has expressed to the author a preference for the Wurlitzer varnish.

> I have examined two of Mr. Green's instruments and I find the workmanship fine and the tone excellent.

GRIFFIN, WILLIAM REID — *Macon, Ga. B. in Macon Dec. 4, 1911.*

His first teachers in violin making were Chas. L. Williams of Chicago, and Frederick Z. Makett of New York City. He made his first violin at the age of 14 and has since made 68 instruments, selling from $75.00 to $200.00. Almost all have one piece backs and a golden brown to reddish brown varnish. They are, for the most part, copied from a Januarius Gagliano which he owns. Mr. Griffin is a good judge of old violins and is also known for his excellent repair work.

GROVES, A. W. — *Fort Worth, Texas. B. at Gordonville, Mo. December 3, 1871.*

He was a teacher of manual training and physics in high schools for a number of years. Through playing the violin, he became interested in its construction and, even more so, in the artistic repairing of old instruments. This, he thinks, is a harder job than making new ones. Mr. Groves states he has discovered Stradivari's methods of producing a perfect outline by using the square and compass as they were used in his day and taught by Galileo. He produces tone by using scientific methods tested in a physical laboratory. He works on the theory that the quality of a musical note depends on the number of overtones that are in harmony with the fundamental tone. He has made 21 violins which have sold from $100.00 to $150.00. He uses an oil varnish of golden brown or natural old wood color.

HALL, ELMER R. — *Port Angeles, Wash. B. March 8, 1869, at Green Prairie, Minn.*

For the first 20 years, he worked as a farmer. It was the late H. H. Heskett of Minneapolis who inspired him to become a violin maker. Some years later, Mr. Hall worked with a Swedish maker, Herman Hagberg of Brainard, Minnesota, a fine craftsman. He left Mr. Hagberg to become a machinist and for 24 years followed this trade, but during this time he continued to make and repair violins. He is now retired and one of his hobbies is still violin making. He uses oil varnish of different colors and, after altering his model several times, he is now using one which he regards as final. He has made about 84 violins, which have sold as high as $150.00.

> I have examined one of Mr. Hall's violins and found it well made. It is his own model, somewhat after a long pattern Stradivari, with wide purfling, rounded edges and a very well cut scroll.

HAMBURG, GEORGE — *New York, N. Y. B. in Russia in 1873.*

He came to America at the age of ten and started violin making as a hobby in Philadelphia when he was 17 years old. He has many favorable testimonials from artists, among them Mr. Elman, commending him on the quality of tone of his instruments. He has made 50 violins, also a number of violin and cello bows. His instruments are well made and deserve recognition.

HARDEN, WALTER H. — *New Plymouth (Orland), Ohio. B. in Southern Hocking Co., Ohio, July 26, 1874.*

He made violins and other instruments of that family as early as 1892, is self-taught and uses models of his own design. He exhibited a violin at the 1941 Ohio State Fair and was praised for his fine workmanship. He uses mostly oil varnish of a golden color. At present, he makes experiments to eliminate the change of tone in violins due to weather conditions. Mr. Harden has not set a fixed price on his instruments.

HARVEY, HOMER A., M.D. — *Batavia, N. Y. B. in Indianapolis, Indiana, October 8, 1884.*

He is purely an amateur maker, without training. Since 1916, he has made about 50 violins, mostly on a Stradivari model, using oil varnish exclusively, generally reddish orange. He has never sold these instruments but gave them to artists and students. Dr. Harvey is the inventor and producer of the Harvey Peg, a patented peg which grasps the end of the string firmly.

HAYDEN, L. G. — *Eldora, Iowa. B. in Hardin County near Eldora, Iowa, Dec. 6, 1889.*

He studied violin making with Hays-Schermerhorn in Seattle, Washington, and violin bow making with William R. Reisinger at Cedar Falls, Iowa. He has made 11 violins, the first one in 1920, and

10 violin bows. He copies the model of the "Paganini" Guarneri and of the "Dolphin" Strad. The varnish he uses is his own, of a light golden orange color.

HEBERLEIN, CONRAD — St. Louis, Mo. B. October 18, 1878 in Markneukirchen, Germany.

Served as an apprentice from 1893-96 under Ernst Reinhold Schmidt in Markneukirchen. He comes from one of the foremost families of violin makers in that town. In 1897-98, he worked in the shop of Heinrich Theodor Heberlein. He then went to Dresden to work for Richard Weichold. In 1903, Mr. Heberlein went to Berlin and worked for Hans Neuner and in the same year, came to the United States and entered the employ of Julius Guetter in Philadelphia. From there, he went to Chicago and for four years worked for Robert Pelz, and one year with Fassauer-Ferron. He started his own business in 1909 in Chicago which he carried on for 25 years. In 1934, moved to St. Louis to work for a music house, but in 1939 he again established his own shop. He has made over 100 instruments, including violins, violas and cellos. They bear his label and are also branded inside and on the lower block. Mr. Heberlein uses mostly a Guarnerius model, sometimes Stradivarius. He uses oil varnish exclusively, orange to orange-red and light brown to red-brown, always shaded. His first violins sold for $150.00; later his instruments sold for $250.00, $350.00 and as high as $500.00.

HECKEL, KARL WILLY — New York, N. Y. B. March 23, 1898, in Markneukirchen, Germany.

From 1912-15 he served his apprenticeship under the violin maker Herman Todt and became foreman of his shop until 1923. He then went to Graslitz, Czechoslovakia, and was in charge of the Varnishing Department of the firm of A. K. Hüttl, violin-makers. Later, he established his own business in Markneukirchen where he dealt only in high class instruments and furnished these instruments to firms in both Germany and the United States. In 1929, Mr. Heckel accepted a position with William Voit Co. in New York City as violin repairer and expert. Upon liquidation of this firm in 1937, he went into business for himself, again, and is, up to the present day, serving both professional and amateur musicians. He follows the models of the old masters and his workmanship is of high standard. He uses oil and spirit varnish, in colors from light yellow to golden reddish brown.

The prices of his violins range from $250.00 to $500.00, violas and cellos proportionately higher.

HEFFLER, JAMES — *New York, N. Y. B. in New York, October 22, 1900.*

In 1919, he began to devote his evenings to the study of violin making under the guidance of W. Wilkanowski. Between 1923 and 1937, he worked for the following companies: Fred Gretsch Mfg. Co., New York Band Instrument Co., Barth-Feinberg Co., and Buegeleisen & Jacobson. Since 1937, he has been employed by The Rudolph Wurlitzer Co. as a violin repairer. Mr. Heffler has made 3 violins on the Stradivari model, covered with golden brown oil varnish.

HEINZ, NICHOLAS — *New York, N. Y. B. May 28, 1892 in Brooklyn, N. Y.*

From 1906-11, he was an apprentice to Frederick Koenig, then worked for Carl Fischer for three years. He also worked for Julius Guetter in Philadelphia, Lyon & Healy in Chicago and other houses. In 1926, he established the business which he is still conducting in New York City. He has made about 150 violins, of his own model. The first ones were built on a medium high arching, but for the last 18 years, it is slightly lower. Mr. Heinz uses an oil varnish of medium brown color. A number of his instruments are today being used by members of the New York Philharmonic Symphony Orchestra and those of the Metropolitan Opera orchestra. They sell from $300.00 to $400.00. At the present time, Mr. Heinz specializes in repairing and restoring old violins. He has quite a collection of his own and is a dealer as well.

HELLAND, GUNNAR — *Fargo, N. D. B. in Telemark, Norway, January 26, 1885.*

An apprentice under his father, he completed his first violin at the age of 12. He came to America in 1905 to join his brother who had established a violin shop in Wisconsin. Mr. Helland worked with his brother until his death in 1919, and then carried on alone until 1927 when he moved to Minneapolis to be with the noted violin maker Jacob O. Lundh, and later moved to Fargo. Up to the present time, he has made 450 violins, on a Guarneri, and occasionally on a Stradivari model, using oil varnish. His instruments sell from $250.00 to $350.00. His forefathers were all violin makers and he had four brothers also engaged in violin making, two of whom are still working in Norway.

Mr. Helland has repaired a great many instruments and has been highly recommended for his work.

HERBRIG, CHARLES EDWARD — *St. Paul, Minn. B. in Montgomery, Minn.*

His forefathers were organ-builders and violin makers in Saxony and he was a pupil of William Herbrig in Germany. He has made about 70 violins, following the models of Stradivari and Guarneri as well as his own. He uses oil and spirit varnish which he prepares himself, the colors being orange red and red brown. His instruments have been sold from $150.00 to $800.00. They are known for their good tone and excellent varnish.

HERRICK, JOHN G. — *Hillsboro, N. H. B. in North Yarmouth, Me. April 3, 1863.*

He was a mechanic in his early life and later turned to cabinet making. He came to New Hampshire in 1899, and took up violin repairing as a hobby and started violin making in 1907. Mr. Herrick has made about 60 instruments, on a Stradivari pattern, varnished with a reddish brown oil varnish, using both native and imported wood, but chiefly American curly maple and spruce from old buildings. During the World War, when it was so difficult to obtain fittings and trimmings, he returned to cabinet making. Mr. Herrick did not work for any master, but by the aid of observation, good books, natural ability and experience he reached the point where others came to him for instruction. His instruments have sold as high as $100.00.

HERRMANN, EMIL — *New York, N. Y.*

The firm of Emil Herrmann—Rare Violins is a house of international reputation, founded in Berlin, 1883; New York house established 1924. Violin maker: Mr. Simone F. Sacconi (see page 169).

HESKETT, CLAUDE L. — *Glendale, Calif. B. April 24, 1869, in Leroy, Ill.*

Learned the trade under his father, H. H. Heskett, a violin maker who was born in Ross County, Ohio, and died in Minneapolis in 1898. He succeeded his father's business in 1905, at which time he finished a number of the instruments his father had started, and retoned some of the finished ones according to his own acoustical discoveries. He opened a new shop in Omaha, Nebraska, where he stayed from 1907 to 1915. Later Mr. Heskett went to Los Angeles and in 1933, settled in Glendale where he is still working. He has made about 100 violins. Of these, a few were after Stradivari and Guarneri, the others, after his own models which he now uses exclusively because he thinks they are more scienific in their proportions and therefore acoustically correct. His varnish ranges in color from Italian yellow to golden brown. His instruments have been priced from $100.00 to $350.00, but since working out to completion a system of acoustical violin making, he now claims them to be worth easily $500.00.

HORNSTEINER, JOHN — *Chicago, Ill. B. in Mittenwald, Bavaria, Dec. 1, 1862.*

Worked as a student in the State School of Violin Making in Mittenwald for a period of 4 years under the direction of Joseph Kriner. Upon graduation, he worked in Mittenwald for another year, then went to Frankfurt-on-Main to work with Edler for 3 years, and later to Berlin with Mathias Neuner (a pupil of J. B. Vuillaume). During the 12 years he stayed with Neuner; he had the opportunity to study famous instruments and bows. There he was the official repairman for such artists as Joachim, Sarasate, Moser, Remenyi and Haussmann. At the suggestion of Max Adler, the well known philanthropist, he came to Chicago and established the firm of Adler & Hornsteiner. This venture lasted 6 years. Mr. Hornsteiner then entered the employ of Lyon & Healy whose violin department was headed by Mr. J. C. Freeman. After 12 years with this firm, he opened his own establishment where he enjoyed a good reputation and did work for many of the world's famous artists. In 1931, The Rudolph Wurlitzer Co. bought his entire stock and, since that time, Mr. Hornsteiner has been with the Old Violin Department of that company in Chicago. He has not made violins in the past 20 years due to the fact that his time was taken up in the artistic repairing of fine instruments. He worked almost entirely on the Stradivari patterns of 1710-15. The varnish used is a typical Mittenwald color and texture, laid on slightly heavier. The selection of wood is invariably plain but acoustically ideal. He has made 4 violas, 10 cellos and approximately 300 violins. An exact copy of the "King Joseph" Guarneri, which he made for Lew Wallace, author of "Ben Hur," is considered the finest violin he ever made. For his regular grade violins, Mr. Hornsteiner has received a price of $200.00, and for violins made to order, $300.00. Some of America's foremost violin makers learned the craft under his guidance. These include Carl Becker, Frank Sindelar, Knute Reindahl, Eugene Knapik and many others.

HOWE, ARTHUR W. — *Union, N. Y. B. February 14, 1878.*

Learned violin making from Sewell L. Boyce in Norwich, N. Y. in 1897. He has made about 40 violins and 1 cello, mostly Stradivari models. He also made 1 Amati and 6 Guarneri copies. In later years, he found a way to color clear oil varnish made especially for him. His purfling is perfectly done and his work accurate, and has been praised by one of the foremost experts in this country. His violins have sold from $100.00 to $250.00.

HUNNICUTT, CHARLES — *Wilmington, Ohio. B. 1867.*

A self-taught violin maker, who has been building violins for the last twenty years. He has studied a large number of European books on violin making and has gathered further information through direct correspondence with violin makers both in Europe and in America. He has made 60 violins, on Stradivari and Guarneri models. The amber varnish he uses is imported from England and it is the best he has been able to find. His violins are priced at $100.00. Mr. Hunnicutt has recently sent two of his violins to the Ohio State Fair and won a prize as the best Ohio Maker of hand-made violins in that state represented at this exhibition. There were about 20 Ohio makers in this competition.

JACKSON, A. E. — *Ogdensburg, N. Y. B. January 2, 1880, in Ogdensburg.*

Served his apprenticeship under his father, L. C. Jackson, who is now 84 years old, and has been making and repairing violins for 60 years.

JACKSON, L. C. — *Rossic, N. Y. B. 1857.*

Made about 100 violins. He and his son are still working together. Mr. Jackson, Jr. has made between 35 and 40 instruments, following mostly the Stradivari model. A few are built on a Gagliano model. He uses oil and spirit varnish, dark red and golden brown. His violins sell from $50.00 to $100.00.

JELLIGA, GEORGE J. — *Minneapolis, Minn. B. in Habovfka (Orava), Czechoslovakia, June 12, 1893.*

Eldest son of George Jelliga, who, like his grandfather, was an amateur violin maker. He studied violin making in Europe, but most of his knowledge was acquired through practical experience. He has made about 30 violins, 6 violas, 5 cellos and 1 viol da gamba. The oil varnish, which is his discovery, varies from yellow gold to dark brown. It is made after a secret formula and differs from other varnishes in that it penetrates completely through the wood. It is composed of rare gums gathered from the mountains of Czechoslovakia. Mr. Jelliga has received many testimonials from fine artists and professionals complimenting him on his fine workmanship and varnish and the excellent tone quality of his instruments. They are built on his own model and sell for $500.00 and up.

JENKS, EDMUND B. — *Whitney Point, N. Y. B. March 16, 1863, at Upper Lisle, N. Y.*

Violin making and repairing has been his hobby all his life, but he is purely an amateur maker and has made but five instruments. His first violin was built on a Stradivari pattern in 1884. He has never sold a violin for money. After making his first violin, he worked out a model for himself based on that of Stradivarius and Guarnerius, but inclining more to that of Guarnerius. He has, thereafter, adhered strictly to this model. He uses an oil varnish of an orange color. Mr. Jenks is self-taught and obtained his information from books and personal experience. He always works on the smaller models with a body length of not over 14″. He has invented a new model bass bar, which was described in the December, 1938 issue of "Violins & Violinists," which has been used by many American and some English violin makers and has met with much favor. Mr. Jenks has had 4 violins made on his model by Mr. Arthur W. Howe, a talented violin maker of Union, N. Y. Number one of this series was sold for $200.00.

KAHLER, FREDERICK E. — *Washington, D. C. B. November 3, 1907 in Washington, D. C.*

He is a violinist and saxophone player and makes violins as a hobby. He has completed 2 instruments and has 5 more in work. He learned this art from other violin makers and repairers he knows. He uses only the finest old spruce and maple and a red amber oil varnish and follows the patterns of Stradivari and Guarneri.

KAPLAN, LADISLAV — *South Norwalk, Conn. B. June 19, 1874 in Moravia, Bohemia, and served his apprenticeship there.*

He came to the United States in 1893 and opened a shop in New York City. Here he worked until 1929, after which he moved to South Norwalk. Mr. Kaplan is the senior partner and founder of the famous Kaplan Musical String Co. He made his first violin in 1895. His practical knowledge is based chiefly on his experience in seeing and repairing fine old masters. He follows the Stradivari pattern, but applying his own principles. He makes his own oil varnish, usually golden yellow or orange. He has made a total of 92 violins, 9 violas and 2 cellos. The violins sell from $300.00 to $500.00, violas from $350.00 to $600.00, and cellos from $500.00 up.

> I have recently inspected one of Mr. Kaplan's 17 inch violas which is one of the finest new instruments that I have seen. His model is graceful and the workmanship such as only a master craftsman could turn out. It is covered with a beautiful golden yellow varnish of excellent texture. The tone of this viola is superb and has great possibilities. Mr. Kaplan is one of the outstanding makers of today and the instruments he creates are something of real and lasting value.

KARR, ALBERT H. — *Independence, Mo. B. March 27, 1885, in Clinton County, Ill.*

He comes from a family of mechanics and wood workers. He studied violin making under Silas P. Benjamin in Bloomington, Ill. and under Hendershot in Chicago. He began making violins under his own name in 1910. Up to 1940, he has made about 1,000 violins and they have sold from $250.00 to $500.00. Since then, he has made 30 violins after new methods which he has discovered. These are priced at $1,000.00 and may be advanced later. Mr. Roth and Mr. Weinstock of the Roth Quartet are using his instruments. The varnish is of a clear and finely textured nature, oil or spirit, the color mostly reddish brown or red. Mr. Karr prefers the Guarneri model but has also in the past worked after Stradivari patterns. He is also a successful bow-maker and has a factory in which he is producing all price bows. His finest Artist Pernambuco sells for $50.00. Musicians claim that his new instruments really sound like old ones, which is the result of three decades of work.

KAYE, JOSEPH — *Pittsburgh, Pa. B. in Reading, Pa. Jan. 3, 1866.*

He is self-taught and none of his ancestors were violin makers. He has made approximately 150 violins, violas and cellos. Mr. Kaye's aim is to build instruments of real merit, both as to tonal quality and appearance. He does not copy the old masters in every detail; he follows his own style of work, but he prefers the Guarneri model. For the past fifteen years, he has been using the finest oil varnish, varying from yellow to orange, light red and red brown. He works alone, has no assistants and has for many years done expert repairing. His instruments have been sold from $800.00 to $1,000.00 and some even higher.

KIRKHAM, S. R. — *Albia, Iowa. B. in Exire, Iowa, 1883.*

Has made 14 violins following the Stradivari model. The oil varnish he uses is generally a brown color. The information he received on violin making came from Leroy F. Geiger of Chicago. Mr. Kirkham has not sold any of his violins, as he makes them for a hobby and not for an income. He makes all his own forms and practically all his own tools.

KLIER, ROMAN JOSEF — *New York, N. Y. B. in Schönbach, Bohemia, January 31, 1904.*

He started violin making in his father's shop, who was a pupil of Georg Winterling, and, who, in turn, was a pupil of Mr. Klier's grandfather. In 1920, he went to work for Walter E. Geipel in Mannheim, Germany, and later for Robert Laumann in Budapest, Hungary. He came to America in 1927. He has made about 40 violins, 10 violas and 8 cellos while in this country and abroad, following the Stradivari and Guarneri models, and using an oil varnish of his own preparation of a golden brown color. In 1933, he entered the employ of The Rudolph Wurlitzer Co. in New York, where he is now working as an expert repairer and restorer.

KNOPF, HENRY RICHARD — *New York, N. Y. B. in Markneukirchen, Germany, December 15, 1860.*

A son of Henry Knopf, who was a bow maker of that town. His family moved to Berlin when he was 12, and two years later, his father died. He then went to live with his Uncle William, a violin maker. At the age of 18, he came to America and worked for John Albert in Philadelphia. In 1879, he established his own business in New York City. During his lifetime, he made about 450 instruments, of which about 50 were cellos and 50 violas. He had a fine reputation as bow maker and made approximately 1,000 bows. These were all stamped "H. R. Knopf, New York." His violins and violas sold for $250.00, his cellos for $500.00. A model which Mr. Knopf often followed in his early years, was a combination of Stradivari and Guarneri patterns, but from 1890 on, he strictly adhered to Stradivari models. He used an oil varnish of his own special formula. In 1930, he retired from business, after which he made about six more instruments at his home. He died in 1939.

KOODLACH, A. — *Los Angeles, Calif. He was born in Russia and came to Canada in 1910.*

After working there until 1920, he established himself in the United States. He discontinued making new violins when he was in Winnipeg and devoted his time to repairing and restoring fine old violins and bows. He began his career as a child in Kiev, Russia, apprenticed to the great master Rakovsky and later to Hillinsky. He worked for some of the famous violin shops in Germany, France and England. He is known as a connoisseur of rare instruments and bows. Mr. Koodlach has worked on instruments in the hands of the greatest artists in the world and many of them are his personal friends.

KOVANDA, FRANK — *Chicago, Ill. B. in Chicago, 1904.*

Bow maker. He has been with William Lewis & Son since 1924, and, during that time, has made approximately 100 bows, for the violin as well as for the viola and cello, most of which are in the hands of professional players. They range in price from $75.00 to $125.00. He also duplicates frogs of any of the great masters. Kovanda bows are being used in the Chicago and many other professional symphony orchestras.

KUGLER, WILLIAM J. — *Minneapolis, Minn. B. September 12, 1899 in Roberts County, S. D.*

Pupil of Charles E. Herbrig of St. Paul, Minn. In 1938, he established his own business. He is keenly interested in the instrumental art and history, particularly in the origins of the violin family, and is now working on early string instruments such as rebabs, vielles, etc. For his violins, he generally follows the patterns of Guarneri and Stradivari, using only the best quality wood. His workmanship is very clean and neat. He uses oil and spirit varnish of a golden yellow color, shaded to red. His instruments have sold from $250.00 to $600.00.

LEAVY, B. J. — *Williamsport, Pa. B. in Lycoming County near Williamsport in 1893, a descendant of a family of fine woodworkers and carvers.*

He started making violins in 1914, and has received many fine comments from some of the best makers and dealers. The late G. M. François of Pittsburgh bought several of his instruments. He has made 12 violins, mostly modelled after Stradivari, but some after Amati and Joseph Guarneri. He uses oil varnish, usually of his own composition and an orange to deep red color. His instruments are priced from $150.00 to $200.00.

LEHMAN, EUGENE — *Sharon Springs, N. Y. B. October 11, 1883 in Sharon Springs.*

He began the study of the violin at the age of six and later took up violin making in Boston and New York. He became a professional musician and teacher. His knowledge of the art of violin making was acquired chiefly through hard work and actual study, and he has made 130 violins and 3 cellos, his favorite models being the "Messie" Strad and a Joseph Guarnerius. He uses oil varnish (Millington), golden yellow and ruby brown. His instruments are made of the finest imported woods and are priced at $150.00.

WILLIAM LEWIS & SON — *Chicago, Ill.*

A musical instrument house established in 1874, one of the largest violin houses in the United States, enjoying an excellent business reputation. The following violin makers are presently employed by this concern: Carl Becker, Ferdinand Pfeiffer, Frank Kovanda, Raymond del Prato, John Emil Carlson and Fritz Truetschler. These will be found listed under their respective names.

LINN, LEWIS F. — *Los Angeles, Calif. B. April 25, 1883 in Philadelphia, Pa.*

Began studying the violin at an early age. He received much help from Mr. Sewell L. Boyce, violin maker in Buffalo, N. Y., where he lived at that time. In later years he became a professional violin maker and repairer. He uses the Stradivari model only and applies various kinds of oil varnish, usually a red and brown combination. He has made about 100 violins and they have sold up to $200.00. While working for Wurlitzer, he had the opportunity of examining fine examples of the great masters. At present, he is teaching instrumental music in a public school and does some repair work on the side.

LITTO, ALBERT S. — *Buffalo, N. Y. B. March 31, 1892, in Budapest, Hungary.*

Learned his trade under Carl Raab of Tombor, Hungary. Mr. Litto's forefathers were all violin makers and the family history has been traced back as far as 1642. He uses conventional materials, colors and models and has made about 1,000 violins. The commercial prices have ranged from a very moderate figure to a top of $800.00.

At the present time, Mr. Litto is directing and supervising operations of the Litto Manufacturing Co. which consists of his son, Albert J. Litto, and Mr. Alfred M. Zisser.

LONGIARU, GIOVANNI — *New York, N. Y. B. 1886 in Venice, Italy.*

He comes from a talented musical family. He devoted several years of his youth to designing and woodcarving under the foremost Italian woodworker, Eduardo Gottardo of Venice. He also studied music and the violin at the Royal Conservatory of Music. These studies completed, he went to Cremona, and there, under the able leadership of Guglielmo V. Pezzoni, he studied the art and secrets of violin making and the methods of restoring old master instruments. On arriving in America in 1904, Mr. Longiaru established himself in the violin business and, during these 38 years, has gained the reputation of being one of the leading modern violin makers. He enjoys the patronage of numerous well-satisfied customers. He has made 210 violins, his reproductions being mainly those of Stradivari, Guarneri, del Gesu and Guadagnini. His oil varnish is a transparent yellow and reddish brown, of warm, glowing texture. Only the finest materials obtainable are used and this, with his great knowledge as an expert craftsman, probably accounts for the rich, solid and appealing tone of his instruments. Prices range from $500.00 to $1,000.00.

> I have seen a number of Mr. Longiaru's instruments and consider him a master craftsman.

LUNDH, JACOB O. — *Minneapolis, Minn. B. in Norway March 15, 1865.*

He is a self-taught craftsman and has been making violins for the past 45 years. He works mostly on the Joseph Guarneri del Gesu model as he prefers that character of tone, but has also made some violins on the Stradivari pattern. Mr. Lundh has made about 400 instruments, including violas and cellos. He finds that his combination of oil and spirit varnish is better than the regular oil varnish, as the instruments respond more freely with this type of varnish and maintain their color better. The future of the instruments, of course, depends much on the filler applied to the wood under the varnish. His colors are orange yellow to various shades of red. His instruments sell from $400.00 to $600.00.

MARKERT, FRED J. — *New York, N. Y.*

Specializes in the restoration of old instruments.

MARKERT, JOHN — *New York, N. Y. B. September 18, 1910.*

He is the son of John Markert, Sr., a well known violin maker. Served his apprenticeship at the State School of Violin Making in Mittenwald, Germany, also with Ludwig Glaesel in Berlin and Markneukirchen. He worked under his father and his uncle, John Friedrich of New York. Mr. Markert has made approximately 150 instruments, among them 20 cellos and 25 violas. He copies mostly the great Italian masters, and uses a light bodied oil varnish, of various colors. His violins sell for $200.00. They are, like those of the older members of this renowned family, well made and deserve the place they have taken in the violin field.

MAURER, NICHOLAS — *Beach City, Ohio. B. in Stark County near Navarre, Ohio, 1858.*

A carpenter and wood carver by trade, he studied books on violin making and found it a valuable experience to experiment on their construction. He made his first violin at the age of 30 and has now made 75. They are all built on a Strad pattern, the last ones being copies of the "Dolphin." The varnish used is a brownish red color. Mr. Maurer has also repaired many violins. His own instruments have sold up to $125.00. He recently made a violin for Mr. Rubinoff and presented it to him at one of his concerts at New Philadelphia, Ohio.

McCORD, C. W. — *St. Louis, Oklahoma. B. July 28, 1886, in Washington County, Arkansas.*

He has studied the standard books on violin making but has not served a regular apprenticeship. He has made 5 violins, for the better ones of which he is asking $500.00. Mr. McCord says that professional players and experts have spoken very highly of his work.

MEADOWS, LYLE JOHN — *Ottumwa, Iowa. B. in Oskalousa, Iowa, December 7, 1898.*

He started violin making about 1925 and has since made 40 violins and 2 violas. He follows the Amati, Stradivari and Guarneri patterns, and uses either pure oil varnish or a mixture of oil and spirit varnish. His instruments have sold from $75.00 to $100.00.

MISNER, RAYMOND R. — *Middletown, N. Y. B. June 19, 1902, in Monticello, N. Y.*

Has attended art schools and has done painting and fine cabinet work, but his ambition is the mastery of the art of violin making. In this he is self-taught, but his work is already being recognized. He follows a Stradivari model, with slight deviation in the shape of the bouts, and uses oil varnish of a golden brown color. Prices have not as yet been established. Mr. Misner, who is a collector of antiques, also repairs violins and has all the work he can handle. Mr. Henry H. Joseph, Secretary of the Middletown Musicians Protective Union, praises his instruments very highly for their beauty and tonal quality.

MOENNIG, WILLIAM, SR. — *Philadelphia, Pa. B. in Markneukirchen, Germany, June 29, 1883.*

Served his apprenticeship under his uncle, Adolf Moennig, who had worked in Budapest, Hungary, where he was well known. He came to America at an early age, and, in 1909, opened a shop in Philadelphia where this business is still conducted by him and his son. He copies Guarneri and Stradivari patterns, and also makes cellos and basses. Mr. Moennig descends from a very old violin making family in Germany, dating back to 1640.

MOENNIG, WILLIAM H., JR. — *B. in Philadelphia, Pa. July 21, 1905.*

He was an apprentice to his father but later went to Europe working for Paul Dörfel in Markneukirchen, and at the Violin Makers' School in Mittenwald, Germany. In 1936, he received his Master's Certificate from the German Guild of Violin Makers and this was the first time that this certificate had ever been issued to an American. He has made many violins, violas and cellos, copies practically every model but prefers Amati, Guarneri and Stradivari patterns. He made for the Curtis String Quartet a copy of each of the Cremonese instruments used by the members of this quartet.

MOGLIE, ALBERT F. — *Washington, D. C. B. in Rome, Italy, Dec. 16, 1890.*

Served his apprenticeship under Antonio Sgarbi of Rome, and Leandro Bisiach of Milan. He also worked for Silvestre of Paris. Mr. Moglie was luthier to the Royal Conservatory, the Costanzi Opera House and the Augusteum Symphony Orchestra of Rome. He came to the United States in 1914 to do fine repairing for The Rudolph

Wurlitzer Co. of Cincinnati. He was transferred to New York in January, 1917, for the opening of their old violin studios there. He was put in charge of the repairing and restoration of the Wurlitzer Collection of Old Violins. He has repaired many of the greatest artists' violins and is known as a very able and skillful craftsman and one of the best of modern makers. To date, he has made 110 violins, 6 violas and 3 cellos. He uses his own models, but also follows the models of Stradivari, Guarneri and Sanctus Seraphin. His varnish is generally golden orange to golden red. Many of the instruments he made are owned by famous artists both in America and Europe. In 1918, he established his own business in New York which he transferred to Washington, D.C. in 1922, where it is still flourishing. Mr. Moglie is not only an excellent craftsman but also a successful dealer. He enjoys a very fine reputation in the business world. His violins and violas sell for $500.00, his cellos for $600.00.

MOYER, GUY H. — *Freeburg, Pa. B. Dec. 22, 1893, in Freeburg, Pa.*

He studied violin at Moyers Musical College in Freeburg, at Susquehanna University Conservatory of Music in Selinsgrove and with Wm. Hoppich of Philadelphia. He later taught violin at Moyers Musical College and had his own studio in Akron, Ohio. For two years, he travelled with the Metropolitan Concert Company as solo violinist. When he became interested in violin making, he was trained by Frederick C. Williams in South Bend, Indiana, with whom he worked for three years. Afterwards, he joined a musical comedy company and toured Europe. While in Paris, he studied violin making under Pierre Vieuxtemps for nine months. He has to date made 62 violins, using Stradivari and Guarneri models and an oil varnish of orange and Italian red colors. They sell from $150.00 to $300.00. Mr. Moyer claims that his method of varnishing, on which he has experimented for years and which is named "welded varnish," is the greatest advance in modern times.

NEBEL, FRED — *Brooklyn, N. Y. B. in New York City, April 14, 1901.*

Served his apprenticeship under his father, Andrew, and his uncle, Martin Nebel, in New York. He went to Mittenwald and worked for Johann Bader, from there to Michael Doetsch and later to Theodor Schrage, both of Berlin. These were excellent workmen, very well known in Germany. Mr. Nebel's forefathers, for many generations, have been violin makers of great renown. He reproduced old masters, especially Stradivari, Guarneri, Guadagnini and Gagliano. He uses both spirit and oil varnish, of various colors. He also makes instruments on his own model, which is entirely individual in outline of body, soundholes and scroll. His instruments retail from $500.00 up. He has made approximately 50 instruments.

NICHOLS, JOHN K. — *Haverhill, Mass. B. 1872 at Fort Edward, N. Y.*

Learned his trade under Robert Pelz of Chicago and E. F. Bryant of Boston. He has made about 50 violins and one viola, his model being mostly the "Messie" Strad, and sometimes a Guarneri. He uses only oil varnish, usually yellow brown. His instruments have sold from $100.00 to $150.00. Mr. Nichols spends a good part of his time repairing and restoring violins from all over the New England States and has customers throughout the country.

NIEBELL, PAUL H. — *Washington, D. C. B. in Scranton, Pa., June 26, 1901.*

An amateur maker who has so far made 4 violins. He follows the Guarneri model and uses oil varnish, either golden brown or orange. For the experience he has acquired, he is indebted to two violin makers, Prof. Flavien Vanderveken of Brussels, Belgium, and Ithaca, N. Y. and Albert Moglie of Washington, D.C. Professional violinists praise his instruments for their tone, responsiveness and carrying power and have valued them at about $1,000.00.

NIELSEN, N. CHRIS — *Omaha, Nebr. B. in Skive, Denmark, 1892.*

Served his apprenticeship in Denmark from 1906-10. Until 1912, he worked with Danish and German makers and repairers. In that year, he came to Omaha and worked for A. Rassmussen who came here at the same time from Copenhagen. Mr. Nielsen established himself in Omaha in 1918 as an importer and dealer in old and new violins and bows. In 1926, he went to Denmark on a purchasing trip to establish contacts in both Denmark and Germany. He has made several violins on the Guarneri pattern, usually using golden orange oil varnish. His instruments have sold for $250.00. He has not made violins since 1920 as he has specialized, since that time, in repairing and restoring old violins, for which he is enjoying a wide reputation.

O'BRIEN, VINCENT — *Ozone Park, Long Island, N. Y.*
B. Oct. 22, 1911, in Brooklyn, N. Y.

A self-taught amateur maker, he is greatly indebted to the work of Ed. Heron-Allen "Violin Making As It Was And Is." He occasionally had the help and advice of Andrew Nebel, a maker from an old Mittenwald family in Germany. Mr. O'Brien has copied Stradivari, Stainer and Guarneri models. He uses oil varnish of a golden color, made after his own formula, and takes only old wood, carefully selected for beauty. His instruments are trimmed with the finest fittings and range from $250.00 up.

OLSEN, LARS JORGEN RUDOLF — *New York, N. Y.*
B. December 11, 1889, in Copenhagen, Denmark.

He served a complete apprenticeship under Emil Hjorth & Sons between 1904 and 1909, then worked for Otto Möckel in Dresden from 1909 to 1912 and another year for the same firm in Berlin after Otto Möckel had taken over the business of his father, Oswald. He was awarded a scholarship and was thus able to travel in France and Holland and visit the violin making industries of these countries. While in Amsterdam, in the summer of 1913, he worked for Karel Van der Meer and at the same time learned bow making under Max Möller, who was then one of Van der Meer's workmen. In the fall of 1913, he came to the United States, and, at first, worked for John Markert, New York. In 1914, he established his own business in New York City, where he has had his workshop ever since. He has made approximately 40 violins, 3 cellos, a viola and a viol d'amour. His violins are mostly built on a Stradivari model, although some are made after Guarneri and Amati. The wood used is practically all imported, the varnish both spirit and oil, and the color a transparent reddish gold and light yellow brown. His violins and violas are priced at $500.00, his cellos at $750.00.

> I have examined one of Mr. Olsen's Amati patterns and a Strad copy. The workmanship in these instruments is excellent, beautifully executed, the soundholes well cut, the scrolls exceptionally well made. The measurements of the Amati are exact and the tone is very responsive. I have also seen his viol d'amour, made in 1916, which is a copy of a famous viol d'amour in the Royal Opera House in Dresden. It is exceptionally well made and proves that Mr. Olsen is a craftsman of extraordinary experience and skill.

OLSON, ANTON — *Worcester, Mass. B. in Vermland, Sweden,*
    Feb. 6, 1883.

He was a cabinet maker and came to America in 1903. Between
1903 and 1926 he made violins as a hobby, from then on, professionally. He has completed 66 violins, 5 violas and 9 cellos. His models
are predominantly Stradivari, occasionally Guarneri. He also reproduced models of Joseph Klotz and Dominicus Montagnana and two
of his violas are modelled after Gasparo da Salo. The last of these
was displayed at Shropshire & Frey, New York. Uses only oil varnish,
colors reddish brown to golden. His instruments retail from $250.00
to $300.00.

OSTROY (OSTROVSKY), JOSEPH — *New York, N. Y.*
    B. April 25, 1897, in Zegestov, Carpathian Russia.

As a boy, he took a great interest in violin making and learned
his trade from local violin makers serving mainly to vacationists and
to members of the symphony orchestra. He came to this country at an
early age and traveled for one of the larger importing houses in the
U. S. A., which brought him together with many violin makers and
players and afforded him valuable knowledge. He has made a few
violins on the Guarneri pattern, and some bows. He is a maker of a
naturally oxidized oil varnish of a rich orange brown color which is
unusually transparent and of a soft silky texture. At present Mr.
Ostroy is employed as a violin repairer with The Rudolph Wurlitzer
Co. of New York.

PARSONS, LLOYD — *Truman, Minn. B. in Webster County,*
    Neb., June 22, 1879.

Has been making violins as an amateur for twenty years, following a Stradivari model of 1708. He uses a good oil varnish of
reddish brown and amber brown colors and selects very old imported
wood. He has made 26 violins all told, which sold up to $200.00.

PFEIFFER, FERDINAND — *Chicago, Ill. B. in the Rhein-*
    pfalz, Germany, 1893.

He learned violin-making with Carl George of Wagner & George
in Chicago. Has at various times been employed as a violin maker
by Wurlitzer, Lyon & Healy, John Hornsteiner and is now with
William Lewis & Son, all of Chicago. He has made approximately 50
violins, mostly patterned after Joseph Guarnerius del Gesu and covered with oil varnish of varying colors. These instruments have been
sold for $250.00.

PHILLIPS, BENJAMIN F. — *Pittsburgh, Pa. B. 1886 in War-*
saw, Poland, descendant of a family of violin makers
that dates back to 1840.

He learned his trade under the guidance of his father and grandfather. At the age of 19 he came to America. From 1902-08 he
worked for Westinghouse. Between 1908 and 1918 he worked for the
violin maker G. M. François of Pittsburgh. He then opened his own
business which he has carried on up to this day, now assisted by his
son Edwin. Mr. Phillips has made 121 violins, 2 cellos and 4 violas.
He follows the Stradivari and Guarneri models, but on order, he
furnishes copies of any other Italian maker. He has perfected an
oil varnish which he uses on all of his instruments. The colors generally used are golden yellow, brown, plum, red and red-brown. Mr.
Phillips enjoys a large reputation for his excellent work and the
fine tonal qualities of his instruments. He is the inventor of a chinrest
which has been successfully used by many of the symphony players
of America. He prices his instruments at $500.00 to $1,000.00.

PINNEY, HAROLD A. — *Plymouth, Vt. B. May 18, 1894 in Ply-*
mouth, Vt.

He studied violin making under George Granger of Rutland, Vt.
He has made 475 violins and 4 cellos up to this time and has copied 14
different models of the old masters. He also uses a model of his own.
He prefers the Stradivari pattern and that of George Klotz. His
varnish is of his own formula and usually an orange shade although
he also recommends Ruben Frost's varnish. He uses only old wood of
fine quality. His instruments are scientifically made and he enjoys a
high reputation as an artistic maker. The price of his instrument
varies from $200.00 to $750.00.

POEHLAND, BERNARD of POEHLAND & FUCHS — *Brook-*
lyn, N. Y. B. in 1869 in Klingenthal, Germany.

Came to America in 1886 and established his business in Brooklyn. He is a self-taught violin maker, his guide having been "Die
Geige" by Paul Otto Apian-Bennewitz. He made about 200 violins,
2 cellos, 1 viola and 2 basses. He follows the Stradivari and Gagliano
models and uses oil varnish in various colors. His instruments have
sold from $100.00 to $250.00.

> I have seen some of Mr. Poehland's instruments and can
> say that they are very well made and certainly well worth the
> prices quoted.

REICHENBERG, W. C. — *Scottsbluff, Nebr. B. in Hannover, Germany, July 16, 1886.*

A cabinet maker by trade, like his father, who was also an amateur maker and repairer. He has made, in his spare time, about 20 violins, 3 violas and 4 cellos and has done considerable repair work. He uses various commercial varnishes as well as his own. Most of his instruments have been given away to friends and very few have been sold. Therefore a commercial value has not been set.

RICARD, ALEXANDER — *Springfield, Mass. B. February 17, 1861 at West Shefford, Canada, d. April 10, 1931.*

Of French descent. Originally a cabinet maker and woodcarver, he developed his hobby of violin making into a full time profession in 1917. He followed the Stradivari, Guarneri and Amati models, later only his own. He used an oil varnish of his own make, in the different shades of yellow, brown and red. His instruments were graded and priced from $100.00 to $300.00. He has made approximately 375 violins and several violas. He has received many fine letters from his clients praising his work, some stating they would not sell their Ricard instruments for many times the price paid because of their beautiful quality and appearance.

RICARD, RAOUL — *Springfield, Mass. B. in Springfield July 6, 1898.*

A cabinet maker by trade, son of Alexander Ricard, from whom he learned the art of violin making and to whom he succeeded at his death in 1931. He made violins in collaboration with his father, all of which bear the elder's label. He now makes an occasional violin or viola under his own name, but the greater part of his time is devoted to artistic repairing, restoring and rebuilding of old and new violins. He enjoys a very high reputation, as his father did, and is well known for his master craftsmanship. He has received numerous testimonials from leading artists on his new instruments as well as his repair work. His violins compare favorably with the best modern French and Italian instruments.

RICKER, JOSEPH F. — *Columbus, Ohio. B. in Austria 1873.*

Came to the United States of America at the age of eight. He received instruction in the making of violins and other stringed instruments from Charles Held of Columbus and Stephen Allison of Chicago between 1893 and 1898. In his early days, he made mostly guitars and mandolins. In 1900, he established his own business in Columbus and since then has devoted much of his time to violin and cello making. He has made 50 violins, 12 cellos and some violin bows. He uses mostly oil varnish in orange to red colors. He has a son, John J. Ricker, who has been associated with him for the past 10 years. While he has not made many instruments, he has become a very fine repairer and has just now started to make a few new violins. His violins sell from $125.00 to $150.00, his cellos for $200.00.

ROCKWELL. HARRY V. — *Providence, R. I. B. in Houlton, Me., 1878.*

Son of Joseph H., violin maker established in Brockton, Mass., and nephew of David B. Rockwell, also a well known maker in Boston and later in New York City. Harry V. Rockwell enjoyed excellent training under these two masters. He entered business with his father at the age of fifteen. About 1900, they transferred the shop to Providence where it is still carried on under the firm name J. H. Rockwell & Son. They are makers, repairers and dealers in fine violins, cellos and musical merchandise and have assembled a collection of the famous old masters' works. Mr. Rockwell has made about 250 violins, violas and cellos, following the patterns of Stradivari, Amati and Guarneri. About 20 years ago he developed a new model on which he makes most of his instruments now. They bear his label as well as a brand mark with his initials under the end-pin. Mr. Rockwell uses only the purest of oil varnishes and he has perfected a filler which he says penetrates the wood and brings out prominently the grain and curl of the woods, giving them the appearance of the old Italian instruments. Violas and violins sell from $250.00 to $350.00, cellos from $350.00 to $500.00.

ROSS, A. C. — *Moscow, Idaho. B. February 6, 1904 near Republic, Wash.*

A self-taught maker who gathered his information from books and from other makers whenever he had an opportunity to meet them. He has made 16 violins, 5 violas, 7 cellos and 3 basses. Besides his own models, he uses the Stradivari patterns, but his basses are built entirely on his own design. He uses oil varnish and his colors are usually dark red. He has not gone into the violin business commercially and therefore does not price his instruments at any specific figure, but they have sold as high as $100.00.

ROSSMASSLER, EDWARD — *Chadds Ford, Pa. B. in Philadelphia, Pa. December 5, 1878.*

He is self-taught but received instruction from the late Louis Drouin of New York. He has made 9 violins, 2 modelled after Amati and 7 after Guarneri; 1 viola and 2 cellos. One of his cellos, a Goffriller model, has back, sides and scroll of Brazilian walnut and the table of spruce. He selects the finest of materials and uses oil varnish only. The color is reddish brown to golden. Mr. Rossmassler made these instruments only as a hobby and therefore prices have not been established. Though he is now retired, he still does a great deal of violin repair work, mostly for friends.

SACCONI, SIMONE F. — *New York, N. Y. B. May 30, 1895, in Rome, Italy.*

He studied the violin with his father, who was a professional violinist. He started his apprenticeship at the age of 8 years under the well-known Venetian violin maker, Giuseppe Rossi, under whose supervision he worked until 1912, when he established his own business in Rome. In 1931, he came to New York to take charge of the repair shop of Emil Herrmann. Most of his time is taken up with the repair and care of fine instruments and he has done work for practically all our great soloists and leading string quartets. He has made approximately 60 violins, 15 violas and 22 cellos. Mr. Sacconi follows the models of the great masters of the Cremonese school and uses oil varnish. He also uses his own original model which is very similar to Strad. His instruments are sold from $400.00 to $1,500.00, depending on the model and the amount of detail work involved. In 1937, Mr. Sacconi attended the Stradivari Bicentennial Exhibition in Cremona, taking over the instruments exhibited by Mr. Emil Herrmann. He was appointed by the Committee of the Exhibition as one of the judges to pass on the exhibits and to appraise the new instruments in a competition for modern violin makers. Mr. Sacconi exhibited a complete quartet of his own make and was awarded a special gold medal for this work apart from the general competition.

SANGSTER, E. H. — *Fitchburg, Mass. B. in Upper Falmouth, N.S., Canada. March 16, 1889.*

Started making violins at the age of 16, as a hobby. He has not been an apprentice to any master, but has gained a great deal of knowledge from Henry Schultz and Harry Haskell who worked for Oliver Ditson of Boston. Mr. Sangster has made about 16 violins. In

1919, he moved to Vineland, N. J. and was employed in the large music store of Jesse Davies, as a repairman. In 1922, he established his own business in Vineland, and after three years returned to Nova Scotia to settle at Grand Pré. From there he opened a business at Halifax, where he remained until 1939. After another stay in Vineland, he is now located in Fitchburg. Mr. Sangster states: "No matter how fine the material, dimensions and construction, no man can produce the old masters' tone unless he varnishes as they did." He uses only oil varnish of his own secret formula. His colors range from reddish yellow to dark brown. Prices are from $250.00 to $350.00.

> Mr. Sangster is a fine craftsman. I have examined his instru-
> ments and have found them to be excellent, and especially
> fine in their tone quality.

SAVAGE, ANTON — *Ashley, Pa. B. January 16, 1896.*

He learned his trade under his father and is a descendant of the well-known Sawicki family of violin makers. Carl Nicholas Sawicki was his great-great-grandfather (see Front Section). He uses American wood and an oil varnish of the finest ingredients, in red, mahogany and golden yellow colors. Mr. Savage specializes in tone production. He is doing research work on high models and is having more than the usual success. His instruments sell from $300.00 to $500.00.

SAVAGE, ELLIOT J. — *Meriden, Conn. B. in Meriden, Conn. January 17, 1890.*

He took up violin making as a hobby when he was about 18. He was never apprenticed to any master but learned by studying and experimenting. His forefathers were skilled mechanical workers, though not violin makers. He has made 20 violins, 1 viola and 1 cello. He uses mostly a model which he has developed himself. He always uses oil varnish, of excellent texture, in amber, brown and red-brown colors. His earlier instruments were sold from $50.00 to $150.00, but his later, and best instruments, have been sold for as high as $300.00.

SCHILBACH, OSWALD ANTON — *New York, N. Y. B. in Schoeneck, Saxony, 1862.*

Pupil of E. W. Neumärker of Schoeneck. He came to America in 1887 and worked for Herman Koenig. In 1894, he established himself in New York as a violin maker and repairer and continued as such until his retirement in 1938. The instruments he made are on the

Stradivari and Guarneri models. The varnish is usually a brilliant reddish brown color.

> I have seen several of Mr. Schilbach's violins and wish to mention one particularly of about 1890, which is a credit to its maker. The measurements are exact, the varnish excellent and the tone of beautiful quality. Only a master craftsman could turn out so perfect an instrument.

SCHILBACH, OSWALD — New York, N. Y. B. in New York 1893.

Son of Oswald A. Schilbach. From 1909 to 1912, he served as apprentice to Paul Ritter in Schoeneck, Saxony, Germany. Upon termination of his apprenticeship, he entered his father's establishment in New York and continued to work there as a violin maker and repairer, until the business was liquidated in 1938. He is now associated with the firm of Deffner & Barandes, Inc., wholesale musical merchandise dealers.

SCHMIDT, ERNEST OSCAR — Cleveland, Ohio. B. April 24, 1891, in Markneukirchen, Germany.

He learned his trade under his father, E. Reinhold Schmidt. In 1908, he passed his examinations and so became a full-fledged violin maker. He came to the United States in 1909, and he and his brother went into business under the name of Schmidt Bros. Co., in Cleveland, Ohio. He has made 30 violins, 2 violas and 3 cellos. He patterned his instruments after Stradivari, Pressenda and Vuillaume. His cellos are patterned after a Stradivari model made by Fiorini. He uses imported wood exclusively and either spirit or oil varnish. Mr. Schmidt has the diploma of the String Instrument Makers Guild of Markneukirchen, which shows him to be a capable maker entitled to teach violin making. At present, he devotes most of his time to the restoration of fine old instruments.

SCHMOLL, RUDOLF F. — Portland, Oregon. B. in Hannover, Germany, February 12, 1904.

He served his apprenticeship under Theodor Berger, Markneukirchen, Germany, from 1921-26, after which he received his journeyman's degree. During the time between 1926 and 1932, he worked in violin shops in the following cities: Utica, N. Y., Salt Lake City, Utah, Los Angeles and San Francisco, California. In 1932, he received his master's degree from the Instrument Makers Guild in

Markneukirchen. On his return to the United States, he established his business in Portland, Oregon. He devotes most of his time to repairing bow instruments and is therefore able to make only a few violins. Mr. Schmoll has made 8 violins, using Stradivari and Guarneri models. He uses both oil and spirit varnish, from orange yellow to reddish brown. His instruments sell from $100.00 to $150.00.

SCHNICKE, HARRY — *Cincinnati, Ohio. B. in Cincinnati 1871.*

He was taught to play the violin by his father, joined the Cincinnati Symphony Orchestra at the age of 26 and was with them for 15 years. When he was 18, he took up violin making as a hobby. While in the orchestra, he studied all the fine old instruments. Later, violin making and repairing became his business. He has, to date, made 63 violins and 4 violas. For violas he followed the Landolphi model and also made a Gasparo da Salo copy. His violins are mainly built after Stradivari, a few after Guarneri and some on his own pattern. Fifteen instruments were bought and used by members of the Cincinnati Symphony Orchestra, which certainly is a commendable record. He uses oil and spirit varnish and prefers that made by himself. The average price of his instruments is $200.00. Not only is Mr. Schnicke a fine violin maker, but also a composer, a portrait painter and a gardener of great repute and he has won many awards in these different fields of activity.

SETTIN, JOSEPH — *New York, N. Y. B. in Crespano (Borough of Treviso), Italy, 1893.*

A self-taught violin maker whose guides were books and fine examples of genuine old Italian violins. At the age of 11, he made his first violin which is still in his possession. He continued to make violins with the exception of the three years during which he served in the first World War. In 1920, he came to the United States where he opened his own shop for violin making and restoring. He uses his own model, a combination of the Stradivari and Guarneri school. He employs the utmost skill in following the old masters and their principles and methods as they have been passed down to our generation. He believes that these methods and principles have stood the test for many decades and does not think it possible to do better than follow these great luthiers. The varnish Mr. Settin uses is a mixture of spirit and oil. He first applies a coat of yellow and over this his color varnish, which is usually reddish brown. Mr. Settin is a sculptor and served his apprenticeship at the Academy of Fine

Arts at Santa Marta, Milan. Some of his works are exhibited at the Public Museum at Tripoli, Africa. In later years, he has devoted most of his time to the restoration and repairing of old violins, as he finds it more profitable than making new violins.

SIMONSON, F. L. — *East Stroudsburg, Pa. B. March 11, 1886, in Rowland, Pike County, Pa.*

Originally a machinist engaged in the automobile field, he has for the past 15 years, together with his brother-in-law, Mr. W. A. Smith, been experimenting on the construction of violins and violas to find out what controls timbre and volume of tone. They have used all kinds of wood and varnish, various models, archings and graduations, because Mr. Simonson says the making of a good violin depends on these various inter-related factors. He has made 57 violins and 3 violas (17"). He uses only old selected wood and prefers oil varnish of a dark brown color. His violins sell for $150.00 to $250.00, his violas for $250.00 to $350.00. Mr. Simonson has also made some very fine bows which sold for $35.00 to $50.00, and after the war he plans to follow up bow-making in preference to violin-making.

SINDELAR, FRANK — *Chicago, Ill. B. 1883 in Czechoslovakia.*

Served his apprenticeship under John Hornsteiner of Chicago and had his own business for many years in that city. Mr. Sindelar has made approximately 300 instruments, chiefly violins, about 25 violas and 2 cellos. He copies the old Italian masters, mostly Stradivari and Guarneri. He uses his own oil varnish, in yellow, orange and red. His instruments sell for $250.00 and up. Most of his time today is spent on repairing and reconstructing the better grade bow instruments. Mr. Sindelar is the originator of the Super Sensitive Stainless Steel strings, which are excellent strings and are becoming more and more popular with the professional musician.

> Mr. Sindelar's work has impressed me very much and I consider him a fine craftsman. His measurements are correct and the varnish of excellent texture. The wood used is of fine quality and the tone large and resonant.

SLAVIK, JOSEPH — *New York, N. Y. B. in Austria March 27, 1880.*

Served his apprenticeship under Johann Schweitzer of Vienna. Worked also in Bucharest and Jasey, Roumania, in Krakau, Poland, and under Liebich, of Leipzig, Germany. He came to America in 1907 and worked for Carl Fischer, Simpson & Fry, Ditsons and Pitt Co., for the following 14 years. In 1921, he established his own business and has been making a series of violins of which he has completed 12 up to the present time, built on Stradivari and Guarneri models. The color of his oil varnish is old brown and dark blood red. The price of his instruments varies from $85.00 to $350.00.

SMITH, WILLIAM J. — *Mt. Kisco, N. Y. B. at Port Hood, Nova Scotia, Canada, February 17, 1880.*

He has been devoted to the study of the violin since childhood. His knowledge of violin making was gained by reading books on the subject and by observing other good violin makers. He has made approximately 100 violins, the first one dating from 1915. He has also done many repairs. His early instruments were built on the Guarneri model, but later he changed to Stradivari which has been his favorite ever since. He uses an oil varnish and prefers golden brown or red brown colors. His instruments have sold from $150.00 to $250.00.

STANLEY, CARLTON F. — *Newton Centre, Mass.*

Comes from a family of violin makers. His great grandfather was Liberty Stanley, b. in 1776. In 1924, Mr. Stanley and his uncle F. O. Stanley began making violins and other stringed instruments for the market, using only the best materials obtainable and selling them at a moderate price. Mr. Stanley has made between 500 and 600 instruments, including violins, violas and cellos. He has many testimonials from fine artists commenting on his great skill as master craftsman. He uses only pure oil varnish, of his own make. He has not served a regular apprenticeship but has picked up violin making when he was associated with his uncle, who, at that time, was in the automobile business and was one of the originators of the Stanley Steamer Automobile. His instruments are exceptionally well made, show beautiful workmanship and have fine tone. His better violins sell for $150.00 and $200.00, violas $150.00 and cellos $600.00.

STASHAK, DR. JOSEPH T. — *Wilkes-Barre, Pa. B. December 23, 1891 in Glen Lyon, Pa.*

The inspiration to make violins came to him through the possession of a fine old violin which was lost and, as he could not afford to buy one equal to it, he decided to make his own. This led him to extensive research work. In this search for proper woods possessing the best acoustical qualities, he finally found them at the Rudolph Wurlitzer Co., where he obtained, in his estimation, the finest, most appropriate materials. In his spare time, he made about ten instruments which he believes possess many of the qualities of rare old instruments. He also has done a number of repair jobs, adjustments and regraduations. He follows the Stradivari model, mostly copying the Messiah and the Betts. He uses only oil varnish of the finest quality, prepared by Hill & Sons, London. He has not placed any commercial value on his instruments and prices therefore cannot be given. Dr. Stashak, as an amateur violin maker, has made some fine instruments and certainly should be given great credit for his work.

STENGER, WILLEBALD CONRAD — *Chicago, Ill. B. at Roanoke, Ill.*

Of German parentage. He began violin making in 1903 at Topeka, Kansas, and he established his own shop in Chicago in 1909. He follows his own model, which is somewhat on the Strad pattern. He also took up bow making in 1920 and now specializes in this. He follows the principles as worked out by the French master, François Tourte, though the head he cuts takes on original character. His best bows, silver mounted, sell for $75.00. His violins are skillfully done. He cuts his own scrolls, which vary in style. His earlier varnish was a pure linseed oil, of a brown color, while the varnish of his present period is soft and transparent, of silky texture, the color, orange red to light brown. From 1930-40, he devoted his time exclusively to research in the propagation of musical sound. His objective in this was to determine the factors that make up the character and shade of fine violin tone. Mr. Stenger works without any assistant. His earlier violins sold for $250.00. Since 1923, they are priced at $500.00.

STEVENS, WALLACE R. — *Stratford, Conn. B. Sept. 15, 1892 in Canaan, Conn.*

An amateur maker, self-taught, who worked out his own forms of graduation and patterns, without following a specific master. He has never set a price on his instruments yet, but expects to do so shortly. He uses American wood, except for the sides and linings.

STOFFEL, WILLIAM PETER — *Milwaukee, Wisconsin. B. 1883 in Racine, Wis.*

Learned his trade in Schoenbach, Czechoslovakia, and is now an American citizen. He discontinued violin making as he now specializes in school work. He has originated an educational plan of service to schools and colleges in the way of repairing and adjusting and with this he combines "shop talks" to students on the care of their instruments. His idea is that a properly adjusted and aligned instrument is essential to the student for correct playing and best results.

STRATON, REV. WARREN B. — *Brooklyn, N. Y. B. December 31, 1907 in Baltimore, Md.*

Mr. Straton, to whose family belong some prominent artists, studied painting and sculpture in Cooper Union, Beaux Arts and is a life member of the Arts Students League in New York. He also studied in Europe. He thus achieved experience and skill in the handling of tools and fine carving. While in Europe, he did a great deal of research regarding paints and varnishes and how to make them by hand as the old masters did, and he was especially interested in the study of the Cremonese varnish. For his own varnishes he uses only the pure gums, no artificial coloring. His colors are from golden yellow to deep red. He first took up violin making as a hobby but has since worked seriously at it. The patterns used are after Antonio Stradivari and Joseph Guarnerius. His instruments range in price from $500.00 up, depending on the wood used.

> I have known Mr. Straton for many years and can say that his work is beautifully done, exact in every detail. His measurements are correct and his artistic ability as a sculptor certainly reflects in his clean carving and fine workmanship.

SWAYSGOOD, D. E. — *Defiance, Ohio. B. June 1, 1866, in Staford Township, Indiana.*

A self-taught violin maker whose guide has been "Violin Making As It Was And Is" by Ed. Heron-Allen. He started out with the Defiance Machine Works as a wood pattern maker. Invented a jig for setting the neck accurately which eliminates the "creep" usually caused by the pressure of the clamps. He has worked on a pattern of a rare master violin received from Mr. Heron-Allen when in London. His violins usually sold for $100.00, but he has received $500.00 for a fine copy of a Peter Guarnerius, 1695. He has also made bows copying the style of François Tourte. Mr. Swaysgood has circularized a blue-print demonstrating the well-made violin and explaining the technical terms used to denote the various parts.

THIERRY, JAMES — *Akron, Ohio.*

An iron-molder by trade, now aged 83 years, he took up violin making as a hobby more than 40 years ago and used Ed. Heron-Allen's book as a guide. He has made about 85 violins, a viola and a cello all on the Stradivari model. He used oil varnish on all but the first few violins as he finds it better than spirit varnish. The colors are mostly "old brown," sometimes red or light brown. In former years, he imported his wood from Czechoslovakia, but as this is very hard to get now, he has turned to American grown maple and spruce, always endeavoring to select old stock. Mr. Thierry receives between $20.00 to $75.00 for his violins but sells them only when he needs material for more.

THOMA, JACOB — *B. 1837 at Raab, Hungary.*

Learned his trade in Vienna, Austria, under Lembeck-Bittner. He made about 75 violins, 20 violas and 15 cellos. He followed the Stradivari, Guarneri, Amati, Bergonzi and Ruggeri models. He secured wood 300 years old which came from an old church door that had been torn down. His varnish is both amber oil and spirit; his colors are yellow golden brown to light red. He made a string quartet for the Vienna Exhibition in 1888 and was awarded a medal and diploma for this fine work. In 1889, he and his son Alexander came to the United States and established themselves in Boston, Mass. where they became the violin repairers for the Boston Symphony Orchestra. Jacob died in Boston 1917, and his son is carrying on the shop in Dorchester, Mass. The prices of Jacob Thoma violins range from $100.00 to $250.00.

THOMA, ALEXANDER — *Dorchester, Mass. B. in Vienna, Austria, 1872, son of Jacob.*

He learned his trade in his father's shop. He received his diploma of approval and acceptance from the Musical Trade Committee. In 1889, he came to America with his father and they opened their shop in the Old Music Hall Building in Boston. He made about 50 violins and numerous violas and cellos. His workmanship is excellent and the tone quality fine. He follows the Stradivari, Guarneri and Amati models, using only old, seasoned wood. The colors of his amber oil varnish are golden brown, orange and red. His violins have a clear and brilliant tone, excellent for orchestra. Prices range from $100.00 to $200.00. Both he and his father received many testimonials from prominent violinists and teachers for their fine instruments.

THOMPSON, THEODOR — *B. in Omaha, Nebraska, d. 1933.*

He was a great violin enthusiast and a pupil of Jacob Lundh of Minneapolis. He established himself as a professional violin maker in this city in 1923. His model was exclusively that of Joseph Guarnerius and he used a spirit varnish of a golden brown color. He made about 60 violins and was known as an excellent craftsman.

THORP, FRANCIS A. — *Houston, Texas. B. 1892 in Holstebro, Denmark.*

At the age of 14, he began his trade as a blacksmith and, during the following four years, attended a technical school studying mechanical drafting and mathematics. He went to sea as a fireman and visited many nations—and their violin makers. In 1912, he came to the United States, and in 1926, went to Houston, where he has been and is still working for a large oil company as layer out in the boiler department. As a violin maker he is self-taught. He began actual construction of violins in 1933 and has now made 32. Of these, 30 are copies of Stradivari, 1 of Guarneri and 1 of Amati. He is now making a Strad pattern cello and three Strad violas. He uses an oil varnish, yellow golden brown and reddish brown. Mr. Thorp is also known for his repairs of which he has done a great number. His instruments have sold from $65.00 to $285.00.

TIETGEN, HANS — *B. April 24, 1857, at Stolpe, Germany.*

He first studied music in Neumünster and later learned violin making in various German cities. In 1886, he came to the United States of America and established himself in New York as a violin maker and dealer. He afterward moved to New Jersey and there died in the early 1930's. He made a great many instruments, following the Stradivari model. The color of his varnish is usually a poor red, not attractive. His work, however, is well done. His instruments have sold from $100.00 to $200.00.

TURNER, NORMAN — *Nassau, N. Y. B. Nov. 25, 1876 in Nassau, N. Y.*

He has no vocational background in violin making and is purely an amateur maker. What he has learned was through experiment and the study of books. His first violin was made in 1908. He is a carpenter and painter by trade and makes violins in his spare time, about fifty up to this time. The first ones were not very valuable, but the later ones he sells from $75.00 to $100.00 and has been advised that his better instruments should bring $125.00. He prefers to work

on a Strad model but does not follow it in every detail. He leaves it
a trifle wider in the waist and with a longer arching. He uses only
oil varnish and his favorite color is yellow brown.

> I have examined two of Mr. Turner's instruments recently
> and find them very well made and beautifully varnished. The
> measurements are good, the tone quality fine and, as a self-
> taught man, he deserves recognition.

TRUETSCHLER, FRITZ — *Chicago, Ill. B. in Markneukirchen, Saxony, 1901.*

Apprenticed to Durschmidt and later worked with Otto Moeckel
and Anton Pilar in Berlin. He has been with William Lewis & Son
since 1928. He has made approximately 200 violins, mostly on a
Strad model and covered with a golden yellow varnish. These instruments are valued at $150.00 and up.

URDAHL, O. N. — *Minneapolis, Minn. B. in Bergen, Norway, 1882.*

He came to America in 1901. In 1924 he again was abroad and
in the same year took up violin making under Sverre Hansen in
Bergen. He returned to the United States in 1925 and resumed his
studies under Jacob Lundh and Mr. Weston of Minneapolis. In 1928,
he established himself as a professional violin maker in this town.
Mr. Urdahl has made 74 violins. He follows exclusively the Stradivari model and he uses a light transparent oil varnish of golden red
and yellowish brown color. He temporarily discontinued his professional work due to business conditions. His violins are priced from
$200.00 to $500.00.

VASICH, NICHOLAS — *Baltimore, Md. B. in Zvornik, Yugo-slavia, 1891.*

He received his training at the State School of Violin Making
in Schoenbach, Czechoslovakia, and Markneukirchen, Saxony, two
famous centers of this industry. One of his masters was Johann
Dvorak, Prague. He formerly maintained violin shops in Petrograd,
Shanghai and Harbring, Manchukuo, also in Seattle, Wash. Besides
his own model, Mr. Vasich uses mostly Guarneri and Stradivari patterns. He applies either an oil or a balsam-spirit varnish. The com-
binations of colors are chiefly red, yellow and brown, shaded or fully
imitated after the old masterpieces on which he specializes. He has
made approximately 350 instruments, including violas and cellos.

The present price range is from $265.00 to $500.00. He has maintained his shop in Baltimore since 1933. Mr. Vasich enjoys a fine reputation as one of the foremost violin makers of today and has many personal letters from great artists commending him on his work. His instruments are excellent both in tone and craftsmanship. They are of the highest artistic quality.

VIRZI, GIOVANNI BATTISTA — *New York, N. Y.*
B. in Palermo, Italy, 1886.

Came to the United States of America in 1912. He learned his trade under his father, Rosario Virzi, who was a violin and cabinet maker and a carver. Mr. Virzi has made 50 violins, 3 violas of 16½" and 16¾" length, and 1 cello which is now being used, together with 2 of his violins and a viola, in the NBC orchestra. The material used is old Italian wood of the finest quality. Mr. Virzi has his own formula for an oil varnish of golden yellow or reddish yellow color. For 16 years, until 1934, he worked with his brother Giuseppe, then established his own business in New York City where he is still conducting it. Up to 1934, he used a Stradivari model and from then on his own model which he prefers. His instruments are well made and are liked for their large tone. Many professional musicians are using his instruments today. Violins sell from $300.00 to $400.00, violas from $400.00 to $500.00 and cellos at $500.00.

WALDRON, HUGH H. — *Froid, Montana.*

An amateur violin maker who learned the art from books and through actual experience and association with other violin makers. He started to build violins in 1936 and has now made 12. Some of these have been sold to leading schools and artists. He follows the "Dolphin" Strad model and uses a fine oil varnish of a beautiful red shaded to golden red. He uses choice old wood imported from Switzerland. His work has been praised very highly by the Juilliard School of Music and the eminent artist, Yehudi Menuhin. His instruments have been found to be very even, smooth and soft yet powerful in tone, with rapid response. They have been sold from $250.00 to $500.00.

WALLER, ALFRED — *Minneapolis, Minn. B. Oct. 4, 1891 in Grant Co., Minn.*

Follows the Stradivari and Guarneri models, using reddish orange oil varnish. His best instruments are priced at $350.00. Mr. Waller has also been active as a professional violinist.

WALLO, JOHN JOSEPH — *Ellerson, Va. B. June 2, 1889 in Lalit, Austria-Hungary, of Slovak parents.*

Since his early childhood, he has been deeply interested in violin making. At the age of nine, he made his first violin independently and did so well that his comrades also gave him orders for instruments. Among his ancestors were musicians, woodcarvers and carpenters. In 1906, Mr. Wallo came to the United States where he continued his study of the violin and its music. He was also interested in the orchestra and between 1910 and 1919 he had his own in Detroit and Flint. In 1915, he built a cello and later started making violins on a Jacobus Stainer pattern; but due to serious illness, he had to interrupt his work until 1932. Since then, he has made many instruments and is assisted by his sons, Joseph and Paul. His models are known as the Wallo Flat and High. The former is priced from $100.00 to $300.00, the latter from $100.00 to $400.00. These are similar in outline to the Strad model, but the bouts are less rounded and the height of the arching is ½", resp. ¾". He also copies the classic models. He uses various kinds of American maple and spruce, beech and redwood, and both oil and spirit varnishes in colors varying from dark red to light yellow. In addition to making violins, Mr. Wallo does repairs and has received numerous testimonials from satisfied customers.

WALTER, JOSEPH A. — *Montclair, N. J. B. September 23, 1902, in New York, N. Y.*

Studied violin and violin making under Adrian Primrose, a European artist. Most of his training and knowledge have been acquired through close contact with reputable violin makers in this country. He has been making violins since 1918 and has to his credit 31 violins and 2 violas. He uses the choicest quality wood and follows the Stradivari and Guarneri models. He uses an oil varnish of golden amber color, at times shaded red. Mr. Walter has given many public exhibitions and lectures on the art of violin making. His prices range from $250.00 to $500.0.

> I have examined an instrument that Mr. Walter made in 1940 and find his measurements to be correct, the model very fine and the tone excellent. He can be honestly classed as one of America's fine craftsmen.

WEAVER, HERMAN A. — *Washington, D. C. B. in Gloucester
     Court House, Va., August 10, 1886.*

He started making violins in 1898, and shortly after moved to
Portsmouth, Va., where he studied violin playing. At the age of 17,
he moved to Denver, Colo. and studied violin making under David
Ruschenberg, with whom he remained until 1907. He then went to
Chicago and continued his work under John Hornsteiner for another
3 years. Seeking new fields, he went to Cincinnati and worked under
Adolph Spicker until 1916. He then conducted shops of his own
in various cities, in Pulaski, Norfolk, Baltimore (1923-1935) and,
since 1935, in Washington, D. C. Mr. Weaver has made approximately 144 violins, 4 cellos, 4 string basses and 3 violas. He used
European wood mostly, but for some instruments has used wood from
different parts of the United States and Canada. He generally followed the Stradivari and Guarneri lines, but the model he has worked
on for the last three years is his own in outline, arching and general
make-up. He makes his own oil varnish, the colors being golden
amber, sometimes nut brown and occasionally reddish gold. The price
of his instruments varies from $100.00 to $500.00; most of them
have sold for $250.00.

WERCHMAN, JOHN — *New York, N. Y. B. January 26, 1900,
     in Berne, Switzerland.*

He served his apprenticeship under Jean Werro, Berne, with
whom he stayed from 1917 to 1921. He then came to America and
worked for John Friedrich & Bro., New York, until 1928, since
which time he has been with The Rudolph Wurlitzer Co. of that
city as an expert repairer and restorer. While in this country, Mr.
Werchman has made 12 violins, of different models, in oil and spirit
varnish. He became a citizen of the United States in June, 1928.
His brother Fritz is a violin maker in Berne, Switzerland.

WHITE, ODD S. — *Asheville, N. C. B. February 11, 1898, in
     Asheville, N. C.*

For the past 15 years, he has been repairing violins and bows.
During this time he made several violins which, however, he did not
consider of any great value. Four years ago he became acquainted
with the process developed by Jack Westall of Asheville for pre-
aging spruce and maple. In his research in connection with this
processed wood known as "Wesmeraged," Mr. Westall had the
collaboration of Mr. E. C. Mertzanoff of New York, from which the

word "Wesmeraged" is derived. The first violin Mr. White made of this wood was so successful that he decided to confine his future efforts to this material. The process claims to produce in a plank of wood, before it is carved, the same chemical and physical changes that atmospheric exposure effects in a thin piece of wood over a period of many decades. Wood so processed has been found to have increased density and stiffness, which means greater vibrancy, while the essential structure of the wood is unimpaired. Violins made by Mr. White of this wood have been judged by competent experts in competitive tests as having power, tonal beauty and a significant similarity in playing quality to those of fine old instruments. The models used by Mr. White are a Strad model and a special Mertz-anoff model designed according to mathemathetical calculations. The colors of his oil varnish are dark red and brown. Mr. White has not established any commercial prices as yet.

WHITE, ZENAS — *Lewiston, Idaho. B. at Lexington, Le Sueur Co., Minn., December 2, 1870.*

As to his knowledge of violin making, experience and observation have been his teachers. He received much information also from Mr. Robert Robinson, a violin maker of Portland, Oregon. Mr. White comes from a woodworking family. He has made 70 violins, 3 cellos, 3 violas, 5 guitars and other instruments. He has also done a great deal of repair work and believes that this, well done, is more difficult to master than new construction. He has used Amati, Stradivari, Guarneri and Guadagnini models and prefers the latter, a broad model with low arching. He prepares his own oil varnish, in various colors. He attaches the greatest importance to the sizing of the wood before applying the varnish. The average price of his violins is $80.00.

WHITEFORD, H. K. — *Darlington, Md. B. in Darlington, Md. June 16, 1878.*

He served his apprenticeship under Walter Goss of Boston and has always faithfully followed his advice and instructions. His ability was soon recognized and developed by his teacher. He has made 83 violins and 5 violas, usually following the Stradivari pattern for the violins and that of Gasparo da Salo for the violas. He uses oil varnish in varied colors; some are rich mahogany; others, mostly of bird's-eye maple, were left in the natural wood slightly colored in gold. The prices vary from $75.00 to $125.00 and up to $225.00 for exceptional specimens. Mr. Whiteford is now making violin bows of Osage orange, which is hard, extremely resilient but light in weight and is not affected by weather conditions; the color is deep yellow.

WILKANOWSKI, W. — *Brooklyn, N. Y. B. in Poland, March 15, 1886.*

He completed his first violin at the age of nine and through much practice and experience he became a full-fledged violin maker when he was 17. The approximate number of violins he made is 5000, 100 violas and 30 guitars. He uses four models: Stradivari, Amati, Guarneri and his own. The selections of wood are of the finest. He uses an oil varnish of his own discovery, made of genuine amber. The color is usually golden-brown amber, shaded to red-brown. His instruments are used by many of the leading professional musicians and are known for their large volume of tone. For over 20 years, Mr. Wilkanowski has made instruments for the Oliver Ditson Co. and is now making them for the Fred Gretsch Mfg. Co. His violins range from $50.00 to $250.00, his violas sell for $100.00, and his guitars for $400.00.

WILSON, R. J. — *Ravenna, Ohio. B. in Edinburg, Ohio, 1887.*

An amatuer violin maker whose interest in this art was first aroused by the late Charles Elliott of Kent. Mr. Wilson's patterns are taken from the "Dolphin" Stradivari. The varnish he uses is Howe's Cremona oil varnish. As he makes violins merely as a hobby, he has not set a commercial value on them.

WUNDERLICH, CURT — *Detroit, Mich. Son of Gustav Wunderlich, Leipzig, a very famous German maker belonging to an old violin making family. Curt was born at Leipzig, Germany, April 25, 1902.*

At the age of 16, he entered his father's shop, where he served five years' apprenticeship. He then worked for one year under August Brueckner of Wernitzgruen, Saxony, on bows exclusively. In 1924, he came to the United States and worked for John Friedrich, Louis Drouin and Walter Gretsch of New York City. After becoming a citizen of the United States in 1931, he worked for The Rudolph Wurlitzer Co. in Detroit for a period of over two years. In 1934, he established his own business in that city. Here he was soon recognized as a maker of true copies of the great Italian masters. Mr. Wunderlich prefers to copy Guarnerius del Gesu and Carlo Bergonzi, although he also uses a Stradivari pattern of 1723. At present he is making a copy of a famous Goffriller cello. He uses oil varnish exclusively and matches the colors of the old masters he is copying. His selections of wood are only the best and of very old seasoned stock. He is known as a very skillful and accurate workman and artists have praised his instruments very highly. His violins sell for $300.00 to $350.00, violas for $400 and cellos for $800.00.

THE RUDOLPH WURLITZER COMPANY — *Founded Cincinnati, Ohio, 1856.*

Internationally known as dealers in rare string instruments. Stores in New York, Los Angeles, Chicago and other cities. They employ the following expert violin makers: John Werchman, Roman Klier, James Heffler, Mario Frosali, Joseph Ostroy.

WURLITZER, RUDOLPH H. — *Cincinnati, Ohio.*

The history of the Wurlitzer family is an extremely interesting one and has been traced back as far as the 16th century. It begins with Henry (1596-1656), John (1629-1679) and Michael (1661-1727), who were lute makers. Hans Andreas (b. 1701) and his nephew Hans Adam Wurlitzer were the first violin makers. Then follow Hans Andreas (1732-1799), John Andreas (1771-1807), Christian Gottfried (1807-1871), and Rudolph Francis (1831-1914) with his sons Howard Eugene (1871-1928), Rudolph Henry (see below, b. 1873) and Farney Reginald (b. 1883). There was also another violin maker, a collateral descendant, John George, b. 1726, and one Frederick Wurlitzer who made a tour of Europe as a child prodigy and became Court Pianist in Prussia at the age of sixteen.

Mr. Rudolph Wurlitzer studied at the University of Berlin and obtained the degree of Doctor of Philosophy. His studies at the university were principally the History of Musical Instruments under Oscar Fleischer. He also heard Helmholtz and Kundt in Acoustics and Physics, and Spitta in the History of Music. While in Berlin, he spent two afternoons a week with August Riechers, a violin maker. He states that at that time, there were more fine violins brought to his shop than any other in Germany and that it was through Riecher's interest in him that he acquired the basic knowledge of violins and violin making. He studied violin playing under Emanuel Wirth of the Joachim Quartet. Mr. Rudolph Wurlitzer is known and recognized as one of the leading connoisseurs of this country.

WURLITZER, REMBERT — *New York, N. Y. B. March 27, 1904, in Cincinnati, Ohio. Son of Rudolph H. Wurlitzer.*

He entered the violin shop of J. R. Carlisle as an apprentice in 1924 and stayed with him for six months. He then went to Europe and spent 18 months with the well known craftsman Amédée Dieudonné in Mirecourt, France, and another year in Italy, Germany and England, studying the works of the old masters as well as the art of modern violin making. While in England, he studied under one of the greatest violin experts, Mr. Alfred Hill. Since 1930, Mr. Wurlitzer has been active in the Violin Department of The Rudolph Wurlitzer Company, founded by his grandfather in 1856, and is the assistant of Mr. J. C. Freeman, the well-known connoisseur.

YURKEVITCH, MISCHA — *New York, N. Y. B. in Sebastopol, Russia, July 20, 1900.*

After the war of 1914-18, he went to Markneukirchen, Germany, to study violin making under Willy Goetz. He also worked in Berlin under the supervision of Alexander Bucher in the Herrmann workshops. He later came to the United States and worked for Emil Herrmann in New York City. In 1933, he opened a studio and workshop in Carnegie Hall, New York. He is a master craftsman and has a thorough knowledge of making and repairing fine instruments. Mr. Yurkevitch has repaired many of the famous violins of the world, such as Stradivaris, Guarneris, Amatis, Bergonzis and others, and has done work for many of the leading artists of this country. Among them are Mr. Heifetz and Mr. Elman, who are his personal friends. The number of new violins he made is small, usually after the models of Stradivarius, Guarnerius del Gesu and Guadagnini. He also made master copies of old instruments. He uses both oil and spirit varnish of his own preparation, only natural colors (not aniline). The reason why Mr. Yurkevitch does not make more instruments is that he works alone and is kept continuously busy with repair work on fine instruments. His violins sold as high as $750.00.

Appendix

CONTEMPORARY ITALIAN VIOLIN MAKERS
As yet little known in America

ALAGIA, NICOLA—works in Lauria Superiore.

ALLAIOLI, FLORINDO—Casteldario (Mantua).

ALOI, CARLO—Rome.

ALOI, DARIO—Rome.

ANNARUMMA, VINCENZO—Salerno. Born there 1892. Pupil of Vincenzo Postiglione.

ARASSI, ENZO—Milan. Born in Trieste 1889. Established since 1914. Uses red oil varnish.

AVERNA, ENRICO—B. in Caltanisetta, works in Palermo.

AVERNA, GESNALDO—Works in Caltanisetta, following the models of Stradivari, Guarneri, Amati and Gagliano.

BANNI, GIUSEPPE—Rapallo (Genoa).

BARBIERI, ARNALDO—B. in Asti 1893, son of Francesco. Works in Forlì, following Stradivari, Amati and his own models.

BEDOCCHI, MARIO—Reggio Emilia. Born there 1880, son of Clemente. Self taught.

BELLA FONTANA, LORENZO—Genoa.
Self taught. Works on models of his own.

BONORA, GIUSEPPE—Bologna. A maker with a fine reputation as an expert restorer.

BOSELLI, ALFREDO—Florence.

BOSI, CARLO—Cremona. Born in Paderno Cremonese 1873. Department manager with Cavalli & Poli. Self taught. Stradivari models.

BOSSI, GIUSEPPE—Stradella (Pavia).

BOTTINI, BENVENUTO—Brescia.

CALACE, GIUSEPPE—Naples. Born there 1899. Member of a family of guitar and mandolin makers.

CANDI, CESARE—Genoa. Born in Bologna 1869. Pupil of Raffaele Fiorini. The models used are Stradivari and Guarneri del Gesu, also his own. Has made fine inlaid specimens.

CANDI, ORESTE—Genoa.

CANTAGALLI, PAOLO—Rome.

CAPALBO, GIOVANNI—Rome.

CAPELLI, ANNIBALE—Cremona.

CAPICCHIONI, MARINO—Rimini.

CARPI, ORESTE—Dosolo di Guastella (Mantua).

CARUANO MARSIGLIESE, BIAGIO—Rome. Born in Santa Elizabetta 1885.

CASINI, LAPO—Florence. Born in Campi Bisenzio 1896, son and pupil of Lapo di Serafino (b. 1863). Follows his own models.

CASTAGNINO, GIUSEPPE—Chiavari (Genoa). B. in Cagorno 1883. Pupil of G. Fiorini. Works on Stradivari and Guarneri models.

CASTELLOTTI, ALDO DI LUIGI—Cremona. Born there 1913. Self taught. Copies Stradivari.

CATANIA, FRANCESCO—Catania (Sicily).

CAVANI, VINCENZO—Spilamberto (Modena). Son and pupil of Giovanni (b. 1851). Also studied under Bisiach. Uses Guarneri model chiefly.

CELANI, COSTANTINO—Monticelli near Ascoli Piceno. Born there 1869. Brother and pupil of Emilio. Amati and Guarneri models.

CHIARAFFA, GUGLIELMO—Rome.

CININO, ANGELO—Vittoria (Ragusa).

COMEL, STEFANO—Gorizia. Born 1890. Pupil of his father Stefano. Strad model.

CONTAVALLI, LUIGI—Imola. Born there 1862. Self taught maker, has received high awards for his excellent work.

CONTINO, ALFREDO—Naples. Born there 1890. Pupil of and successor to Vincenzo Postiglione.

COTUGNO, GIOVANNI—Ancona. Born 1894 in Pizzo Calabro. Self taught.

D'AMORE, GIUSEPPE—Rome.

DE BARBIERI, PAOLO—Genoa. Born there 1889. Pupil of Cesare Candi.

DEL FIUME, FAUSTO—Rome.

DE LUCCA, ANTONIO—Rotello.

DE PECCATI, UMBERTO—Milan. Born in Soncino (Cremona).

DESPOSITO, LORENZO—Rome.

DIGIUNI, LUIGI—Cremona. Born in Casalbuttano (Cremona) 1878. Self taught. Works on his own model. Invented in 1922 a "violetto," an instrument between viola and cello, played on the shoulder.

DI LEO, DOMENICO—Palermo. Pupil of Antonio Sgarbi.

DI STEFANO, GIUSEPPE—Catania, Sicily.

DOLCINI, RENATO DI QUINTO—Marina di Ravenna. Born in Forlì 1903. Self taught. Has his own models.

EMBERGHER, LUIGI—Rome. Born in Aprio 1856. Self taught. Specializes in the making of mandolins, mandolas and zithers.

FABIANI, ANTONIO—Ascoli Piceno. Born there 1898. Pupil of Andrea Bisiach and of F. Sacconi. Stradivari model.

FAROTTI, CELESTINO—Milan. B. in San Germano Monferrato 1905. Pupil of his uncle Celeste Farotti. Copies Stradivari, Rocca and Pressenda.

FERRARIS, ORESTE—Vigevano (Pavia).

FERRONI, FERNANDO—Florence. Born there 1868. Pupil of Zorzi. Uses a model of his own.

FONTANINI, ARISTIDE—Rome. Native of Cremona.

GADDA, GAETANO—Mantua. B. 1900 in Sorgà (Verona). Pupil of Stefano Scarampella. Copies Stradivari.

GALIMBERTI, LUIGI—Milan. B. 1880 in Seveso (Milan). Pupil of Innocente Rottola and of Romeo Antoniazzi.

GALLINOTTI, PIETRO—Salero (Piemonte). Born there 1885. Follows the models of Stradivari and Guarneri.

GEROSA, GIOVANNI—Morbegno (Sondrio). Born there 1895. Self taught. Stradivari and Guarneri models.

GIARONI, ELVIRO—Villa San Maurizio (Reggio Emilia).

GIORDANI, ENRICO—Rome.

GIRARDI, MARIO—Trieste.

GIUSQUIANI, RAFFAELLO—Arezzo.

GOTI, ORSOLO—Ascoli Piceno. Born in Pieve di Cento 1867. Studied under Carlo Carletti. Now in business for himself.

GUADAGNINI, PAOLO—Turin.

GUERRA, EVASIO—Turin. Maker of violins and mandolins.

GULINO, SALVATORE—Pinerolo (Turin). B. 1910 in S. Cataldo, Sicily. Pupil of Gesnaldo Averna.

KRESNICK, DR. FRANCESCO—Fiume. Born in Vienna 1865. A connoisseur of many years' experience. The author of a treatise on how to obtain powerful yet sweet tone. Works on Stradivari and Guarneri del Gesu models.

LEPRI, GIUSEPPE—S. Arcangelo di Romagna (Forlì).

LOMBARDI, COLOMBO—Rome.

MAGGIALI, CESARE—Carrara. B. 1886 in Ruderi di Moneta (Tuscany).

MARCONI, LORENZO—Cremona.

MARTINENGHI, MARCELLO—Milan. Pupil of his father Stelio.

MASETTI, FRATELLI—Modena.

MASSARA, PIETRO—Ivrea (Aosta).

MASTRACCI, AMEDEO—Paganica (Abbruzzi).

MELEDANDRI, ADOLFO—Viareggio.

MIGLINO, CARLO—Turin.

MIRONI, PIETRO—Catania.

MONTERUMICI, ARMANDO—Bologna. Born in Vendriana 1875. Pupil of Raffaele Fiorini whose successor he became in 1898.

MOZZANI, G.—Bologna. Conducts his own school for violin making.

MUTTI, VITTORIO—Castiglione (Mantua). Self taught.

OLIVIERI, FRANCESCO—Rome and Catania. Makes also mandolins and guitars.

PALUMBO, FRANCESCO—Seminara (Calabria).

PARMEGGIANI, ROMOLO—Modena. Born there 1889. Self taught. Stradivari model.

PECCHINO, VASCO—Suzzara (Mantua).

PEDRAZZINI, GIUSEPPE—Milan. B. 1879 in Pizzighettone (Cremona). Pupil of Riccardo Antoniazzi. Follows Stradivari patterns as well as his own.

PINHEIRO, ERNESTO—Trieste.

PITETTI, LORENZO—Ivrea (Aosta).

POGGINI, MILTON—Anghiari (Arezzo). Born there 1911. Self taught. Follows classical models as well as his own.

POLITI, A.—Rome.

POLITI, ENRICO—Rome. Born there 1885. Son and pupil of Eugenio. Follows Stradivari models. Transparent varnish.

PUCCI, D.—Florence.

PUCCINI, ELIGIO—Empoli. Born 1900 in Castelfiorentino. Pupil of Fernando del Perugia of Florence. Stradivari model.

RADRIZZANI, ANGELO—Born 1870 in Milan. Pupil of G. Rossi and L. Bisiach. Went to Switzerland 1898 and established his business in Vevey.

ROCCHI, SESTO DI ERMINIO—San Paolo d'Enza (Reggio Emilia). Studied at the Parma School of Violin Making, also under Leandro Bisiach. Uses the "Amatisé" Strad model.

ROVESCALLI, AZZO—Cremona. Born there 1880. Learned under his father Teodoro. Stradivari model.

SCEVCENKO, VLADIMIR—Bologna. Born in St. Petersburg 1889. Self taught. Uses his own models.

SCHIAVI, CARLO—Cremona. Born in San Bassano 1908. Pupil of Dr. F. Kresnick. Stradivari and Guarneri models.

SDERCI, NICOLO IGINIO—Florence. B. 1884 in Gaiole in Chianti. Pupil of L. Bisiach. He follows the classical models. He received the first award for violin construction at the Stradivari Exhibition in Cremona 1937.

SGARABOTTI, GAETANO—Parma. Born in Vicenza 1878. Self taught. Uses the "Amatisé" Strad model. He is the director of the Parma School of Violin Making.

SGARBI, ANTONIO—Palermo.

SISTO, SISTO—Milan. B. 1870 in Mirabello Monferrato. Self taught. Has his own model and methods of construction.

SOLFERINI, REMO—Mantua.

STELLUTO, LORENZO—Mantua. Born 1886 in Vico Garganico (Foggia). Pupil of Stefano Scarampella. Works on a Strad model. Invented an instrument which he calls "Controviolino" which sounds like a cello.

TIVOLI, FIORINI ARRIGO—San Remo. Born 1894 in Mogliano Veneta. Nephew and pupil of Giuseppe Fiorini. Uses Stradivari models.

TRAMONTI, RODOLFO—Forlì.

TUA, SILVIO—Born in Turin 1894. Pupil of Radrizzani. Established himself in Vevey, Switzerland, and transferred his business to Nice in 1929. Follows Guarneri patterns.

UBERT, EMILIO—Genoa.

UTILI, NICOLA—Ravenna. Born in Castelbolognese 1888. A self taught and successful maker.

VACHIER, GALILEO—Catania, Sicily. Born in Messina 1874.

VALENTINI, ARTURO—Rimini (Forlì).

VENEZIA, PROVINO—Crescentino (Piemonte).

VISTOLI, LUIGI—Lugo (Ravenna).

ZANI, ALDO—Cesena (Forlì).

ZANI, DOMENICO—Cesena (Forlì).

ZANIER, DR. FERRUCIO—Trieste. B. 1889. Self taught. Originated a special modern streamline model, with flat top and back. He published a booklet on "How I Construct a Violin."

ZINK, ANTONIO—Zara (Venezia Giulia).

SUPPLEMENTARY APPENDIX CONCERNING CONTEMPORARY (1973) PRICES

by Harold M. Chaitman

These past thirty years have seen a remarkable increase in monetary value for all true art objects; and string instruments — particularly those of fine artistic quality — have risen greatly and without exception. From the records for prices paid, we can see that the rate of increase is almost always in direct proportion to the artistic value of the particular instruments. So that, the figures of slightly over $200,000 for the Lady Blunt Stradivarius of 1721, and the approximately $250,000 paid for the Cessol Stradivarius of 1716 (instruments sold within the last four years) reflect the concept that singularly outstanding instruments can secure outstanding prices.

The vicissitudes of the stock markets, the uncertainty of the international monetary values, spiraling inflation have all contributed to an appreciation for the intrinsic value of a string instrument that has been crafted by talent, if not genius. Moreover, let us note that this artistic craft does not come to the artisan without devoted attention to the violin-maker's art, plus years of study and work.

What should be kept in mind is that the violin, viola, cello and bass must be able to perform; that is to say, the instrument must be able to sing, to have a brilliant voice or a sweet voice, an intense voice or a melancholy voice, perhaps a quietly refined voice, or perhaps an articulately assertive voice, but it must have that special quality of voice that the performing artist will employ. So that, the valuable violin, viola or cello is something like a beautiful statue that can dance, or a beautiful portrait that can sing (when in the hands of an artistic performer); and this performability plus the health (the state of preservation) of the instrument gives the violin, viola, cello or bass a type of value that differs from the monetary caprices of art objects that often fetch high figures because of short-lived fads.

Of course, what has been said for quality violin makers can be said for quality bow makers; with the understanding that the bow is not as complicated or as time consuming in the crafting. However, the prices for bows from the hands of the great bow makers have shown the same leaping prices as quality violins. A bow made by Francois Tourte will bring nine, ten or twelve thousand dollars. Bows made by Dominique Pecatte and F. N. Voirin will

193

be eight thousand dollars and more, depending upon the state of preservation and the innate quality of the bow. Fetique, Lamy, LaFleur, Viullaume, W. E. Hill and Sons, Henry, Persoit, Vigneron, Satory, James Tubbs, John Kew Dodd, Otto Bauch, Ludwig Bauch, E. Ouchard, Retford (father and son), A. R. Bultitude, Taylor, Watson, are but a handful of names (of both the past and present) that continue to rise in value.

A reading of *Known Violin Makers* will familiarize the player or collector with the relative merits of the outstanding bow makers of the past. Today such makers as W. E. Hill and Sons, L. Thomassin, Maline, Fetique, Lamy, Sartory, Vigneron, Bultitude, Retford, and Watson will be in the price range of 500 dollars to 900 dollars; keeping in mind that exceptional examples will always go for higher prices. James Tubbs, John Kew Dodd, Persoit, J. B. Viullaume, Adam, will be in the price range starting at 800 dollars and going up to approximately 2,000 dollars.

The first half of the twentieth century (to aproximately the late 1950's and early 1960's) saw a continual movement of quality instruments and bows to the United States. The World Wars, the revolutions in Europe, the strength of the American dollar, the arrival to these shores of many violin, viola, cello players were all factors contributing to Americans acquiring most of the best examples of the luthier's art. Now, the trend seems to show that many instruments are going back to Europe, and there is the new trend of instruments going to Japan and the orient. One does not have to spend much time explaining the recovery of the European economies and the outstanding recovery of the Japanese economy. Also, it should be noted that violin playing has become popular in Japan, with many commercial instruments being made there, and Europe has retained its interest in the violin, viola and cello as an instrument for the amateur player.

At this time, the future of the violin-maker's craft is difficult to ascertain. There are those who see the future pessimistically: too many young men preferring to join the employ of the large European automobile works, taking an immediate salary to the years of apprenticeship necessary to become a skilled luthier. On the other hand, there are now many opportunities for skilled luthiers and bow makers to enjoy comfortable salaries — with the added possibility of, at times, acquiring a valuable instrument at a relatively modest price.

If the golden age of violin making began with Andrea Amati (c. 1535 to c. 1581) and seemed to end with Lorenzo Storioni (born 1751, died after 1801), it should be noted that quality luthiers continued the smaller but steady stream of artistic instruments up until the present time. The names of Francesco Pressenda, Giuseppe Rocca, Enrico Rocca, Giovanni Baptista Ceruti, Giuseppe Ceruti, Enrico Ceruti, Jean Baptiste Viullaume, Eugenio Degani, V. Postiglioni, Giuseppe B. Lecchi, the Antoniazzi family, the Scarampella family, Enrico Politi, Caesare Candi, H. Fagnola, the Bisiach family being just a few of the nineteenth and early twentieth century makers that produced very fine instruments; instruments that are now coming into their own, some having already gained the necessary maturity with time to show outstanding tonal properties, and the others made from approximately 1900 on arriving now to full tonal maturity. Then too, there has been the renewed interest in the makers of the 18th century Neopolitan school, particulary the works of Allessandro, Nicolo and Gennaro Gagliano.

The 18th and 19th century English school of makers, notably Richard Duke, Benjamin Banks, John Johnson, Wm. Forster, Daniel Parker, Vincenzo Panormo and his sons, Betts, Hill and sons, Craske, John Lott, Fendt have all gained in favor and demand. The Stradivari modeled instruments of Daniel Parker will now fetch $4000 and upwards. Vincenzo Panormo's instruments are superb and can bring $8000 and upwards. The Stainer and Amati styled instruments of Richard Duke, Benjamin Banks, Nathaniel Cross, J. Johnson will fall in the price range of $1200 to $2000 and affords the buyer beautifully crafted instruments with a mellow, though not exceptionally powerful voice.

Two makers of the French school — Nicolas Lupot and J. B. Viullaume — have joined the special circle of makers whose best work is referred to as "masterpieces": N. Lupot's best violins being priced now at ten to twelve thousand dollars and J. B. Viullaume's best violins being seven and eight thousand dollars (cellos priced higher than violins or violas).

The violin makers of the French school have not accelerated in price with the same rapidity as the best of the Italian school. It should be noted that French bows have risen in price very markedly; but French violins, generally speaking, have made continual and steady gains. The instruments of Gand and Bernadel are now priced from two thousand to three thousand dollars; while the instruments made by Gand, Pierray, Boquay are now priced between three thousand and four thousand dollars.

In conclusion, let us state that while the tonal trend is generally in favor of the robust, powerful sounding, flatter arched instruments, many good buys can be had in acquiring instruments of the higher arched Stainer, and Amati type of violin. The Tyrolian, Bavarian, Viennese schools have produced many beautifully crafted and beautiful sounding violins, violas, and cellos of this type. A reading of *Known Violin Makers* will inform the prospective buyer of the luthiers of the aforementioned schools who produced quality instruments.

The following is a list of violin, viola, cello, bass and bow makers whose last names begin with the letters A, T and V. These letters were chosen arbitrarily and the makers are listed alphabetically, with their dates and contemporary (1973) prices paid for their instruments and bows. By comparing this section with the earlier European violin makers section, one can ascertain the prices and ratio of prices for the diverse luthiers and schools of violin making.

A

Achner, Michael — Worked between 1764 and 1773.
    $500 to $1000 — depending upon state of preservation.

Acton, William J. — Born 1848, died 1931.
    Violins: $800 to $1500.
    Bows: $250 to $500.

Albani, Matthias Bolzano, or Bober (Latin: Bulsani) Born about 1620, died about 1712.
    Violins, violas: $2000 to $4000.
    Cellos: $3000 to $6000.

Albani, Johann Michael — Graz, Austria
    Born about 1677, died 1730.
    Violins, violas: $2000 to $4000
    Cellos: $3500 to $6000.

Albani, Joseph — Bozen, Tyrol.
    Born 1680, died 1722.
    Prices: $2500 to $3500.
    Exceptional specimens much higher.

Albani, Nicolas — Mantua, Italy
    Worked between 1763 and 1770.
    Prices: $4000 to $6000.

Alberti, Ferdinand — Worked in Milan, Italy, 1737 to about 1760.
    Prices: $3000 to $4000.

Aldric, Jean Francois — Born in Mirecourt, France, 1765, died 1843.
    Prices: $3000 to $4500.
    Exceptional instruments around $7000.

196

Amati, Andrea — Cremona, Italy.
Born about 1535, died before 1581.
There are few examples of his work remaining.
One violin made for a King of France has been
valued at $50,000. Others should sell from $10,000 upwards.

Amati, Antonio — Creomona, Italy.
Born about 1555, died before 1630.
He worked together with his brother Girolamo (Hieronymus) ;
Hieronymus considered the slightly better maker.
Prices for violins: $8000 to $15,000.
Violas: $12,000 to $15,000.
Cellos: $20,000 upwards.

Amati, Nicolo — Cremona, Italy
Born 1596, died 1684. Son of Girolamo.
Prices: $10,000 to $20,000. Exceptional instruments higher.

Ambrosi, Petrus — Worked in Brescia and Rome, Italy between
1712 and 1748.
Violins: $4000 to $6000; violas a little higher.

Andres, Domenicus -- Worked in Bologna, Italy between
1740 and 1750.
Prices: around $5000.

Antoniazzi, Gaetano — Cremona, Italy.
Born 1823, died in Milan, 1897.
Prices: $2500 to $3500.

Antoniazzi, Riccardo — Son of Gaetano.
Prices: $2000 to $3000.

Antoniazzi, Romeo — Born in Cremona in 1862.
Also a son of Gaetano.
Prices: $2000 to $3000.

Arlow, Heinrich — Worked in Brunn, Czechoslovakia 1850 to 1865.
Prices: $800 to $1500.

Artelli, Giuseppe — Milan, Italy.
Worked about 1765.
Prices: $4000 to $6000

Ascensio, Vincenzo — Worked in Madrid, Spain, between
1775 and 1790.
Prices: $3000 to $4000.

Audinot, Nestor Dominique — Paris, France.
Born 1842, died 1920.
Prices: $1500 to $2500.

Tanegia, Carlo Antonio — Worked in Milan, Italy, about
1725 to 1737.
Prices: $5000 to $8000.

Tassini, Bartolomeo — Worked in Venice, Italy, about 1740 - 1756.
Prices: $6000 to $8000.

Tecchler, David — Born 1666, worked in Rome, Italy, about
1705 to 1743.
Prices: early violins of the Stainer type approximately $4000.
Later violins of the broad pattern approximately $6000-$10,000.
Cellos $20,000 and upwards.

Tedesco, Leopoldo Il — Rome, Italy.
Born around 1625.
Prices: $5000 to $6000.

Testore, Carlo Giuseppe — Born about 1660 in Novara, Italy,
died about 1717.
Prices: $7000 to $12,000.

Testore, Carlo Antonio — Milan, Italy.
Born about 1688, died after 1764.
Prices: $7000 to $9000.

Testore, Paolo Antonio — Milan, Italy.
Born about 1690, died after 1760.
Prices: $2500 to $4500.

Thibouville-Lamy, Louis Emile Jerome
Mirecourt and Paris, France, Born 1833.
Commercial instruments.
Prices: $150 to $300.

Thir, Anton I. Worked in Pressburg, Slovakia, about 1750 to 1790.
Prices: $700 to $1200.

Thir, Andreas — Pressburg. Born 1765, died after 1798.
Prices: $700 to $1200.

Thir (Thier), Johann Georg — Vienna, Austria.
Worked approximately from 1738 to 1781.
Prices: $700 to $1500.

Thir, Mathias — Worked in Vienna, Austria about 1770 - 1795.
Prices: $800 to $1500.

Thomassin, Louis — Born 1855, in Mirecourt, France.
Prices of bows from $400 to $700.

Thouvenel, Henry — Worked in Mirecourt, France
about 1850 to 1869.
Prices: $600 to $1,000.

Tobin, Richard — Worked in London, England, about 1790,
died about 1836.
Prices for violins: $800 to $1600.
Prices for cellos: $1200 to $2000.

Tononi, Felice — Worked in Bologna, Italy, about 1670-1710.
Prices for violins: $9,000 to $18,000
Prices for cellos: $20,000 and upwards.

Tononi, Giovanni (Joannes) — Worked in Bologna and Venice,
Italy, about 1689 - 1713, the date of his death.
Prices for violins: $10,000 to $18,000.
Prices for cellos: $20,000 and upwards.

Tononi, Carlo — Worked in Bologna and Venice, Italy,
about 1689 to 1717.
Prices: $10,000 to $18,000.
Some exceptional instruments higher.

Toppani, Angelo (De) — Worked in Rome, Italy, about 1735-1750.
Prices for violins: $4,000 to $5,000.
Prices for cellos: $6,000 and upwards.

Tourte, Xavier — Worked in Paris, France, about 1770-1786.
Prices for bows: $3,000 and upwards depending on the
individual bow.

Tourte, Francois — Paris, France. Born 1747, died 1835.
Prices for bows: $6,000 to $12,000 depending on the
individual bow.

Tubbs, James — London, England. Born 1835, died 1919.
Prices for bows: $600 to $1,200. Most of his bows are
steadily rising in price.

V

Valenzano (Valenciano), Giovanni Maria — Worked in Valenza,
Rome and Trieste, Italy about 1771 to 1825.
Prices for violins: $3,000 to $4,000.

Vandelli, Giovanni — Worked in Modena, Italy
about 1796 to 1839.
Prices for violins: $2,500.

VanDerSlaghmeulen, Johannes Baptist — Worked in
Antwerp, Belgium, about 1660-1697.
Prices: $1,000 to $1,500.

Varotti, Giovanni — Worked in Bologna, Italy, about 1786-1815.
Prices: $1,500 to $2,500.

Vatelot, Marcel — Born 1884. Came from a small town
near Mirecourt, France.
Prices: $1,500 to $2,000.

Vauchel, Jean — Worked in Mainz, Wurzburg and Damm,
Germany. Born 1782, died 1856.
Prices for violins around $2,500 to $3,500.

Ventapane, Vincenzo — Worked in Naples, Italy,
between 1750 and 1799.
Prices for violins: $3,500 to $4,500 and some higher.
Prices for violas and cellos above: $5,000.

Ventapane, Pasquale — Worked in Naples, Italy, in
the 18th century.
Prices for violins: $3,000 to $4,000, some higher.
Prices for cellos: $5,000 and up.

Ventapane, Lorenzo — Worked in Naples, Italy about 1809-1828.
Prices for violins: $4,000 to $5,000.
Prices for cellos: $6,000 and up.

Verzella, Francesco — Worked in Constantinople, Turkey,
toward the end of the 19th century.
Prices for violins around $1,500.

Viedenhofer, Bernard — Worked in Budapest, Hungary
about 1790 to 1812.
Prices for violins around $400 to $450.

Vignali, Giuseppe — Born 1888 in Verucchio, Italy,
established in 1910, died very young.
Prices for violins: $2,000 to $3,000.

Vigneron, Joseph Arthur — Paris, France.
Born 1851 in Mirecourt, France.
Prices for bows $400 and upwards.
These bows are rising in price.

Vinaccia, Antonio — Worked in Naples, Italy, about 1760-1775.
Prices for violins: $4,000 to $5,000.

Vinaccia, Antonio II — Worked in Naples, Italy about 1770 to 1815
Prices for violins: $4,000 to $5,000.

Vincenzi, Luigi — Born 1775, died about 1820 at Capri, Italy.
Prices for violins: $3,500 and up.

Vogler, Johann Georg — Wurzburg, Germany.
Born 1692, died 1750.
Prices for violins: $400 to $600.

Voirin, Joseph — Born 1830 in Mirecourt, France.
Prices for bows $700 and up.
His bows continue to rise in value.

Voirin, Francois Nicolas — Born 1833, died 1885.
Prices for bows: $800 and up. His bows continue to rise in value, and $3,000 for a bow is not unusual.

Voller, William — London, England. Born 1860.
Prices for violins: $3,000 and upwards.

Vuillaume, Jean Baptist — Paris, France. Born 1798, died 1875.
He produced violins in three grades and employed a number of craftsmen to aid him in his shop. Vuillaume's best violins — those he made himself and devoted his best efforts to — are now priced around $7,000. His St. Cecelia model violins are approximately $2,500, and his Stentor model violins are $1,500 to $2,000 in price. The prices for J. B. Vuillaume bows are $800 and up; some very much higher.

Vuillaume, Nicolas Francois — Born 1807, died 1876.
Prices for violins: $2,500 to $3,500.

Vuillaume, Sebastien — Paris, France. Born about 1835, died 1875.
Prices for violins: $2,000 to $3,000.

The publishers wish to thank Mr. Jacques Francais—the well known violin dealer of New York City, New York—for his generous efforts in compiling the entire list of 1980 prices for the following European section of violin makers and bow makers.

1980 Price Guide for the European Section

Achner, Michael	$2,000 to $2,500	Alberti, Ferdinand	$16,000 to $20,000
Acton, William J.	NO PRICE GIVEN	Albrecht, Johannes	$1,800 to $2,000
Albani, Matthias	$15,000 to $20,000	Aldric, Jean Francois	$8,000 to $12,000
Albani, Johann Michael	$12,000 to $18,000	Alletsee, Paul	$2,000 to $3,000
Albani, Joseph	$12,000 to $18,000	Amati, Andrea	$60,000 to $80,000
Albani, Nicolas	NO PRICE GIVEN	Amati, Antonio	$50,000 to $75,000
Albert, Charles Francis	$1,000 to $1,500	Amati, Nicolo	$50,000 to $100,000
		Ambrosi, Petrus	$6,000 to $8,000

Andres, Domenicus	NO PRICE GIVEN
Antoniazzi, Gaetano	$8,000 to $10,000
Antoniazzi, Riccardo	$6,000 to $8,000
Antoniazzi, Romeo	$6,000 to $8,000
Arlow, Heinrich	$500 to $800
Artelli, Giuseppe Antonio	$8,000 to $10,000
Ascensio, Vencenzo	$5,000 to $8,000
Aubert, Claude	$1,500 to $2,000
Audinot, Nestor Dominique	$6,000 to $8,000
Baader (Bader)	$500 to $800
Bagatella, Antonius	$12,000 to $18,000
Bailly, Paul	$6,000 to $8,000
Bairhoff, Giorgio	$16,000 to $20,000
Bajoni, Luigi	$6,000 to $8,000
Baldantoni, Giuseppe	$14,000 to $16,000
Balestrieri, Tommaso	$60,000 to $80,000
Banks, Benjamin	$6,000 to $8,000
Barbe, Telesphore Amable	$6,000 to $8,000
Bartl	$1,200 to $1,500
Bassot, Joseph	$1,200 to $1,500
Bausch, Ludwig	$800 to $1,200
Bausch, Otto	$600 to $800
Bellone, Pietro Antonio	$15,000 to $18,000
Bellosio, Anselmo	$25,000 to $28,000
Benoit, Eugene	$2,000 to $2,500
Benoit, Pierre	$1,000 to $1,500
Benti, Matteo	$15,000 to $18,000
Beretta, Felice	$20,000 to $25,000
Bergonzi, Carlo	$100,000 to $120,000
Bargonzi, Michel Angelo	$50,000 to $60,000
Bergonzi, Nicola	$50,000 to $60,000
Bernardel, Auguste Sebastien Phillipe	$12,000 to $15,000
Bernardel, Leon	$800 to $1,200
Bertolotti, Gasparo	$40,000 to $45,000
Bertucci, F. M.	$2,000 to $2,500
Betts, John Edward	$6,000 to $8,000
Bianchi, Nicolo	$10,000 to $12,000
Bimbi, Bartolomeo	$18,000 to $20,000
Bisiach, Leandro	$5,000 to $8,000
Blanchard, Paul Francois	$6,000 to $8,000
Bogner, Ambrosius Joseph	$1,000 to $1,500
Bohmann, Joseph	$1,000 to $1,200
Boivin, Claude	$6,000 to $8,000
Boller (or Poller), Michael	$2,000 to $2,500
Bollinger, Joseph	$1,500 to $2,000
Boquay, Jacques	$8,000 to $10,000
Borelli, Andrea	$18,000 to $20,000
Borgia, Antonio	$16,000 to $20,000
Boumeester, Jan	$8,000 to $12,000
Brandilioni (Brandiglioni), Filippo	NO PRICE GIVEN
Brandini, Jacopo	$15,000 to $20,000
Brandstaetter, Mathaeus Ignaz	$2,000 to $2,500
Breton, Joseph Francois	$1,000 to $1,500
Buchstetter, Gabriel David	$2,000 to $2,500
Bull, Ole	$300 to $350
Busan, Domenico	$20,000 to $25,000
Bussetto, Giovanni Maria (del)	$35,000 to $40,000
Buthod	$5,000 to $8,000
Calcanius, Bernardo	$20,000 to $25,000
Calvarola, Bartolommeo	$20,000 to $25,000
Camilli, Camillo	$30,000 to $40,000
Campostano, Antonio	$20,000 to $25,000
Cappa, Gioffredo	$25,000 to $35,000
Carcassi	$20,000 to $25,000
Cardi, Luigi	$6,000 to $8,000
Caressa, Felix Albert	$4,000 to $5,000
Carletti, Carlo	$2,000 to $2,500

Carter, John	$4,000 to $5,000
Casini (Cassini), Antonio	$25,000 to $30,000
Castagneri, Andrea	$6,000 to $8,000
Castellani, Pietro	$8,000 to $12,000
Castello, Paolo	$25,000 to $30,000
Cavalli, Aristide	$2,000 to $2,500
Celani, Emilio	$2,000 to $2,500
Cerin, Marco Antonio	$30,000 to $35,000
Ceruti, Giovanni Baptista	$20,000 to $25,000
Ceruti (Cerutti), Giuseppe	$15,000 to $20,000
Ceruti, Enrico	$16,000 to $18,000
Chanot	$6,000 to $8,000
Chanot, Georges	$5,000 to $6,000
Chappuy, Nicolas Augustin	$4,000 to $6,000
Chardon, Joseph Marie	$4,000 to $5,000
Charotte	$1,500 to $2,000
Charles, Jean	$1,500 to $2,000
Chevrier	$1,000 to $1,500
Chiocchi (Ciocchi), Gaetano	$15,000 to $20,000
Clark, A. B.	$500 to $800
Claudot	$1,000 to $1,500
Clement, Jean Laurent	$1,000 to $1,500
Coletti, Alfred	$500 to $800
Collin-Mezin, Charles Jean Baptiste	$3,000 to $3,500
Collin-Mezin	$2,000 to $2,500
Comuni, Antonio	$10,000 to $12,000
Contreras, Joseph	$10,000 to $12,000
Costa, Felix Mori	$16,000 to $20,000
Costa, Giovanni Baptista	$16,000 to $18,000
Couturieux, N.	$1,500 to $2,000
Craske, George	$1,200 to $1,500
Cross, Nathaniel	$5,000 to $6,000
Crowther, John	$2,000 to $2,500
Cuypers, Johannes	$8,000 to $10,000
Dalinger, Sebastian	$2,000 to $2,500
Dalla Corte, Alfonso	$8,000 to $12,000
Dalla Costa, Pietro Antonio	$25,000 to $28,000
Dall'Aglio, Giuseppe	$20,000 to $22,000
Darche, Nicolas	$3,000 to $3,500
Darte, Auguste	$4,000 to $5,000
Davidson, Peter	$800 to $1,000
Dearlove, Mark William	$3,000 to $3,500
De Comble, Ambroise	$5,000 to $6,000
Deconet, Michael	$25,000 to $30,000
Degani, Eugenio	$6,000 to $8,000
Deleplanque, Gerard J.	$5,000 to $6,000
Delunet, Auguste Leon	$800 to $1,200
De Planis, August	$20,000 to $22,000
Derazey, Jean Joseph Honore	$6,000 to $8,000
Despine (D'Espine), Alexander	$18,000 to $20,000
De Vitor, Petrus Paulus	$14,000 to $16,000
Didelot, Dominique	$2,000 to $2,500
Didion, Gabriel	$2,000 to $2,500
Diehl, Nokolas	$800 to $1,200
Diener, Franz	$800 to $1,200
Dieudonne, Amedee Dominique	$1,200 to $1,500
Dodd, Edward	$3,000 to $4,000
Dodd, Thomas	$3,000 to $4,000
Dodd, John Kew	$4,000 to $5,000
Doerffel	$2,000 to $2,500
Doetsch, Michael	$6,000 to $7,000
Dolling	$500 to $800
Dollenz, Giovanni	$6,000 to $8,000
Drouin, Charles	$1,500 to $2,000
Drouin, Louis	$1,000 to $1,200
Duchesne (Duchene), Nicolas	$1,500 to $2,000
Duiffoprugcar, see Tieffenbrucker	NO PRICE GIVEN
Duke, Richard	$5,000 to $6,000
Duncan,	

Robert	$1,000 to $1,500
Durfell, J.	
Gottlob	$1,500 to $1,800
Dvorak,	
Johann	
Baptist	$2,500 to $3,000
Dykes, George	
L.	$800 to $1,200
Eberle,	
Johannes	
Udalricus	$3,000 to $4,000
Eberle, Magnus	$2,000 to $3,000
Eberle,	
Tomaso	$20,000 to $22,000
Edlinger,	
Thomas	NO PRICE GIVEN
Ellersieck,	
Albert	$2,000 to $2,500
Enders, F. & R.	$500 to $800
Enel, Charles	$2,000 to $2,500
Ernst, Franz	
Anton	$800 to $1,200
Eury, Nicolas	$5,000 to $6,000
Fabbricatore,	
Gennaro	$3,500 to $4,000
Fabris, Luigi	$6,000 to $8,000
Fagnola,	
Hannibal	$8,000 to $10,000
Farotti, Celeste	$5,000 to $6,000
Fent, Francois	$5,000 to $6,000
Fendt,	
Bernhard	$5,000 to $6,000
Fetique, Victor	$1,500 to $2,000
Fichtl, Martin	$2,000 to $2,500
Ficker, Johann	
Christian	$2,500 to $3,000
Fillion,	
Georges	
Charles	$1,000 to $1,500
Finolli,	
Giuseppe	
Antonio	$16,000 to $18,000
Fiorini,	
Raffaele	$8,000 to $10,000
Fiorini,	
Giuseppe	$10,000 to $12,000
Fischer	$800 to $1,000
Fischer, Anton	$2,500 to $3,000
Fleury, Benoit	$5,000 to $6,000
Floriani, Pietro	$5,000 to $6,000
Forster,	
William, Sr.	Violins $5,000 to $6,000
	Cellos $18,000 to $20,000
Fourrier,	
Francois	
Nicolas	$3,000 to $4,000
Francias, Henri	$4,000 to $5,000
Frank,	
Meinrad	$3,000 to $3,500
Fredi, Rodolfo	$4,000 to $5,000
Furber	$3,000 to $3,500

Gabrielli,	
Giovanni	
Baptista	$25,000 to $30,000
Gaffino,	
Joseph	$4,000 to $5,000
Gagliano,	
Alexander	$35,000 to $40,000
Gagliano,	
Nicolo	$35,000 to $40,000
Gagliano,	
Gennaro	
(Januarius)	$35,000 to $40,000
Gagliano,	
Ferdinando	$25,000 to $30,000
Gagliano,	
Giuseppe	
(Joseph)	$25,000 to $30,000
Gagliano,	
Antonio	$20,000 to $25,000
Gagliano,	
Giovanni	
(Joannes)	$18,000 to $20,000
Gagliano,	
Raffaele	$12,000 to $15,000
Gaillard,	
Charles	$6,000 to $8,000
Galbusera,	
Carlo	
Antonio	$3,000 to $4,000
Gand, Charles	
Francois	$14,000 to $16,000
Gand,	
Guillaume	
Charles	$6,000 to $8,000
Gand, Charles	
Adolphe	$6,000 to $8,000
Gand, Charles	
Nicolas	
Eugene	$6,000 to $8,000
Gasparo Da	
Salo, see	
Bertolotti	
Gavinies,	
Francois	$4,000 to $5,000
Gedler, Johann	
Anton	$2,500 to $3,000
Gedler, Joseph	
Benedikt	$1,500 to $2,000
Geipel	NO PRICE GIVEN
Geissenhof,	
Franz	$6,000 to $8,000
Gemunder,	
August	
Martin	
Ludwig	$1,000 to $1,500
Gemunder,	
George	$6,000 to $8,000
Germain,	
Joseph Louis	$5,000 to $6,000
Gibertini,	
Antonio	$18,000 to $20,000
Gigli, Giulio	
Cesare	$18,000 to $20,000

204

Gilkes, Samuel	$2,000 to $2,500	Wilhelm Theodor	$500 to $800
Glaesel	$500 to $800	Hamm, Johann Gottfried	$1,500 to @,000
Glass	$300 to $350	Hammig, Johann Georg	$1,500 to $2,000
Glier	$500 to $800	Hammig, Wilhelm Hermann	$2,500 to $3,000
Glier, Robert	$500 to $800	Hardie, Matthew	$2,000 to $2,500
Gobetti, Francesco	$40,000 to $50,000	Hardie, James	$1,000 to $1,500
Goetz, Johann Michael	$1,500 to $1,800	Hare, Joseph	$2,000 to $2,500
Goffriller, Matteo	$40,000 to $50,000	Harris, Charles I	$2,500 to $3,000
Goffriller, Francesco	$30,000 to $35,000	Harris, Griffith	$1,000 to $1,200
Gosselin, Jean	$1,500 to $2,000	Hart, John Thomas	$3,000 to $3,500
Gragnani, Antonio	$20,000 to $25,000	Havelka, Johann Baptist	$2,500 to $3,000
Grancino, Paolo	$30,000 to $32,000	Havemann, David Chrisian	$2,000 to $2,500
Grancino, Giovanni Baptista	$35,000 to $40,000	Heberlein	$800 to $1,000
Grand, Gerard	$1,500 to $2,000	Heinicke, Mathias	$500 to $800
Grandjon	$2,000 to $2,500	Hel, Pierre Joseph	$5,000 to $6,000
Grienberger, Joseph	$2,000 to $2,500	Hellmer, Johann Georg	$3,000 to $3,500
Grimm, Karl	$2,000 to $2,500	Hellmer, Carl Joseph	$2,000 to $2,500
Guadagnini, Lorenzo	$75,000 to $100,000	Henry, J.	$5,000 to $6,000
Guadagnini, Giovanni Baptista	$80,000 to $120,000	Hentschel, Johann Joseph	$1,500 to $2,000
Guadagnini, Giuseppe (Joseph)	$30,000 to $40,000	Herold, Conrad Gustav	$500 to $800
Guadagnini, Gaetano I	$8,000 to $10,000	Herzlieb, Franciscus	$2,000 to $2,500
Guarnerius, Andreas	$60,000 to $65,000	Hesketh, Thomas Earle	$1,200 to $1,500
Guarnerius, Petrus	$80,000 to $120,000	Hill, Joseph	Violins $5,000 to $6,000
Guarnerius, Giuseppe (Joseph)	$75,000 to $85,000		Cellos $5,000 to $6,000
Guarnerius, Joseph (Del Gesu)	$250,000 to $400,000	Hill, William	$5,000 to $6,000
Guarnerius, Petrus II	$75,000 to $100,000	Hill, Henry Lockey	$5,000 to $6,000
Guarini, see Menesson		Hill, William Ebsworth	$4,000 to $5,000
Guerra, Evasio Emiliano	$6,000 to $8,000	Hjorth, Emil	$1,000 to $1,500
Guersan, Louis (Ludovicus)	$6,000 to $8,000	Hoffmann, Martin	$2,500 to $3,000
Guetter	$600 to $800	Hofmann, Anton	$2,500 to $3,000
Guidantus, Joannes Florenus	$20,000 to $25,000	Homolka	$2,500 to $3,000
Guillami, Joannes	$6,000 to $8,000	Hopf	$1,200 to $1,500
Gusetto, Nicolas	$16,000 to $18,000		
Gutermann,			

Hopf, Carl Friedrich	NO PRICE GIVEN
Hopf, David	$500 to $1,000
Horil, Jakob	$16,000 to $18,000
Hornsteiner	$1,200 to $1,500
Hornsteiner, modern commercial	$500 to $1,000
Hoyer	$1,500 to $2,000
Huber, Johann Georg	$2,000 to $2,500
Hunger, Christoph Friedrich	$2,000 to $2,500
Jacobs, (Jacobsz) Hendrick	$15,000 to $18,000
Jacquot, Charles	$6,000 to $8,000
Jacquot, Charles Albert	$6,000 to $8,000
Jaeger	$500 to $600
Jais, Andreas	$3,000 to $3,500
Jais, Anton	$3,000 to $3,500
Johnson, John	$3,000 to $3,500
Jorio, Vincent	$6,000 to $8,000
Kaembl, Johann Andreas	$2,000 to $2,500
Karner, Bartholomaeus	$2,000 to $2,500
Keffer, Johann	$2,000 to $2,500
Kempter, Andreas	$2,000 to $2,500
Kennedy, Thomas	$3,000 to $3,500
Kessler	$400 to $500
Khoegl, Hanns	
Kittel, Nikolaus	$8,000 to $12,000
Klier	
Klotz, Egidi	$3,000 to $3,500
Klotz (Kloz), Mathias	$3,000 to $3,500
Klotz, Sebastian	$3,000 to $3,500
Klotz, Aegidius	$3,000 to $3,500
Klotz, Johann Carol	$3,000 to $3,500
Klotz, Joseph	$3,000 to $3,500
Knilling	$2,000 to $2,500
Knitl, Franz	$2,500 to $3,000
Knopf, Henry Richard	
Knorr, Arthur	Violins: $500 to $800 Bows: $200 to $300
Kolditz, Matthias Johann	$2,500 to $3,000
Kollmer	$2,500 to $3,000
Krausch, Georg Adam	
Krell, Albert	$500 to $800
Kretzschmann	$2,000 to $2,500
Kriner, Simon	$2,000 to $2,500
Kriner, Matthaeus	$1,000 to $1,500
Kulik, Johannes	$3,000 to $3,500
Laberte & Magnie	$1,500 to $2,000
Lafleur, Jacques	$5,000 to $6,000
Lagetto, Louis	$1,200 to $1,500
Lamy, Alfred Joseph	$2,500 to $3,000
Landolfi, Carlo Ferdinando	$25,000 to $35,000
Landolfi, Pietro Antonio	$25,000 to $30,000
La Prevotte, Etienne	$2,000 to $2,500
Laske (Laschke), Joseph Anton	$1,500 to $2,000
Laurent, Emile	$3,000 to $4,000
Lavazza, Antonio Maria	$20,000 to $25,000
Lecchi, Giuseppe	$2,000 to $2,500
Leeb, Johann Georg I	$2,500 to $3,000
Leeb, Johann Georg II	$2,500 to $3,000
Leeb, Andreas Carl	$3,000 to $4,000
Lefebvre, Jacques B.	$3,000 to $4,000
Lefebre (Lefebvre), Toussaint Nicolas Germain	$3,000 to $3,500
Leidolff, Nicolas	$2,500 to $3,000
Leidolff, Johann Christoph	$2,500 to $3,000
Leidolff, Joseph Ferdinand	$3,000 to $3,500
Le Jeune, Francois	$2,000 to $2,500
Lemboeck, Gabriel	$3,000 to $4,000
Lenoble, Auguste	$3,000 to $4,000
Lepri, Luigi	$1,500 to $2,000
Lewis, Edward	$1,000 to $1,500
Liebich, Johann Gottfried	$1,000 to $1,500

206

Lippold, Johann Georg	$1,000 to $1,500
Lippold, Carl Friedrich	$1,000 to $1,500
Lippold, Johann Gottlob	$1,000 to $1,500
Lolio, Giovanni Battista	$10,000 to $12,000
Lorange, Paul Victor	$1,000 to $1,500
Lott, John Frederick	$12,000 to $15,000
Louvet, Jean	$3,000 to $4,000
Lowendall Star Works	$500 to $800
Lupot, Francois I	$3,000 to $4,000
Lupot, Nicolas	$35,000 to $50,000
Lupot, Francois II	$5,000 to $6,000
Maggini, Giovanni Paolo	$35,000 to $40,000
Maire, Nicolas	$5,000 to $6,000
Maline, Guillaume	$4,000 to $5,000
Maline, Francois Alexis	$1,000 to $1,500
Malvolti, Pietro Antonio	$10,000 to $15,000
Mann, John Alexander	$1,000 to $1,500
Mansuy, Pierre	$3,000 to $4,000
Mantegazza (Mantegatia), Pietro Giovanni	$20,000 to $25,000
Marchetti, Abbondio	$10,000 to $15,000
Marchi, Giovanni Antonio	$12,000 to $15,000
Marconcini, Giuseppe	$15,000 to $20,000
Martin	$800 to $1,200
Mast, Joseph Laurent	$1,500 to $2,000
Maucotel	$4,000 to $5,000
Maussiell, Leonhard	$1,500 to $2,000
Mayr	$1,500 to $2,000
Mayson, Walter H.	$1,000 to $1,500
Medard	$5,000 to $8,000
Meinel	$500 to $800
Meisel	$500 to $800
Melegari, Enrico Clodoveo	$10,000 to $12,000
Mennegand, Charles	$3,000 to $3,500
Mennesson, Jean Emile	$4,000 to $5,000
Merighi, Pietro	$12,000 to $15,000
Meyer, Magnus Andreas	$500 to $800
Mezzadri, Allesandro	$20,000 to $25,000
Michelot, Jacques Pierre	$4,000 to $5,000
Milton, Louis Frank	$1,000 to $1,200
Miremont, Claude Augustin	$6,000 to $8,000
Moeckel, Oswald	$1,500 to $2,000
Moitessier, Louis	$5,000 to $6,000
Mongel, A.	$1,000 to $1,500
Montagnana, Dominicus	$100,000 to $120,000
Morelli	$500 to $800
Morrison, Archibald	$1,200 to $1,500
Mougenot, Georges	$1,000 to $1,500
Mougento, Leon	$1,000 to $1,500
Muncher, Romedio	$1,500 to $2,000
Nadotti, Giuseppe	$15,000 to $20,000
Nemessanyi, Samuel Felix	$10,000 to $12,000
Neuner, Mathias	$1,500 to $2,000
Neuner, Ludwig Neuner & Hornsteiner	$800 to $1,000
Nicolas, Didier	$1,200 to $1,500
Niggell, Sympertus	$2,000 to $2,500
Novello, Pietro Valentino	$10,000 to $15,000
Nurnberger	$400 to $800
Obici, Bartolomeo	$15,000 to $20,000
Oddone, Carlo Giuseppe	$10,000 to $12,000
Odoardi, Giuseppe	$18,000 to $20,000
Olry, J.	$2,000 to $2,500
Omond, James	$1,000 to $1,500
Ornati, Giuseppe	$10,000 to $12,000
Pacherel (E), Pierre	$16,000 to $20,000
Padewet, Johann	$1,000 to $1,500
Pageot, Louis	

207

Simon	$5,000 to $6,000
Pailliot (Paillot)	$1,000 to $1,500
Pallotta, Pietro	$15,000 to $20,000
Pamphilon, Edward	$10,000 to $12,000
Pandolfi, Antonio	$18,000 to $20,000
Panormo, Vincenzo	$15,000 to $20,000
Panormo, Joseph	$8,000 to $12,000
Panormo, Georges Louis	$8,000 to $12,000
Pantzer, Johann Karl	$1,000 to $1,500
Paquotte, Jean Baptiste	$1,000 to $1,500
Parker, Daniel	$15,000 to $20,000
Pasta	$12,000 to $15,000
Pauli, Joseph	$1,000 to $1,200
Paulus	$100 to $500
Pazzini, Giovanni Gaetano	$15,000 to $18,000
Peccatte (Peccate), Dominique	$7,000 to $8,000
Peccatte, Francois	$4,000 to $5,000
Peccatte, Charles	$4,000 to $5,000
Pedrinelli, Antonio	$15,000 to $20,000
Pellizon	$6,000 to $8,000
E. Perrin Fils	$800 to $1,000
Perry, Thomas	$1,000 to $1,500
Pfretzschner	$400 to $800
Piegendorfer, Georg	$1,000 to $1,500
Pieroni, Luigi	$2,000 to $2,500
Pierray, Claude	$8,000 to $10,000
Pillement, F.	$2,000 to $2,500
Pique, Francois Louis	$15,000 to $16,000
Pirot, Claude	$1,200 to $1,500
Pizzurnus, David	$2,000 to $2,500
Placht	$500 to $800
Platner, Michael	$20,000 to $25,000
Poggi, Ansaldo	$5,000 to $6,000
Pohland	$800 to $1,000
Poirson, Justin	$1,000 to $1,500
Pollastri, Augusto	$5,000 to $8,000
Pollastri, Gaetano	$4,000 to $6,000
Posch (Bosch), Antonio	$2,000 to $2,500
Postacchini, Andrea	$20,000 to $25,000
Postiglione,	
Vincenzo	$10,000 to $12,000
Prager, Gustav	$300 to $500
Pressenda, Joannes Franciscus	$30,000 to $35,000
Preston	$1,000 to $1,200
Prevot, P. Charles	$2,000 to $2,500
Railich, Giovanni	
Rambaux, Claude Victor	$5,000 to $6,000
Rauch, Sebastian	$1,500 to $2,000
Rauch, Joseph	$1,500 to $2,000
Rauch, Thomas	$1,000 to $1,500
Reichel	$500 to $800
Reiter, Johann Baptist	$1,200 to $1,500
Remy, Mathurin Francois	$2,000 to $2,500
Renaudin, Leopold	$5,000 to $6,000
Riechers, August	$1,000 to $1,500
Rief, Anton	$2,500 to $3,000
Rief, Dominicus	$2,000 to $2,500
Rieger, Johann	$1,500 to $2,000
Rieger, Georg	$1,500 to $2,000
Rinaldi, Gioffredo Benedetto	$8,000 to $12,000
Rivolta, Giacomo	$15,000 to $18,000
Rocca, Giuseppe Antonio	$20,000 to $25,000
Rocca, Enrico	$14,000 to $16,000
Rodiani, Giovita	$15,000 to $20,000
Rogeri, Giovanni Battista	$50,000 to $65,000
Rogeri, Pietro Giacomo	$50,000 to $60,000
Rombouts, Pieter	$10,000 to $12,000
Ronchetti, Domenico	$30,000 to $40,000
Roscher, Christian Heinrich Wilhelm	$1,500 to $2,000
Rossi, Enrico	$6,000 to $8,000
Roth	$500 to $1,200
Ruggeri, Franciscus	$60,000 to $65,000
Ruggeri, Giacinto	

Giovanni Battista	$50,000 to $60,000
Ruggeri, Vincenzo	$60,000 to $65,000
Ruprecht, Wilhelm	$1,500 to $2,000
Sacquin	$1,000 to $1,200
Saint Paul, Pierre	$4,000 to $5,000
Salo, Gasparo Da, see Bertolotti	
Sajot	$2,000 to $2,500
Salomon, Jean Baptiste	$5,000 to $6,000
Salzard	$1,500 to $2,000
Santagiuliana, Gaetano	$18,000 to $20,000
Santagiuliana, Giacinto	$10,000 to $12,000
Santucci, Sebastian	$1,500 to $2,000
Sartory, Eugene	$2,500 to $3,000
Sawicki, Carl Nikolaus	$1,500 to $2,000
Scarampella, Paolo	$6,000 to $8,000
Scarampella, Giuseppe	$6,000 to $8,000
Scarampella, Stefano	$10,000 to $12,000
Schaller, Oswald	$300 to $500
Schandl, Anton	$2,000 to $2,500
Scheverle, Johann	$2,000 to $2,500
Schlosser	$2,000 to $2,500
Schmidt	$800 to $1,200
Schneider	$800 to $1,200
Schonfelder	$2,000 to $2,500
Schonger, Franz	$1,500 to $2,000
Schorn, Johann Paul	$1,500 to $2,000
Schuster	$500 to $800
Schuster, Kurt	$1,500 to $2,000
Schweitzer, Johann Baptist	$2,000 to $2,500
Seidel	$1,500 to $2,000
Seraphin, Sanctus	$50,000 to $65,000
Sgarabotto, Gaetano	$5,000 to $6,000
Sgarbi, Antonio	$4,000 to $5,000
Silvestre, Pierre	$6,000 to $8,000
Silvestre & Maucotel	$4,000 to $5,000
Simon, P.	$5,000 to $6,000
Simoutre, Nicolas	$5,000 to $6,000
Sitt, Anton	$800 to $1,000
Skomal, Nikolaus Georg	$1,500 to $2,000
Smith, Thomas	$3,500 to $4,000
Socquet, Louis	$5,000 to $6,000
Soffritti, Ettore	$5,000 to $6,000
Soliani, Angelo	$10,000 to $12,000
Soriot, D.	$1,000 to $1,500
Spidlen, Franz	$800 to $1,000
Stadlmann, Johann Joseph	$5,000 to $6,000
Stainer, Jacobus	$30,000 to $35,000
Stainer, Marcus	$5,000 to $6,000
Staininger, Jacob	$500 to $800
Stauffer, Johann Georg	$1,500 to $2,000
Storck, Johannes Friedrich	$1,500 to $2,000
Storioni, Lorenzo	$40,000 to $45,000
Stoss, Martin	$5,000 to $6,000
Stradivari, Antonio	$200,000 to $350,000
Stradivari, Francesco	$120,000 to $150,000
Stradivari, Omobono	$120,000 to $150,000
Strnad, Caspar	$3,000 to $3,500
Strobl, Johann	$2,000 to $2,500
Suss, Johann Christian	$600 to $800
Szepessy, Bela	$4,000 to $5,000
Tanegia, Carlo Antonio	$15,000 to $18,000
Tassini, Bartolomeo	$18,000 to $20,000
Tecchler, David	Violins: $18,000 to $20,000 Cellos: $100,000 to $120,000
Tedesco, Leopoldo II	NO PRICE GIVEN
Testore, Carlo Giuseppe	$25,000 to $28,000
Testore, Carlo Antonio	$25,000 to $28,000
Testore, Paolo Antonio	$20,000 to $25,000
Thibouville-Lamy, Louis Emile Jerome	$1,000 to $1,500
Thir, Anton I	$3,000 to $3,500
Thir, Andreas	NO PRICE GIVEN
Thir (Thier), Johann	

Georg	$3,000 to $3,500
Thir, Mathias	$3,000 to $3,500
Thomassin, Louis	$1,500 to $2,000
Thouvenel, Henry	$800 to $1,200
Tieffenbrucker, Caspar	$800 to $1,200
Teiffenbrunner, Georg	$500 to $800
Tobin, Richard	$2,000 to $2,500
Tononi, Felice	$50,000 to $60,000
Tononi, Giovanni	$50,000 to $60,000
Tononi, Carlo	$50,000 to $60,000
Toppani, Angelo	$18,000 to $20,000
Tourte, Pere	$5,000 to $6,000
Tourte, Xavier	$5,000 to $6,000
Tourte, Francois	$16,000 to $20,000
Trucco, Girolamo	$4,000 to $5,000
Tubbs, James	$2,500 to $3,000
Tubbs, Edward	
Valenzano (Valenciano), Giovanni Maria	$10,000 to $12,000
Vandelli, Giovanni	$8,000 to $10,000
Van Der Slaghmeulen, Johannes Baptist	$4,000 to $5,000
Varotti, Giovanni	$18,000 to $20,000
Vatelot, Marcel	$2,000 to $2,500
Vauchel, Jean	$2,000 to $2,500
Ventapane, Vincenzo	$18,000 to $20,000
Ventapane, Pasquale	$25,000 to $30,000
Ventapane, Lorenzo	Violins: $18,000 to $20,000
	Cellos: $40,000 to $50,000
Varzella, Francesco	$800 to $1,000
Viedenhofer, Bernard	$800 to $1,000
Vignali, Giuseppe	$2,000 to $2,500
Vigneron, Joseph Arthur	$1,800 to $2,000
Vinaccia, Antonio	$16,000 to $18,000
Vinaccia, Gennaro	$16,000 to $18,000
Vincenzi, Luigi	$18,000 to $20,000
Vogler, Johann Georg	$2,000 to $2,500
Voigt, Johann Georg	$1,500 to $2,000
Voigt, Carl Hermann	$1,000 to $1,500
Voigt, Arnold	$500 to $800
Voirin, Joseph	$2,000 to $2,500
Voirin, Francois Nicolas	$4,000 to $5,000
Voller, William	$6,000 to $8,000
Vuillaume, Jean Baptiste	$20,000 to $25,000
Vuillaume, Nicolas Francois	$6,000 to $8,000
Vuillaume, Sebastien	$6,000 to $8,000
Wagner, Benedict	$2,000 to $2,500
Wamsley, Peter	$8,000 to $10,000
Weichold, August	$600 to $800
Weigert, Johann Blasius	$2,000 to $2,500
Weis, Jacob	$2,000 to $2,500
Werner, Franz	$3,000 to $4,000
Widhalm, Leopold	$6,000 to $8,000
Widhalm, (Martin) Leopold	$4,000 to $5,000
Willems, Hendrick	$6,000 to $8,000
Winterling, Georg	$1,000 to $1,500
Withers, George	$1,000 to $1,500
Wunderlich	$300 to $400
Wutzelhofer, Sebastian	$1,500 to $2,000
Zach, Thomas	$1,500 to $2,000
Zach, Carl	$800 to $1,200
Zacher, Maximilian	$800 to $1,200
Zanoli, Giovanni Battista	$20,000 to $25,000
Zanoli, Giacomo	$20,000 to $25,000
Zanotti (Zanotus), Antonio	$25,000 to $30,000
Zanti, Alessandro	$18,000 to $20,000
Zianni, Pietro	$18,000 to $20,000

The publishers wish to thank Mr. Jacques Francais—the well known violin dealer of New York City, New York—for his generous efforts in compiling the entire list of 1983 prices for the following European section of violin makers and bow makers.

1983 Price Guide for the European Section

Achner, Michael	$2,500 to $3,500
Albani, Matthias	$20,000 to $30,000
Albani, Johann Michael	$18,000 to $25,000
Albani, Joseph	$18,000 to $25,000
Albert, Charles Francais	$1.500 to $2,000
Alberti, Ferdinand	$20,000 to $25,000
Albrecht, Johannes	$2,000 to $2,500
Aldric, Jean Francois	$12,000 to $16,000
Alletsee, Paul	$3,000 to $6,000
Amati, Andrea	$80,000 to $140,000
Amati, Antonio	$75,000 to $85,000
Amati, Nicolo	$100,000 to $140,000
Ambrosi, Petrus	$12,000 to $20,000
Antoniazzi, Gaetano	$12,000 to $16,000
Antoniazzi, Riccardo	$8,000 to $12,000
Antoniazzi, Romeo	$8,000 to $12,000
Arlow, Heinrich	$500 to $800
Artelli, Giuseppe Antonio	$12,000 to $15,000
Ascensio, Vencenzo	$5,000 to $8,000
Aubert, Claude	$1,500 to $2,000
Audinot, Nestor Dominique	$6,000 to $8,000
Baader (Bader)	$500 to $800
Bagatella, Antonius	$18,000 to $20,000
Bailly, Paul	$6,000 to $8,000
Bairhoff, Giorgio	$16,000 to $20,000
Bajoni, Luigi	$6,000 to $8,000
Baldantoni, Giuseppe	$16,000 to $20,000
Balestrieri, Tommaso	$80,000 to $100,000
Banks, Benjamin	$6,000 to $8,000
Barbe, Telesphore Amable	$6,000 to $8,000
Bartl	$1,200 to $1,500
Bassot, Joseph	$5,000 to $8,000
Bausch, Ludwig	$800 to $1,200
Bausch, Otto	$600 to $800
Bellone, Pietro Antonio	$15,000 to $18,000

Bellosio, Anselmo	$28,000 to $30,000
Benoit, Eugene	$2,000 to $2,500
Benoit, Pierre	$1,000 to $1,500
Benti, Matteo	$18,000 to $20,000
Beretta, Felice	$25,000 to $30,000
Bergonzi, Carlo	$175,000 to $250,000
Bergonzi, Michel Angelo	$60,000 to $85,000
Bergonzi, Nicola	$60,000 to $80,000
Bernardel, Auguste Sebastien Phillipe	$15,000 to $18,000
Bernardel, Leon	$1,200 to $1,500
Bertolotti, Gasparo	$45,000 to $65,000
Bertucci, F. M.	$2,500 to $5,000
Betts, John Edward	$6,000 to $8,000
Bianchi, Nicolo	$10,000 to $12,000
Bimbi, Bartolomeo	$20,000 to $25,000
Bisiach, Leandro	$5,000 to $8,000
Blanchard, Paul Francois	$6,000 to $8,000
Bogner, Ambrosius Joseph	$1,000 to $1,500
Bohmann, Joseph	$1,000 to $1,200
Boivin, Claude	$6,000 to $8,000
Boller (or Poller), Michael	$2,000 to $2,500
Bollinger, Joseph	$1,500 to $2,000
Boquay, Jacques	$10,000 to $12,000
Borelli, Andrea	$18,000 to $20,000
Borgia, Antonio	$16,000 to $20,000
Boumeester, Jan	$8,000 to $12,000
Brandini, Jacopo	$15,000 to $20,000
Brandstaetter, Mathaeus Ignaz	$2,000 to $2,500
Breton, Joseph Francois	$1,500 to $2,000
Buchstetter, Gabriel David	$2,000 to $2,500
Bull, Ole	$300 to $350
Busan, Domenico	$20,000 to $25,000
Bussetto, Giovanni Mario (del)	$35,000 to $40,000
Buthod	$5,000 to $8,000
Calcanius, Bernardo	$25,000 to $30,000
Calvarola, Bartolommeo	$25,000 to $30,000

211

Camilli, Camillo	$40,000 to $60,000
Campostano, Antonio	$20,000 to $25,000
Cappa, Gioffredo	$35,000 to $50,000
Carcassi	$25,000 to $30,000
Cardi, Luigi	$6,000 to $8,000
Caressa, Felix Albert	$4,000 to $5,000
Carletti, Carlo	$3,500 to $5,000
Carter, John	$5,000 to $6,000
Casini (Cassini), Antonio	$30,000 to $35,000
Castagneri, Andrea	$6,000 to $8,000
Castellani, Pietro	$8,000 to $12,000
Castello, Paolo	$25,000 to $30,000
Cavalli, Aristide	$3,000 to $5,000
Celani, Emilio	$8,000 to $12,000
Cerin, Marco Antonio	$35,000 to $40,000
Ceruti, Giovanni Baptista	$25,000 to $40,000
Ceruti (Cerutti), Giuseppe	$20,000 to $25,000
Ceruti, Enrico	$18,000 to $20,000
Chanot	$6,000 to $8,000
Chanot, Georges	$6,000 to $8,000
Chappuy, Nicolas Augustin	$6,000 to $8,000
Chardon, Joseph Marie	$4,000 to $5,000
Charotte	$2,000 to $3,500
Charles, Jean	$1,500 to $2,000
Chevrier	$1,000 to $1,500
Chiocchi (Ciocchi), Gaetano	$15,000 to $20,000
Clark, A. B.	$500 to $800
Claudot	$1,500 to $2,000
Clement, Jean Laurent	$1,500 to $2,000
Coletti, Alfred	$500 to $800
Collin-Mezin, Charles Jean Baptiste	$3,000 to $3,500
Collin-Mezin	$2,000 to $2,500
Comuni, Antonio	$10,000 to $12,000
Contreras, Joseph	$14,000 to $16,000
Costa, Felix Mori	$20,000 to $25,000
Costa, Giovanni Baptista	$18,000 to $25,000
Couturiex, N.	$1,500 to $2,000
Craske, George	$1,500 to $3,500
Cross, Nathaniel	$5,000 to $6,000
Crowther, John	$2,000 to $2,500
Cuypers, Johannes	$15,000 to $20,000
Dalinger, Sebastian	$3,500 to $6,000
Dalla Corte, Alfonso	$12,000 to $16,000
Dalla Costa, Pietro Antonio	$28,000 to $30,000
Dall'Aglio, Giuseppe	$25,000 to $30,000
Darche, Nicolas	$4,000 to $5,000
Darte, Auguste	$4,000 to $5,000
Davidson, Peter	$800 to $1,000
Dearlove, Mark William	$3,500 to $5,000
De Comble, Ambroise	$6,000 to $8,000
Deconet, Michael	$30,000 to $35,000
Degani, Eugenio	$10,000 to $12,000
Deleplanque, Gerard J.	$6,000 to $8,000
Delunet, Auguste Leon	$800 to $1,200
De Planis, August	$20,000 to $22,000
Derazey, Jean Joseph Honore	$6,000 to $8,000
Despine (De'Espine), Alexander	$20,000 to $28,000
De Vitor, Petrus Paulus	$14,000 to $16,000
Didelot, Dominique	$3,000 to $5,000
Didion, Gabriel	$2,000 to $2,500
Diehl, Nikolas	$800 to $1,200
Diener, Franz	$800 to $1,200
Dieudonne, Amedee Dominique	$2,000 to $2,500
Dodd, Edward	$4,000 to $6,000
Dodd, Thomas	$4,000 to $6,000
Dodd, John Kew	$5,000 to $6,000
Doerffel	$2,000 to $2,500
Doetsch, Michael	$7,000 to $8,000
Dolling	$500 to $800
Dollenz, Giovanni	$8,000 to $12,000
Drouin, Charles	$1,500 to $2,000
Drouin, Louis	$1,000 to $1,200
Duchesne (Duchene), Nicolas	$2,000 to $3,500
Duke, Richard	$6,000 to $8,000
Duncan, Robert	$2,500 to $3,000
Durfell, J. Gottlob	$1,800 to $3,000
Dvorak, Johann Baptist	$5,000 to $8,000
Dykes, George L.	$2,500 to $4,500
Eberle, Johannes Udalricus	$6,000 to $8,000
Eberle, Magnus	$3,000 to $5,000
Eberle, Tomaso	$25,000 to $28,000
Ellersieck, Albert	$2,000 to $2,500
Enders, F. & R.	$500 to $800
Enel, Charles	$3,000 to $5,000
Ernst, Franz Anton	$800 to $1,200
Eury, Nicolas	$5,000 to $6,000
Fabbricatore, Gennaro	$10,000 to $12,000
Fabris, Luigi	$6,000 to $8,000
Fagnola,	

212

Hannibal	$12,000 to $16,000
Farotti, Celeste	$6,000 to $8,000
Fent, Francois	$6,000 to $8,000
Fendt, Bernhard	$6,000 to $8,000
Fetique, Victor	$3,000 to $3,500
Fichtl, Martin	$5,000 to $6,000
Ficker, Johann	
Christian	$5,000 to $6,000
Fillion, Georges	
Charles	$3,000 to $3,500
Finolli, Giuseppe	
Antonio	$16,000 to $18,000
Fiorini, Raffaele	$10,000 to $12,000
Fiorini, Giuseppe	$12,000 to $16,000
Fischer	$2,000 to $3,000
Fischer, Anton	$2,000 to $3,000
Fleury, Benoit	$6,000 to $8,000
Floriani, Pietro	$5,000 to $6,000
Forster,	
William Sr.	Violins $6,000 to $8,000
	Cellos $20,000 to $25,000
Fourrier, Francois	
Nicolas	$3,000 to $4,000
Francais, Henri	$4,000 to $5,000
Frank, Meinrad	$3,000 to $3,500
Fredi, Rodolfo	$6,000 to $8,000
Furber family,	
London,	
England	$3,500 to $4,000
Gabrielli,	
Giovanni	
Baptista	$25,000 to $30,000
Gaffino, Joseph	$4,000 to $5,000
Gagliano,	
Alexander	$35,000 to $40,000
Gagliano, Nicolo	$40,000 to $50,000
Gagliano, Gennaro	
(Januarius)	$40,000 to $50,000
Gagliano,	
Ferdinando	$30,000 to $35,000
Gagliano,	
Giuseppe	
(Joseph)	$30,000 to $35,000
Gagliano,	
Antonio	$25,000 to $30,000
Gagliano,	
Giovanni	
(Joannes)	$20,000 to $25,000
Gagliano, Raffaele	$15,000 to $20,000
Gaillard, Charles	$10,000 to $12,000
Galbusera, Carlo	
Antonio	$3,000 to $4,000
Gand, Charles	
Francois	$16,000 to $20,000
Gand, Guillaume	
Charles	$10,000 to $12,000
Gand Charles	
Adolphe	$8,000 to $10,000
Gand, Charles	
Nicolas Eugene	$8,000 to $10,000
Gasparo Da Salo,	
see Bertolotti	

Gavinies, Francois	$5,000 to $6,000
Gedler, Johann	
Anton	$3,000 to $4,000
Gedler, Joseph	
Benedikt	$2,000 to $3,000
Geissenhof, Franz	$6,000 to $8,000
Gemunder,	
August	
Martin	
Ludwig	$1,000 to $1,500
Gemunder,	
George	$6,000 to $8,000
Germain, Joseph	
Louis	$6,000 to $8,000
Gibertini,	
Antonio	$20,000 to $25,000
Gigli, Guilio	
Cesare	$20,000 to $30,000
Gilkes, Samuel	$2,500 to $3,000
Glaesel	$500 to $800
Glass	$300 to $350
Glier	$500 to $800
Glier, Robert	$500 to $800
Gobetti,	
Francesco	$65,000 to $85,000
Goetz, Johann	
Michael	$1,500 to $1,800
Goffriller,	
Matteo	$75,000 to $100,000
Goffriller,	
Francesco	$35,000 to $50,000
Gosselin, Jean	$2,000 to $4,000
Gragnani,	
Antonio	$25,000 to $30,000
Grancino, Paolo	$35,000 to $40,000
Grancino,	
Giovanni	
Baptista	$40,000 to $50,000
Grand, Gerard	$2,000 to $3,000
Grandjon	$2,500 to $3,500
Grienberger,	
Joseph	$2,500 to $4,000
Grimm, Karl	$2,500 to $4,000
Guadagnini,	
Lorenzo	$100,000 to $140,000
Guadagnini,	
Giovanni	
Baptista	$120,000 to $150,000
Guadagnini,	
Giuseppe	
(Joseph)	$40,000 to $65,000
Guadagnini,	
Gaetano I	$15,000 to $18,000
Guarnerius,	
Andreas	$75,000 to $100,000
Guarnerius,	
Petrus	$120,000 to $150,000
Guarnerius,	
Giuseppe	
(Joseph)	$85,000 to $140,000
Guarnerius,	
Joseph	
(Del Gesu)	$250,000 to $800,000

213

Guarnerius, Petrus II	$100,000 to $140,000
Guarini, see Menesson	
Guerra, Evasio Emiliano	$8,000 to $12,000
Guersan, Louis (Ludovicus)	$6,000 to $8,000
Guetter	$600 to $800
Guidantus, Joannes Florenus	$40,000 to $50,000
Guillami, Joannes	$12,000 to $15,000
Gusetto, Nicolas	$16,000 to $18,000
Gutermann, Wilhelm	$2,500 to $3,500
Hamm, Johann Gottfried	$6,000 to $8,000
Hammig, Johann Georg	$2,000 to $3,000
Hammig, Wilhelm Hermann	$3,000 to $5,000
Hardie, Mathew	$2,000 to $2,500
Hardie, James	$1,000 to $1,500
Hare, Joseph	$2,000 to $2,500
Harris, Charles I	$2,500 to $3,000
Harris, Griffith	$1,000 to $1,200
Hart, John Thomas	$3,000 to $5,000
Havelka, Johann Baptist	$2,500 to $3,000
Havemann, David Christian	$2,000 to $2,500
Heberlein	$1,000 to $2,000
Heinicke, Mathias	$500 to $800
Hel, Pierre Joseph	$8,000 to $12,000
Hellmer, Johann Georg	$5,000 to $8,000
Hellmer, Carl Joseph	$3,000 to $6,000
Henry, J.	$5,000 to $6,000
Hentschel, Johann Joseph	$1,500 to $2,000
Herold, Conrad Gustav	$500 to $800
Herzlieb, Franciscus	$2,000 to $2,500
Hesketh, Thomas Earle	$1,200 to $1,500
Hill, Joseph	Violins $6,000 to $8,000 Cellos $10,000 to $15,000
Hill, William	$6,000 to $8,000
Hill, Henry Lockey	$6,000 to $8,000
Hill, William Ebsworth	$5,000 to $8,000
Hjorth, Emil	$4,000 to $5,000
Hoffmann, Martin	$2,500 to $3,000
Hofmann, Anton	$5,000 to $6,000
Homolka	$5,000 to $6,000

Hopf	$1,500 to $2,000
Hopf, Carl Friedrich	$1,500 to $2,000
Hopf, David	$500 to $1,000
Horil Jakob	$20,000 to $25,000
Hornsteiner	$1,500 to $2,000
Hornsteiner, modern commercial	$1,000 to $1,500
Hoyer	$2,000 to $3,000
Huber, Johann Georg	$2,500 to $3,000
Hunger, Christoph Friedrich	$2,500 to $3,000
Jacobs, (Jacobsz) Hendrick	$18,000 to $20,000
Jacquot, Charles	$8,000 to $12,000
Jacquot, Charles Albert	$8,000 to $12,000
Jaeger	$800 to $1,200
Jais, Andreas	$6,000 to $8,000
Jais, Anton	$6,000 to $8,000
Johnson, John	$5,000 to $6,000
Jorio, Vincent	$8,000 to $12,000
Kaembl, Johann Andreas	$2,500 to $3,000
Karner, Bartholomaeus	$2,500 to $3,000
Keffer, Johann	$2,500 to $3,000
Kempter, Andreas	$2,000 to $2,500
Kennedy, Thomas	$5,000 to $6,000
Kessler	$400 to $500
Kittel, Nikolaus	$8,000 to $12,000
Klier	$4,000 to $5,000
Klotz, Egidi	$5,000 to $6,000
Klotz (Kloz), Mathias	$5,000 to $8,000
Klotz, Sebastian	$5,000 to $6,000
Klotz, Aegidius	$5,000 to $6,000
Klotz, Johann Carol	$5,000 to $6,000
Klotz, Joseph	$5,000 to $6,000
Knilling	$2,500 to $3,000
Knitl, Franz	$2,500 to $3,000
Knoph, Henry Richard	$1,200 to $1,500
Knorr, Arthur	Violins $800 to $1,200 Bows $300 to $500
Kolditz, Matthias Johann	$2,500 to $3,000
Kollmer	$2,500 to $3,000
Krausch, Georg Adam	$2,500 to $3,000
Krell, Albert	$500 to $800
Kretzschmann	$3,500 to $4,000
Kriner, Simon	$3,500 to $4,000
Kriner, Matthaeus	$5,000 to $6,000

214

Kulik, Johannes	$3,000 to $3,500	Lupot,	
Laberte &		Francois II	$5,000 to $6,000
Magnie	$1,500 to $2,000	Maggini, Giovanni	
Lafleur,		Paolo	$40,000 to $60,000
Jacques	$6,000 to $8,000	Maire, Nicolas	$6,000 to $8,000
Lagetto, Louis	$1,200 to $1,500	Maline,	
Lamy, Alfred		Guillaume	$5,000 to $6,000
Joseph	$3,000 to $5,000	Maline,	
Landolfi, Carlo		Francois Alexis	$4,000 to $5,000
Ferdinando	$35,000 to $40,000	Malvolti, Pietro	
Landolfi, Pietro		Antonio	$10,000 to $15,000
Antonio	$30,000 to $35,000	Mann, John	
La Prevotte,		Alexander	$1,000 to $1,500
Etienne	$2,000 to $2,500	Mansuy, Pierre	$3,000 to $4,000
Laske (Laschke),		Mantegazza	
Joseph Anton	$1,500 to $2,000	(Mantegatia),	
Laurent, Emile	$4,000 to $6,000	Pietro Giovanni	$20,000 to $25,000
Lavazza, Antonio		Marchetti,	
Maria	$20,000 to $25,000	Abbondio	$10,000 to $15,000
Lecchi, Giuseppe	$4,000 to $5,000	Marchi, Giovanni	
Leeb, Johann		Antonio	$12,000 to $15,000
Georg I	$3,000 to $3,500	Marconcini,	
Leeb, Johann		Giuseppe	$20,000 to $30,000
Georg II	$3,000 to $3,500	Martin	$800 to $1,200
Leeb, Andreas		Mast, Joseph	
Carl	$5,000 to $6,000	Laurent	$2,000 to $2,500
Lefebvre,		Maucotel	$4,000 to $5,000
Jacques B.	$4,000 to $5,000	Maussiell,	
Lefebre (Lefebvre),		Leonhard	$5,000 to $6,000
Toussaint		Mayr	$5,000 to $6,000
Nicolas		Mayson,	
Germain	$3,500 to $4,000	Walter H.	$1,000 to $1,500
Leidolff, Nicolas	$4,000 to $5,000	Medard	$5,000 to $8,000
Leidolff, Johann		Meinel	$500 to $800
Christoph	$4,000 to $5,000	Meisel	$500 to $800
Leidolff, Joseph		Melegari,	
Ferdinand	$3,500 to $4,500	Enrico	
Le Jeune,		Clodoveo	$15,000 to $16,000
Francois	$2,000 to $2,500	Mennegand,	
Lemboek, Gabriel	$4,000 to $5,000	Charles	$5,000 to $6,000
Lenoble, Auguste	$3,000 to $4,000	Mennesson, Jean	
Lepri, Luigi	$2,000 to $2,500	Emile	$4,000 to $5,000
Lewis, Edward	$1,000 to $1,500	Merighi, Pietro	$12,000 to $15,000
Liebich, Johann		Meyer,	
Gottfried	$1,000 to $1,500	Magnus	
Lippold, Johann		Andreas	$500 to $800
Georg	$1,500 to $2,500	Mezzadri,	
Lippold, Carl		Allesandro	$25,000 to $30,000
Friedrich	$1,500 to $2,500	Michelot, Jacques	
Lippold, Johann		Pierre	$4,000 to $5,000
Gottlob	$1,500 to $2,500	Milton, Louis	
Lolio, Giovanni		Frank	$1,000 to $1,200
Battista	$10,000 to $12,000	Miremont,	
Lorange, Paul		Claude	
Victor	$4,000 to $5,000	Augustin	$8,000 to $12,000
Lott, John		Moeckel, Oswald	1,500 to $2,000
Frederick	$15,000 to $20,000	Moitessier, Louis	$6,000 to $8,000
Louvet, Jean	$4,000 to $5,000	Mongel, A.	$1,000 to $1,500
Lowendall Star		Montagnana,	
Works	$500 to $800	Dominicus	$140,000 to $200,000
Lupot,		Morelli	$500 to $800
Francois I	$3,000 to $4,000	Morrison,	
Lupot, Nicolas	$35,000 to $65,000	Archibald	$1,200 to $1,500

Mougenot, Georges	$1,500 to $2,000
Mougento, Leon	$1,000 to $1,500
Muncher, Romedio	$1,500 to $2,000
Nadotti, Giuseppe	$15,000 to $20,000
Nemessanyi, Samuel Felix	$16,000 to $20,000
Neuner, Mathias	$2,000 to $3,500
Neuner & Hornsteiner	$1,000 to $2,000
Nicolas, Didier	$1,200 to $1,500
Niggell, Sympertus	$5,000 to $6,000
Novello, Pietro Valentino	$10,000 to $15,000
Nurnberger	$400 to $800
Obici, Bartolomeo	$15,000 to $20,000
Oddone, Carlo Giuseppe	$12,000 to $15,000
Ordoardi, Giuseppe	$20,000 to $25,000
Olry, J	$2,000 to $2,500
Omond, James	$1,000 to $1,500
Ornati, Giuseppe	$10,000 to $12,000
Pacherel (E), Pierre	$20,000 to $25,000
Padewet, Johann	$1,000 to $1,500
Pageot, Louis Simon	$6,000 to $8,000
Pailliot (Paillot)	$1,000 to $1,500
Pallotta, Pietro	$15,000 to $20,000
Pamphilon, Edward	$10,000 to $12,000
Pandolfi, Antonio	$18,000 to $20,000
Panormo, Vincenzo	$20,000 to $28,000
Panormo, Joseph	$8,000 to $12,000
Panormo, Georges Louis	$8,000 to $12,000
Pantzer, Johann Karl	$1,000 to $1,500
Paquotte, Jean Baptiste	$1,000 to $1,500
Parker, Daniel	$15,000 to $20,000
Pasta	$15,000 to $20,000
Pauli, Joseph	$1,000 to $1,200
Paulus	$100 to $500
Pazzini, Giovanni Gaetano	$15,000 to $18,000
Peccatte (Peccate), Dominique	$8,000 to $15,000
Peccatte, Francois	$5,000 to $6,000
Peccatte, Charles	$5,000 to $6,000
Pedrinelli, Antonio	$15,000 to $20,000

Pellizon	$8,000 to $12,000
E. Perrin Fils	$800 to $1,000
Perry, Thomas	$4,000 to $5,000
Pfretzschner	$600 to $1,500
Piegendorfer, Georg	$1,000 to $1,500
Pieroni, Luigi	$2,000 to $2,500
Pierray, Claude	$10,000 to $12,000
Pillement, F.	$5,000 to $6,000
Pique, Francois Louis	$16,000 to $22,000
Pirot, Claude	$1,500 to $2,000
Pizzurnus, David	$20,000 to $25,000
Placht	$500 to $800
Platner, Michael	$25,000 to $30,000
Poggi, Ansaldo	$6,000 to $8,000
Pohland	$800 to $1,000
Poirson, Justin	$3,000 to $4,000
Pollastri, Augusto	$8,000 to $10,000
Pollastri, Gaetano	$6,000 to $8,000
Posch (Bosch), Antonio	$6,000 to $8,000
Postacchini, Andrea	$20,000 to $25,000
Postiglione, Vincenzo	$10,000 to $12,000
Prager, Gustav	$300 to $500
Pressenda, Joannes Franciscus	$35,000 to $50,000
Preston	$1,000 to $1,200
Prevot, P. Charles	$3,000 to $4,000
Rambaux, Claude Victor	$5,000 to $6,000
Rauch, Sebastian	$2,000 to $3,000
Rauch, Joseph	$2,000 to $3,000
Rauch, Thomas	$1,500 to $2,000
Reichel	$800 to $1,500
Reiter, Johann Baptist	$1,200 to $1,500
Remy, Mathurin Francois	$2,000 to $2,500
Renaudin, Leopold	$6,000 to $8,000
Reichers, August	$1,000 to $1,500
Rief, Anton	$4,000 to $6,000
Rief, Dominicus	$4,000 to $6,000
Rieger, Johann	$1,500 to $2,000
Rieger, Georg	$1,500 to $2,000
Rinaldi, Gioffredo Benedetto	$12,000 to $15,000
Rivolta, Giacomo	$18,000 to $25,000
Rocca, Giuseppe Antonio	$25,000 to $30,000

216

Rocca, Enrico	$16,000 to $20,000
Rodiani, Giovita	$15,000 to $20,000
Rogeri, Giovanni Battista	$65,000 to $85,000
Rogeri, Pietro Giacomo	$60,000 to $65,000
Rombouts, Pieter	$12,000 to $16,000
Ronchetti, Domenico	$30,000 to $40,000
Roscher, Christian Heinrich Wilhelm	$1,500 to $2,000
Rossi, Enrico	$6,000 to $8,000
Roth	$500 to $1,200
Ruggeri, Franciscus	$65,000 to $85,000
Ruggeri, Giacinto Giovanni Battista	$60,000 to $85,000
Ruggeri, Vincenzo	$65,000 to $75,000
Ruprecht, Wilhelm	$1,500 to $2,000
Sacquin	$1,200 to $1,500
Saint Paul, Pierre	$5,000 to $8,000
Salo, Gasparo Da, see Bertolotti	
Sajot	$2,000 to $2,500
Salomon, Jean Baptiste	$6,000 to $8,000
Salzard	$1,500 to $2,000
Santagiuliana, Gaetano	$18,000 to $20,000
Santagiuliana, Giacinto	$10,000 to $12,000
Santucci, Sebastian	$1,500 to $2,000
Sartory, Eugene	$4,000 to $5,000
Sawicki, Carl Nikolaus	$1,500 to $2,000
Scarampella, Paolo	$8,000 to $12,000
Scarampella, Giuseppe	$14,000 to $16,000
Scarampella, Stefano	$10,000 to $12,000
Schaller, Oswald	$300 to $500
Schandl, Anton	$2,000 to $2,500
Scheverle, Johann	$2,000 to $2,500
Schlosser	$2,000 to $2,500
Schmidt	$800 to $1,200
Schneider	$800 to $1,200
Schonfelder	$2,000 to $2,500
Schonger, Franz	$1,500 to $2,000
Schorn, Johann Paul	$1,500 to $2,000
Schuster	$500 to $800
Schuster, Kurt	$1,500 to $2,000
Schweitzer, Johann Baptist	$2,000 to $2,500

Seidel	$1,500 to $2,000
Seraphin, Sanctus	$65,000 to $100,000
Sgarabotto, Gaetano	$6,000 to $8,000
Sgarbi., Antonio	$5,000 to $8,000
Silvestre, Pierre	$6,000 to $8,000
Silvestre & Maucotel	$5,000 to $8,000
Simon, P.	$6,000 to $8,000
Simoutre, Nicolas	$6,000 to $8,000
Sitt, Anton	$1,000 to $1,500
Skomal, Nikolaus Georg	$1,500 to $2,000
Smith, Thomas	$3,500 to $4,000
Socquet, Louis	$5,000 to $6,000
Soffritti, Ettore	$6,000 to $8,000
Soliani, Angelo	$12,000 to $16,000
Soriot, D.	$1,000 to $1,500
Spidlen, Franz	$1,000 to $2,500
Stadlmann, Johann Joseph	$6,000 to $8,000
Stainer, Jacobus	$40,000 to $65,000
Stainer, Marcus	$5,000 to $6,000
Staininger, Jacob	$500 to $800
Stauffer, Johann Georg	$3,000 to $3,500
Storck, Johannes Friedrich	$4,000 to $5,000
Storioni, Lorenzo	$60,000 to $80,000
Stoss, Martin	$6,000 to $8,000
Stradivari, Antonio	$250,000 to $700,000
Stradivari, Francesco	$200,000 to $250,000
Stradivari, Omobono	$200,000 to $250,000
Strnad, Caspar	$4,000 to $5,000
Strobl, Johann	$2,500 to $3,000
Suss, Johann Christian	$800 to $1,500
Szepessy, Bela	$5,000 to $6,000
Tanegia, Carlo Antonio	$18,000 to $25,000
Tassini, Bartolomeo	$20,000 to $25,000
Tecchler, David	Violins $20,000 to $30,000
	Cellos $120,000 to $150,000
Tedesco, Leopold II	$1,500
Testore, Carlo Giuseppe	$28,000 to $35,000
Testore, Carlo Antonio	$28,000 to $35,000
Testore, Paolo Antonio	$25,000 to $35,000
Thibouville-Lamy, Louis Emile Jerome	$1,000 to $1,500

Thir, Anton I	$5,000 to $6,000	Voigt, Johann	
Thir, Andreas	$5,000 to $6,000	Georg	$1,500 to $2,000
Thir (Thier),		Voigt, Carl	
Johann Georg	$6,000 to $8,000	Hermann	$1,000 to $1,500
Thir, Mathias	$3,000 to $3,500	Voigt, Arnold	$500 to $800
Thomassin,		Voirin, Joseph	$2,000 to $2,500
Louis	$3,000 to $4,000	Voirin,	
Thouvenel,		Francois	
Henry	$800 to $1,200	Nicolas	$5,000 to $6,000
Teiffenbrucker,		Voller, William	$6,000 to $8,000
Caspar	$800 to $$1,200	Vuillaume, Jean	
Teiffenbrunner,		Baptiste	$35,000 to $40,000
Georg	$500 to $800	Vuillaume,	
Tobin, Richard	$2,000 to $2,500	Nicolas	
Tononi, Felice	$50,000 to $60,000	Francois	$6,000 to $8,000
Tononi,		Vuillaume,	
Giovanni	$50,000 to $60,000	Sebastien	$6,000 to $8,000
Tononi, Carlo	$60,000 to $85,000	Wagner,	
Toppani, Angelo	$18,000 to $20,000	Benedict	$2,000 to $2,500
Tourte, Pere	$6,000 to $8,000	Wamsley, Peter	$8,000 to $10,000
Tourte, Xavier	$5,000 to $6,000	Weichold, August	$600 to $800
Tourte,		Weigert, Johann	
Francois	$20,000 to $25,000	Blasius	$2,000 to $2,500
Trucco,		Weis, Jacob	$2,000 to $2,500
Girolamo	$4,000 to $5,000	Werner, Franz	$3,000 to $4,000
Tubbs, James	$3,000 to $5,000	Widhalm,	
Valenzano		Leopold	$6,000 to $8,000
(Valenciano),		Widhalm,	
Giovanni		(Martin)	
Maria	$12,000 to $16,000	Leopold	$4,000 to $5,000
Vandelli,		Willems,	
Giovanni	$8,000 to $10,000	Hendrick	$8,000 to $12,000
Van Der		Winterling,	
Slaghmeulen,		Georg	$1,000 to $1,500
Johannes		Withers, George	$1,500 to $3,500
Baptist	$4,000 to $5,000	Wunderlich	$300 to $400
Varotti,		Wutzelhofer,	
Giovanni	$20,000 to $25,000	Sebastian	$1,500 to $2,000
Vatelot, Marcel	$2,500 to $4,000	Zach, Thomas	$1,500 to $2,000
Vauchel, Jean	$2,000 to $2,500	Zach, Carl	$800 to $1,200
Ventapane,		Zacher,	
Vincenzo	$20,000 to $25,000	Maximilian	$800 to $1,200
Ventapane,		Zanoli,	
Pasquale	$18,000 to $20,000	Giovanni	
Ventapane,		Battista	$25,000 to $30,000
Lorenzo	Violins $20,000 to	Zanoli,	
	$25,000	Giacomo	$20,000 to $25,000
	Cellos $40,000 to	Zanotti	
	$50,000	(Zanotus),	
Varzella,		Antonio	$25,000 to $30,000
Francesco	$800 to $1,000	Zanti,	
Viedenhofer,		Alessandro	$18,000 to $20,000
Bernard	$800 to $1,000	Zianni, Pietro	$18,000 to $20,000
Vignali,			
Giuseppe	$2,000 to $2,500		
Vigneron,			
Joseph Arthur	$2,000 to $3,500		
Vinaccia,			
Antonio	$18,000 to $25,000		
Vinaccia,			
Gennaro	$18,000 to $25,000		
Vincenzi, Luigi	$18,000 to $20,000		
Vogler, Johann			
Georg	$2,000 to $2,500		

How to Choose a Bow
By William Salchow

The French term for "bow," "baguette," connotes a slender, delicate wand nevertheless capable of evoking a full range of expression from a violin, viola or cello — from the merest whisper to a full-throated roar. And what an incredible difference in sound two different bows can have on the same instrument! Musicians know this, and are constantly seeking a bow that will enable them both to play better and to sound better. Whatever reason you may have for acquiring a bow, selecting the right one requires knowledge and judgement.

This article has been prepared to guide you in the art of bow buying so that you may select, with discernment, the right bow for you.

A BOW FOR EACH SEASON

No string player should be limited to one bow. Additional bows can be more than just a spare for emergencies. Here are some reasons for owning more than one bow.

• One bow might be fine for orchestral playing, another more suitable for chamber music, a third perfect for practising (lighter in weight to conserve energy), a fourth good for recitals, a fifth more secure for performing concerti with orchestra.

• A bow can be matched to a particular music style:
  - Baroque music is more easily played with a baroque type of bow. The lack of curve makes vigorous detaché bowing demanded by this music easier to do.
  - Some of the older modern type bows (Père Tourte, Adam) are ideally suited for early classical music (Mozart, Shubert and Beethoven). Their lighter weight and less curve at the head lend a certain ease and grace to this type of music.
  - And for Paganini and Wieniawski, bows from the more modern makers such as Voirin and Sartory are capable of flying staccato and other brilliant effects.

A fine bow by a known bowmaker is an excellent investment. Over the years, fine old French bows have outpaced the stock market and have risen in price faster than violins.

SOUND AND FEEL

Different Strokes from Different Bows

There's one thing all bows have in common: they are all strung with horse hair. But the similarity ends there.

What makes one bow different from every other bow?

It is one of the wonders of nature that every bow stick is acoustically unique, with each bow varying according to the cellular structure of the wood. The quality and volume of the sound produced depends on the acoustical properties of the wood. If the wood does not vibrate sympathetically with every note on the instrument, the bow will mute the sound. Your ideal bow resonates to produce overtones which enhance the sound of your particular instrument.

Along with the sound, you must be comfortable with the feel of your bow. You must be able to perform all the required bowings and to shape the sound artistically with it. This means that the bow must respond well throughout its entire length. Three things combine to determine the feel of a bow: weight, balance and strength or resistance of the stick. Normal weights are:

Violin	55 to 65 grams
Viola	68 to 74 grams
Cello	78 to 88 grams

Normal balance is from 6 1/2 inches to 7 1/2 inches from the front of the frog when the frog is all the way forward (16.5 to 19 cm.).

Weight and balance together determine the feel of a bow, so that both must be taken into account. As the balance moves out toward the head, the bow will feel heavier, and as it moves back toward the frog, the bow will feel lighter.

You should not depart too far from what you are accustomed to using. If you have played for years with a medium weight bow with normal balance, you probably will be uncomfortable with a much heavier bow or one that is top-heavy in balance. Sometimes a top-heavy bow will be seductive, and will seem to perform certain bowings easier, especially sautille and bouncing bowings, but after a time will be very tiring to play.

A heavier bow will not necessarily produce more sound. A strong stick is one that produces a large sound with little effort and is not necessarily stiff.

STRENGTH OF THE STICK

The stick must be supple enough to give tonal gradation and control, but strong enough to resist playing pressure without the stick rubbing the hair.

AUDITIONING YOUR BOW
Do's and Don't's

When choosing from among several bows, you should give primary consideration to the sound. You can adjust your playing to differences in weight and feel, but the sound is a product of the cellular structure of the wood, and can not be altered. Weight and balance can be manipulated quite a lot. A bow can always be made heavier and the balance changed by adding weight to the head or to the frog. For instance, the original ivory tip can always be replaced with silver or gold, for changing the tip does not affect the value of a bow. But the strength or resistance of a stick can not be altered, except if a stick is not curved fully down to the hair; adding that curve will increase the resistance of a stick. If a stick is warped to the wrong side, straightening or warping to the opposite side will also increase the strength of a stick. But a stick that feels like a "club" should not be considered.

In trying out various bows, the following guidelines are recommended:

1. Do not play long passages: the ear quickly becomes accustomed to the sound of a particular bow and then the differences between bows are lost for purposes of comparison.

2. Do no play difficult music; doing so makes it harder to concentrate on the quality of the bow.

3. Pick very simple short passages and even open strings.

4. Do not play only fortissimo; a bow should be capable of pianissimo and all shades in between.

5. Change trial bows frequently and do not attempt to choose from more than two or at most three bows at a time. In this way you can narrow your choices to one or two bows in a relatively brief period of time. To attempt to choose from a large number of bows by playing them one after another leads only to confusion.

PRICE
Having found the Bow of all Bows for you, what should you pay?

Modern Bows
(Those made by living or recently deceased makers)

Modern bows are priced according to the reputation of the maker, which is dependent on the success his or her bows have had with players. Nevertheless, this does not guarantee that every bow by the maker will play equally well. It does imply a certain standard of workmanship and materials.

The materials used also affect the price. Brazilwood is never used by fine makers; it is an inferior substitute for pernambuco. Bows made from this wood are commercial and of lowest quality.

Normally, frogs are made of ebony with silver mountings. Frogs of ivory or tortoise shell with gold mountings will double the price of a bow, since bowmakers save their finest wood for these bows. Fancy inlays and jewels do not add anything except their own value to a bow, although they may appeal to collectors.

Bows without a name or with an unknown name must be regarded as commercial or factory bows and will not appreciate in value like name bows. They must be judged on their own merits; they can be a surprisingly good value.

Antique Bows

Bows by known makers made one hundred years ago or more will have considerable value as antiques. Aside from the fact that fine bows improve with age and use, antique bows will be many times more expensive than modern bows. This increased price does not necessarily indicate a correspondingly better performance in playing but instead indicates value as a work of art.

Bows do improve and mellow with age and use, and the sound they produce improves considerably. But new bows made with old wood, and even some made with new wood, can sometimes produce a sound equal or superior to some old bows. Since the sound produced by a bow seems to be a function of the cellular structure of the wood, a bow which is bad today will still be bad one hundred years from now. But a bow with a great sound will develop to its full potential rather quickly if played regularly, probably within ten years or less.

Nationality

French bows are legendary. Tourte, Peccatte, Voirin are the makers who represent the pinnacle of bowmaking, and are the models by which all bows are judged. They are also the most expensive, being much sought after by musicians. All other things being equal, a French bow will always cost more than an equivalent German or English bow, so if you are looking for the most playing value for the money, do not buy a French bow. A fine German or English bow of the same quality will cost less.

Conclusion

Ultimately, the price of a bow is determined by supply and demand in the market place. There is a very active trade in bows, with an increasing demand meeting a diminishing supply, and this determines price. Since bows are fragile, the rate of attrition is high, and therefore the price of old bows has nowhere to go but up. An authentic bow of established value can always be traded in against a bow of equal or greater value, minus any necessary repairs.

In buying a bow, the only substitute for comprehensive knowledge is to deal with a reputable maker, dealer or expert.

CODA: Bow Maintenance

Bows require constant, skilled attention if they are to be preserved in good condition. And condition is an important factor in determining price and salability. So if fine condition is not maintained, the value of your investment will decline.

Thus, for example, if a bow is warped to one side, kinked, or unevenly curved, it will not respond as well as it could. But a skilled bowmaker can easily and permanently correct these faults. Because of large abrupt changes in weather typical of our American climate, any bow can warp; it can also be straightened. But beware the amateur repairman who can permanently damage or burn your bow. Straightening a bow requires great skill and experience.

William Salchow, Ltd.
Bowmaker and Dealer
250 West 54th St.
New York, N.Y. 10019
(212) 586-4805

Welcome to William Salchow's showroom, open Monday—Friday, 9:30—5:30, and Saturday, September—May.

William Salchow got his start in bowmaking at the violin house of Rembert Wurlitzer where he worked as a cello salesman. Here, under the guidance of Simone F. Sacconi, he began to make and repair bows. Befriended and encouraged by the great cello pedagogue Luigi Silva, he received a Fulbright Grant to study bowmaking as an apprentice in France. In Mirecourt, cradle of the French violin and bowmaking art, he learned traditional French bowmaking techniques which had been handed down unaltered from master to apprentice since the time of Tourte c.1800. His teacher, Georges Barjonnet, had been an apprentice together with Andre Richaume and Emile Ouchard, Fils. in the shop of Emile Ouchard, Père.

After serving his apprenticeship in France, Salchow returned to New York and opened his own studio where he has been making fine bows in the French tradition since 1960. Here he has assembled the raw materials: logs of pernambuco, snakewood and ebony, and ivory tusks from elephants, blocks of tortoise shell. Each bow is crafted individually according to the wood. Each stick is carefully graduated for strength and flexibility and balanced for optimum playability according to the player's preference, with frogs of ebony, ivory and tortoise shell and inlays of ocean pearl shell and mountings of gold and silver. While he often copies classical French designs, he also has his own model which has been designed to give greater flexibility at the head.

In addition to bowmaking, Salchow maintains a large stock of old and new bows, instruments, and accessories for sale.

Some of the world's finest players have used Salchow bows, including Joseph Fuchs, Oscar Shumsky, Benno Rabinof, Samuel Mayes, Joseph Silverstein, Leonard Rose, Lynn Harrell, Raya Garbousova, Jules Eskin, Joseph DiPasquale, Mischa Mischakoff, Zara Nelsova, Ida Kavafian and Pierre D'Archambeau.

To: Harold Chaitman
    Cape Coral, Florida

Dear Harold,

Enclosed are the changes I have made in bow prices, the others I believe should stay the same. I think the bowmakers should be separated from the violin makers because in some case they did both so there could be confusion.

You have my permission to use "How To Choose A Bow".

Bausch, Ludwig	$800.00 to $2000.00
Bernardel, Leon	2000.00 to 3000.00
Eury, Nicholas	8000.00 to 10000.00
Lupot, Francois II	8000.00 to 10000.00
Maire, Nicholas	8000.00 to 10000.00
Albert Nurnberger	1000.00 to 2000.00
Pajeot	8000.00 to 10000.00
Dominique Peccatte	12000.00 to 15000.00
H R Pfretzschner	1000.00 to 2000.00
Tourte, Louis	8000.00 to 12000.00
Vigneron, J A	3000.00 to 4000.00

With kindest regards,

William Salchow

P.S. Xavier Tourte should be removed -- he never existed.

PUBLISHER'S FOREWORD

A careful reading will note that Mr. Chorberg and Mr. Pineiro have left the 1983 prices of certain violin makers unchanged. This is due to the honest disclosure that these particular makers were not often encountered and hence a reluctance to make any monetary evaluation for them. While these names are not many in number, it can be generally assumed that these makers' prices have increased by twenty per cent or more from the 1983 evaluations.

Mr. Chorberg and Mr. Pineiro, while very qualified to assess bows, did not price bows because Mr. Robert Ames has throughly done so in his subsequent chapter.

HORACIO PIÑEIRO
VIOLIN-MAKER & RESTORER
34-43 75TH STREET
JACKSON HEIGHTS, NEW YORK 11372
718-639-7541

HORACIO PIÑEIRO

Horacio Piñeiro was born in Buenos Aires, Argentina on January 18th 1939. He studied in the school of Arts and Crafts for the wood in Buenos Aires. Piñeiro began working on stringed instruments at the age of fourteen under Franco Ponza. He continued working and studying with Henry Viret. His workmanship was perfected with Pierre Gaggini in France.

In 1963 Piñeiro opened his own workshop in Buenos Aires. He emigrated to the United States in 1977 to work for Jacques Francais Inc. and worked for the firm for fourteen years. He was involved in the restoration on some of the most important and valuable instruments available.

Currently he is established in his own shop in Jackson Heights, New York where he is engaged in making new instruments and restoration of old masters' works.

Until the present he has made 160 new instruments (violins, violas, cellos) following the styles of the classical Italian instruments. Piñeiro has participated in numerous competitions receiving several gold medals.

MEMBER: - Entente International of Violin and Bow Makers
                - American Federation of Violin and Bow Makers
                - Violin Society of America

Israel Chorberg
New York. New York
212-765-7390

Israel Chorberg was born in Montevideo, the capital of Uruguay, where he studied the violin. He was a member of the National Quartet, and of the OSSODRE (the National Symphony Orchestra), both government sponsored and concertized exclusively.

In 1959, having won the first prize in a National Competition among 40 instrumentalists,
he was invited by the Ministry of Culture of the Soviet Union to study in the Chaikowsky Conservatory, thus becoming the first South-American violinist to receive a scholarship directly from the Soviet Government. He studied there from 1960 through 1963.

Upon his arrival in the United States in 1966, Mr. Chorberg auditioned for Leopold Stokowsky who immediately hired him as a member of the American Symphony Orchestra. A few years afterwards, Mr. Chorberg became Assistant Concertmaster for the New York City Opera Orchestra and Concertmaster for several ballets orchestras including American Ballet Theater Orchestra and all the foreign ballets that were brought by Sol Hurok to perform at the Metropolitan Opera House. He started dealing with violins in 1973 and has since shifted his activities mostly to the sale of stringed instruments. Mr. Chorberg is a member of the Appraisers Association of America and the Violin Society of America.

FOREWORD by ISRAEL CHORBERG and HORACIO PIÑEIRO

It is not an easy task to try to assess accurately the value of any object, particularly when it falls into the category of art or artisanship, be it a piece of furniture, a painting, or a musical instrument. In this particular case, it becomes even more difficult because a musical instrument has, aside from all other values common to other art or artisan made objects, an intrinsic value as a sound producing tool. Therefore, the personal taste and ability of the prospective buyer plays a very important role. It is a well known fact that the same instrument will please enormously one player and displease enormously another player, even though both players may be equally talented and the instrument extraordinarily made. The instrument may also seem easy to play to one and extremely difficult to another. The basic factors taken into account in the present assessment are:

1. The most important — We only assess instruments that are certified or can be certified, as being **MADE IN ALL ITS PARTS BY ONE AND ONLY ONE MAKER**. We are not assessing composite instruments or instruments in which any of its parts have ben replaced for whatever reason.
2. Country of origin — Of course, Italian instruments are the most valuable.
3. Age — In general, it may be said that a 200 year old instrument is more valuable than a 100 year old instrument.
4. Name of the maker — In general, a Stradivarius violin is more valuable than an Amati or Guadagnini.
5. State of preservation — An instrument of a given maker in poor condition will have a lower value than an instrument of the same maker in good condition and a much lower value than an instrument of that maker in excellent condition. We know of a Gagliano violin which sold for more than double the going price at the time because of its immaculate condition. Conversely, an instrument which is in poor condition my sell for half of its normal price.
6. Basic sound qualities — Power, projection, evenness, clarity, quality, all of which are, however, as stated above, very subjective.
7. State of the market — Country where the instrument is being sold, relationship of the local currencies to the most accepted international currencies such as the Dollar, the Pound, or the Deutsche Mark; causing fluctuations of the market value of instruments over the years.
8. Statistics — Prices at which instruments have been sold, be it by dealers,

privately or at auctions (this last source being taken with a grain of salt since it has happened that in auctions, both have occurred: an instrument sold at a much higher price than its market value at the time, and another one sold for much less than its market value.)

9. Specialty of the maker — In many cases, the cellos of a given maker are more valuable then his violins, e.g. Matteo Goffriller. Or, as in the case of Gasparo da Salo, his violas are more valuable than his violins.

10. Finally — We, Israel Chorberg and Horacio Piñeiro, the underwriters of the Appendix have also our personal experiences of many years as appraisers and dealers and, therefore, even though we did our best to be extremely objective, our opinions may have a small degree of subjectivity.

Achner,		Bagatella,	
Michael	$2,500 to $3,500	Antonius	$30,000 to $40,000
Albani,		Bailly,	
Matthias	$50,000 to $70,000	Paul	$12,000 to $18,000
Albani, Johann		Bairhoff,	
Michael	$35,000 to $45,000	Giorgio	$16,000 to $20,000
Albani,		Bajoni,	
Joseph	$35,000 to $45,000	Luigi	$12,000 to $18,000
Albert, Charles		Baldantoni,	
Francais	$4,000 to $5,000	Giuseppe	$45,000 to $55,000
Alberti,		Balestrieri,	
Ferdinand	$50,000 to $60,000	Tommaso	$175,000 to $275,000
Albrecht,		Banks,	
Johannes	$2,000 to $2,500	Benjamin	$15,000 to $25,000
Aldric, Jean		Barbe,	
Francois	$20,000 to $25,000	Telesphore	
Alletsee,		Amable	$10,000 to $12,000
Paul	$3,000 to $6,000	Bartl	$1,200 to $1,500
Amati,		Bassot,	
Andrea	$200,000 to $300,000	Joseph	$8,000 to $10,000
Amati,		Bellone, Pietro	
Antonio	$100,000 to $150,000	Antonio	$20,000 to $25,000
Amati,		Bellosio,	
Nicolo	$200,000 to $400,000	Anselmo	$40,000 to $50,000
Ambrosi,		Benoit,	
Petrus	$15,000 to $25,000	Eugene	$3,000 to $5,000
Antoniazzi,		Benoit,	
Gaetano	$30,000 to $50,000	Pierre	$2,000 to $2,500
Antoniazzi,		Benti,	
Riccardo	$35,000 to $50,000	Matteo	$18,000 to $20,000
Antoniazzi,		Beretta,	
Romeo	$35,000 to $50,000	Felice	$100,000 to $160,000
Arlow,		Bergonzi,	
Heinrich	$500 to $800	Carlo	$700,000 to $900,000
Artelli,		Bergonzi, Michel	
Giuseppe		Angelo	$200,000 to $300,000
Antonio	$15,000 to $18,000	Bergonzi,	
Ascensio,		Nicola	$200,000 to $350,000
Vencenzo	$5,000 to $8,000	Bernardel,	
Aubert,		Auguste	
Claude	$1,500 to $2,000	Sebastien	
Audinot, Nestor		Phillipe	$20,000 to $35,000
Dominique	$12,000 to $15,000	Bernardel,	
Baader (Bader)	$500 to $800	Leon	$5,000 to $12,000

Bertolotti, Gasparo	Violas: $500,000 to $1,000,00
Bertucci, F. M.	$2,500 to $5,000
Betts, John Edward	$10,000 to $25,000
Bianchi, Nicolo	$20,000 to $35,000
Bimbi, Bartolomeo	$60,000 to $75,000
Bisiach, Leandro	$30,000 to $50,000
Blanchard, Paul Francois	$10,000 to $18,000
Bogner, Ambrosius Joseph	$2,000 to $2,500
Bohmann, Joseph	$1,000 to $1,200
Boivin, Claude	$10,000 to $12,000
Boller (Poller), Michael	$7,000 to $10,000
Bollinger Joseph	$2,000 to $2,500
Boquay, Jacques	$20,000 to $30,000
Borelli, Andrea	$20,000 to $25,000
Borgia, Antonio	$18,000 to $22,000
Boumeester, Jan	$25,000 to $35,000
Brandini, Jacopo	$20,000 to $30,000
Brandstaetter, Mathaeus Ignaz	$2,000 to $2,500
Breton, Joseph Francois	$1,500 to $3,000
Buchstetter, Gabriel David	$2,000 to $2,500
Bull, Ole	$300 to $350
Busan, Domenico	$100,000 to $150,000
Bussetto, Giovanni Mario (del)	$120,000 to $150,000
Buthod	$7,000 to $10,000
Calcanius, Bernardo	$80,000 to $110,000
Calvarola Bartolommeo	$80,000 to 110,000
Camilli, Camillo	$130,000 to $200,000
Campostano Antonio	$30,000 to $40,000
Cappa, Gioffredo	$120,000 to $185,000
Carcassi	$60,000 to $80,000
Cardi, Luigi	$12,000 to $15,000
Caressa, Felix Albert	$8,000 to $12,000
Carletti, Carlo	$20,000 to $25,000
Carter, John	$5,000 to $6,000
Casini (Cassini) Antonio	$60,000 to $80,000
Casatagneri, Andrea	$12,000 to $15,000
Castellani, Pietro	$12,000 to 15,000
Castello, Paolo	$75,000 to $110,000
Cavalli Aristide	$8,000 to $15,000
Celani Emilio	$18,000 to $25,000
Cerin, Marco Antonio	$75,000 to 95,000
Ceruti, Giovanni Baptista	$110,000 to $145,000
Ceruti, (Cerutti) Giuseppe	$50,000 to $70,000
Ceruti, Enrico	$70,000 to 110,000
Chanot	$6,000 to $8,000

Chanot, Georges	$30,000 to $45,000
Chappuy, Nicolas Augustin	$18,000 to $22,000
Chardon, Joseph Marie	$8,000 to $12,000
Charotte	$3,000 to $5,000
Charles, Jean Chevrier	$1,500 to $2,500
Chiocchi (Ciocchi), Gaetano	$50,000 to $80,000
Clark, A. B.	$500 to $800
Claudot	$6,000 to $9,000
Clement, Jean Laurent	$5,000 to $7,500
Coletti, Alfred	$500 to $800
Collin-Mezin	$4,000 to $6,000
Collin-Mezin, Charles Jean Baptiste	$7,000 to $12,000
Comuni, Antonio	$20,000 to $25,000
Contreras, Joseph	$35,000 to $60,000
Costa, Felix Mori	$50,000 to $85,000
Costa, Giovanni Baptista	$40,000 to 75,000
Couturiex, N.	$3,000 to $4,000
Craske, George	$3,000 to $5,000
Cross, Nathaniel	$15,000 to $25,000
Crowther, John	$10,000 to $18,000
Cuypers, Johannes	$35,000 to $50,000
Dalinger, Sebastian	$6,000 to $7,500
Dalla Corte, Alfonso	$30,000 to $55,000
Dalla Costa, Pietro Antonio	$45,000 to $70,000

Dall' Aglio, Giuseppe	$45,000 to $70,000
Darche, Nicolas	$15,000 to $25,000
Darte, Auguste	$4,000 to $5,500
Davidson, Peter	$1,000 to $2,000
Dearlove, Mark William	$3,000 to $4,500
De Comble, Ambroise	$15,000 to $20,000
Deconet, Michael	$80,000 to $110,000
Degani Eugenio	$30,000 to $50,000
Deleplanque, Gerard J.	$6,000 to $8,000
Delunet, Auguste Leon	$800 to $1,200
De Planis, August	$40,000 to $60,000
Derazey, Jean Joseph Honore	$12,000 to $20,000
Despine (De' Espine) Alexander	$50,000 to $75,000
De Vitor, Petrus Paulus	$20,000 to $25,000
Didelot, Dominique	$3,000 to $5,000
Didion, Gabriel	$2,500 to $3,000
Diehl, Nikolas	$800 to $1,200
Diener, Franz	$800 to $1,200
Dieudonne, Amedee Dominique	$5,000 to $10,000
Dodd, Thomas	$18,000 to $35,000
Doerffel	$2,000 to $2,500
Doetsch, Michael	$15,000 to $20,000
Dolling	$500 to $800

233

Dollenz, Giovanni	$25,000 to $40,000
Drouin, Charles	$1,500 to $2,000
Drouin, Louis	$1,000 to $1,200
Duchesne (Duchene) Nicolas	$2,500 to $4,000
Duke, Richard	$8,000 to $15,000
Duncan, Robert	$2,500 to $3,500
Durfell, J. Gottlob	$2,500 to $3,500
Dvorak, Johann Baptist	$8,000 to $13,500
Dykes, George L.	$3,000 to $6,000
Eberle, Johannes Udalricus	$8,000 to $10,000
Eberle, Magnus	$4,000 to $7,500
Eberle, Tomaso	$60,000 to $80,000
Ellersieck, Albert	$2,000 to $3,000
Enders, F & R.	$500 to $800
Enel, Charles	$10,000 to $15,000
Ernst, Franz Anton	$800 to $1,200
Fabbricatore, Gennaro	$30,000 to $40,000
Fabris, Luigi	$20,000 to $30,000
Fagnola, Hannibal	$50,000 to $80,000
Farotti, Celeste	$18,000 to $30,000
Fent, Francois	$15,000 to $20,000
Fendt, Bernhard	$15,000 to $20,000
Fichtl, Martin	$5,000 to $6,000
Ficker, Johann Christian	$10,000 to $15,000
Fillion, Georges Charles	$5,000 to $7,500
Finolli, Giuseppe Antonio	$25,000 to $35,000
Fiorini, Giuseppe	$35,000 to $45,000
Fiorini, Raffaele	$25,000 to $30,000
Fischer Zacharias	$8,000 to $15,000
Fischer, Anton	$2,000 to $3,000
Fleury, Benoit	$20,000 to $25,000
Floriani, Pietro	$15,000 to $20,000
Forster, William Sr.	Violins: $10,000 to $15,000 Cellos: $35,000 to $55,000
Fourrier, Francois Nicolas	$5,000 to $6,000
Francais, Henri	$8,000 to $12,000
Frank, Meinrad	$3,000 to $3,500
Fredi, Rodolfo	$20,000 to $35,000
Furber Family, London, England	$5,000 to $7,000
Gabrielli, Giovanni Baptista	$80,000 to $110,000
Gaffino, Joseph	$4,000 to $5,000
Gagliano, Alexander	$200,000 to $300,000
Gagliano, Antonio	$80,000 to $120,000
Gagliano, Ferdinando	$120,000 to $150,000

Gagliano, Gennaro (Januarius)	$50,000 to $200,000
Gagliano, Giovanni (Joannes)	$90,000 to $125,000
Gagliano, Nicolo	$150,000 to $250,000
Gaglaino, Giuseppe (Joseph)	$125,000 to $150,000
Gagliano Raffaele	$75,000 to $90,000
Gaillard, Charles	$15,000 to $20,000
Galbusera, Carlo Antonio	$6,000 to $10,000
Gand, Charles Adolphe	$25,000 to $35,000
Gand, Charles Francois	$30,000 to $50,000
Gand, Charles Nicolas Eugene	$25,000 to $35,000
Gand, Guillaume Charles	$20,000 to $25,000
Gasparo Da Salo, see Bertolotti	$750,000 to $1,000,000
Gavinies, Fancois	$7,000 to $10,000
Gedler, Johann Anton	$3,000 to $4,000
Gedler, Joseph Benedikt	$2,000 to $3,000
Geissenhof, Franz	$12,000 to $22,000
Gemunder, August Martin Ludwig	$6,000 to $10,000
Gemunder, George	$12,000 to $20,000
Germain, Joseph Louis	$12,000 to $18,000
Gibertini, Antonio	$35,000 to $50,000

Gigli, Guilio, Cesare	$40,000 to $75,000
Gilkes, Samuel	Violins $15,000 to $25,000
	Cellos $40,000 to $50,000
Glaesel	$500 to $800
Glass	$4,000 to $6,000
Glier	$500 to $800
Glier, Robert	$3,000 to $5,000
Gobetti, Francesco	$150,000 to $230,000
Goetz, Johann Michael	$3,000 to $6,000
Goffriller, Francesco	Violins: $150,000 to $200,000
	Cellos: $300,000 to $500,000
Goffriller, Matteo	Violins: $300,000 to $400,000
	Cellos: $800,000 to $1,300,000
Gosselin, Jean	$2,000 to $4,000
Gragnani, Antonio	$80,000 to $120,000
Grancino, Paolo	$35,000 to $40,000
Grancino, Giovanni Baptista	$150,000 to $200,000
Grand, Gerard	$4,000 to $5,000
Grandjon	$6,000 to $10,000
Grienberger, Joseph	$2,500 to $4,000
Grimm, Karl	$2,500 to $4,000
Guadagnini, Gaetano I	$75,000 to $95,000

235

Guadagnini, Giovanni Baptista	$400,000 to $800,000
Guadagnini, Giuseppe (Joseph)	$150,000 to $220,000
Guadagnini, Lorenzo	$400,000 to $600,000
Guarnerius, Andreas	$300,000 to 400,000
Guanerius, Giuseppe (Joseph)	$300,000 to $400,000
Guarnerius, Joseph (Del Gesu)	$1,500,000 to 4,500,000
Guarnerius, Petrus	$400,000 to $600,000
Guarnerius, Petrus II	$350,000 to $500,000
Guarini, see Menesson	$8,000 to $10,000
Guerra, Evasio Emiliano	$25,000 to $35,000
Guersan, Louis (Lodovicus)	$12,000 to $18,000
Guetter	$600 to $800
Guidantus, Joannes Florenus	$90,000 to $100,00
Guillami, Joannes	$35,000 to $40,000
Gusetto, Nicolas	$40,000 to $60,000
Gutermann, Wilhelm	$4,000 to $6,000
Hamm, Johann Gottfried	$6,000 to $8,000
Hammig, Johann Georg	$2,000 to $3,000
Hammig, Wilhelm Hermann	$3,000 to $5,000
Hardie, James	$1,000 to $1,500
Hardie, Mathew	$15,000 to $20,000

Hare, Joseph (when working for Daniel Parker)	$20,000 to $30,000
Harris, Charles I	$7,000 to $12,000
Harris, Griffith	$1,000 to $1,200
Hart, John Thomas	$6,000 to $10,000
Havelka, Johann Baptist	$2,500 to $3,000
Havemann, David Christian	$2,000 to $2,500
Heberlein	$3,000 to $5,000
Heinicke, Mathias	$10,000 to $15,000
Hel, Pierre Joseph	$20,000 to $25,000
Hellmer, Carl Joseph	$3,000 to $6,00
Hellmer, Johann Georg	$5,000 to $8,000
Hentschel, Johann Joseph	$1,500 to $2,000
Herold, Conrad Gustav	$500 to $800
Herzlieb, Franciscus	$3,500 to $5,000
Hesketh, Thomas Earle	$8,000 to $10,000
Hill, Henry Lockey	$10,000 to $15,000
Hill, Joseph	Violins: $10,000 to $15,000
	Cellos: $20,000 to $28,000
Hill, William	$10,000 to $15,000
Hill, William Ebsworth	$8,000 to $10,000
Hjorth, Emil	$6,000 to $10,000
Hoffmanm, Anton	$7,000 to $12,000

Hoffman, Martin	$2,500 to $3,000
Homolka	$8,000 to $13,000
Hopf	$3,000 to $6,000
Hopf, Carl Friedrich	$3,000 to $8,000
Hopf, David	$3,500 to $6,000
Horil, Jakob	$50,000 to $60,000
Hornsteiner	$4,500 to $10,000
Hornsteiner, modern commercial	$1,000 to $1,500
Hoyer	$2,000 to $3,000
Huber, Johann Georg	$3,500 to $5,000
Hunger, Christoph Friedrich	$3,500 to $5,000
Jacobs, (Jacobsz) Hendrick	$40,000 to $50,000
Jacquot, Charles	$15,000 to $20,000
Jacquot, Charles Albert	$15,000 to $20,000
Jaeger	$800 to $1,200
Jais, Andreas	$10,000 to $15,000
Jais, Anton	$10,000 to $15,000
Johnson, John	$8,000 to $10,000
Jorio, Vincent	$30,000 to $40,000
Kaembl, Johann Andreas	$2,500 to $3,000
Karner, Bartholomaeus	$3,000 to $5,000
Keffer, Johann	$3,000 to $5,000
Kempter, Andreas	$2,500 to $3,500
Kennedy, Thomas	Violins: $8,000 to $12,000
Kennedy, Thomas	Cellos: $25,000 to $35,000
Kessler	$400 to $500
Klier	$4,000 to $5,000
Klotz, Aegidius	$8,000 to $12,000
Klotz, Egidi	$8,000 to $12,000
Klotz, Johann Carol	$8,000 to $12,000
Klotz, Joseph	$10,000 to $15,000
Klotz, Sebastian	$8,000 to $12,000
Klotz (Kloz) Mathias	$10,000 to $15,000
Knilling	$3,000 to $4,000
Knitl, Franz	$2,500 to $3,000
Knoph, Henry Richard	$1,200 to $1,500
Knorr, Arthur	Violins: $4,000 to $6,000
	Bows: $300 to $500
Kolditz, Matthias Johann	$2,500 to $3,000
Kollmer	$2,500 to $3,000
Krausch, Georg Adam	$2,500 to $3,000
Krell, Albert	$500 to $800
Kretzschmann	$3,500 to $4,000
Kriner, Simon	$3,500 to $4,000
Kriner, Matthaeus	$5,000 to $6,000
Kulik, Johannes	$15,000 to $20,000
Laberte & Magnie	$5,000 to $7,000
Lagetto, Louis	$1,200 to $1,500
Landolfi, Carlo Ferdinando	$175,000 to $200,000

Landolfi, Pietro Antonio	$120,000 to $150,000	Lippold, Johann Gottlob	$1,500 to $2,500
La Prevotte, Etienne	$2,000 to $2,500	Lolio, Giovanni Battista	$25,000 to $35,000
Laske (Laschke), Joseph Anton	$1,500 to $2,000	Lorange, Paul Victor	$10,000 to $12,000
Laurent, Emile	$5,000 to $7,000	Lott, John Frederick	$40,000 to $50,000
Lavazza, Antonio Maria	$75,000 to $90,000	Louvet, Jean	$7,000 to $10,000
Lecchi, Giuseppe	$25,000 to $35,000	Lowendall Star Works	$800 to $1,500
Leeb, Andreas Carl	$5,000 to $6,000	Lupot, Francois I	$10,000 to $20,000
Leeb, Johann Georg I	$3,500 to $5,000	Lupot, Francois II	$5,000 to $6,000
Leeb, Johann Georg II	$3,500 to $5,000	Lupot, Nicolas	$120,000 to $150,000
Lefebre (Lefebvre), Toussaint Nicolas Germain	$5,000 to $7,500	Maggini, Giovanni Paolo	Viola: $400,000 to $800,000
Lefebvre, Jacques B.	$7,000 to $10,000	Maline, Francois Alexis	$4,000 to $5,000
Liedolff, Johann Christoph	$7,000 to $12,000	Malvolti, Pietro Antonio	$40,000 to $60,000
Leidolff, Joseph Ferdinand	$7,000 to $12,000	Mann, John Alexander	$1,000 to $1,500
Leidolff, Nicolas	$7,000 to $12,000	Mansuy, Pierre	$5,000 to $7,000
Le Jeune, Francois	$4,000 to $6,000	Mantegazza (Mantegatia) Pietro Giovanni	$80,000 to $100,000
Lemboek, Gabriel	$10,000 to $15,000	Marchetti, Abbondio	$25,000 to $30,000
Lenoble, Auguste	$3,000 to $4,000	Marchi, Giovanni Antonio	$30,000 to $50,000
Lepri, Luigi	$5,000 to $7,500	Marconcini, Giuseppe	$80,000 to $100,000
Lewis, Edward	$1,000 to $1,500	Martin	$800 to $1,200
Leibich, Johann Gottfried	$1,000 to $1,500	Mast, Joseph Laurent	$2,000 to $2,500
Lippold, Carl Friedrich	$1,500 to $2,500		
Lippold, Johann Georg	$1,500 to $2,500		

238

Maucotel	$7,000 to $12,000	Mougenot, Georges	$5,000 to $7,000
Maussiell, Leonard	$5,000 to $6,000	Mougenot, Leon	$3,500 to $5,000
Mayr,Andreas Ferdinand	$12,000 to $15,000	Muncher, Romedio	$10,000 to $15,000
Mayson, Walter H.	$1,000 to $1,500	Nadotti, Giuseppe	$25,000 to $35,000
Medard	$7,000 to $15,000	Nemessanyi, Samuel Felix	$40,000 to $60,000
Meinel	$500 to $800		
Meisel	$500 to $800	Neuner, Mathias	$8,000 to $10,000
Melegari, Enrico Clodoveo	$30,000 to $40,000	Neuner & Hornsteiner	$6,000 to $8,000
Mennegand, Charles	$6,000 to $7,500	Nicolas, Didier	$3,000 to $5,000
Mennesson, Jean Emile	$8,000 to $10,000	Niggell, Sympertus	$5,000 to $6,000
Merighi, Pietro	$20,000 to $30,000	Novello, Pietro Valentino	$20,000 to $30,000
Meyer, Magnus Andreas	$500 to $800	Obici Bartolomeo	$15,000 to $20,000
Mezzadri, Allesandro	$75,000 to $90,000	Oddone, Carlo Giuseppe	$30,000 to $40,000
Michelot, Jacques Pierre	$5,000 to $7,500	Ordoardi, Giuseppe	$30,000 to $50,000
Milton, Louis Frank	$1,000 to $1,200	Olry, J.	$2,000 to $2,500
Miremont, Claude Augustin	Violins: $10,000 to $15,000	Omond, James	$1,000 to $1,500
	Cellos: $35,000 to $50,000	Ornati, Giuseppe	$30,000 to $40,000
Moeckel, Oswald	$1,500 to $2,000	Pacherel (E), Pierre	$20,000 to $25,000
Moitessier, Louis	$6,000 to $8,000	Padewet, Johann	$1,000 to $1,500
Mongel, A.	$1,000 to $1,500	Pailliot (Paillot)	$1,000 to $1,500
Montagnana, Domenicus	Violins: $200,000 to $600,000	Pallotta, Pietro	$25,000 to $35,000
	Cellos: $1,300,000 $1,800,000	Pamphilon, Edward	$10,000 to $12,000
Morelli	$500 to $800	Pandolfi, Antonio	$30,000 to $35,000
Morrison, Archibald	$1,200 to $1,500	Panormo, Georges Louis	$60,000 to $70,000

(handwritten:). Warren 65 to 85 11/15/06)

239

Panormo, Joseph	$60,000 to $70,000
Panormo, Vincenzo	$75,000 to $85,000
Pantzer, Johann Karl	$1,000 to $1,500
Paquotte, Jean Baptiste	$1,000 to $1,500
Parker, Daniel	$20,000 to $30,000
Pasta	$35,000 to $70,00
Pauli, Joseph	$1,000 to $1,200
Paulus	$100 to $500
Pazzini, Giovanni Gaetano	$15,000 to $18,000
Pedrinelli, Antonio	$25,000 to $40,000
Pellizon	$20,000 to $30,000
Perrin, E., Fils	$800 to $1,000
Perry, Thomas	$4,000 to $5,000
Piegendorfer, Georg	$1,000 to $1,500
Pieroni, Luigi	$7,000 to $10,000
Pierray, Claude	$15,000 to $25,000
Pillement, F.	$5,000 to $6,000
Pique, Francois Louis	$50,000 to $60,000
Pirot, Claude	$3,500 to $5,000
Pizzurnus, David	$20,000 to $25,000
Placht	$500 to $800
Platner, Michael	$40,000 to $50,000
Poggi, Ansaldo	$35,000 to $50,000
Pohland	$800 to $1,000
Poirson, Justin	$3,000 to $4,000
Pollastri, Augusto	$40,000 to $50,000
Pollastri, Gaetano	$35,000 to $40,000
Posch (Bosch), Antonio	$6,000 to $8,000
Postacchini, Andrea	$45,000 to $50,000
Postiglione, Vincenzo	$50,000 to $70,000
Prager, Gustav	$300 to $500
Pressenda, Joannes Franciscus	$200,000 to $250,000
Preston, John	up to $6,000
Prevot, P. Charles	$3,000 to $4,000
Rambaux, Claude Victor	$7,500 to $12,000
Rauch, Joseph	$2,000 to $3,000
Rauch, Sebastian	$2,000 to $3,000
Rauch, Thomas	$1,500 to $2,000
Reichel	$800 to $1,500
Reiter, Johann Baptist	$1,200 to $1,500
Remy, Mathurin Francois	$6,000 to $9,000
Renaudin, Leopold	$10,000 to $15,000
Reichers, August	$1,000 to $1,500
Rief, Anton	$4,000 to $6,000
Rief, Dominicus	$4,000 to $6,000
Rieger, Johann	$1,500 to $2,000
Rieger, Georg	$1,500 to $2,000
Rinaldi, Gioffredo Benedetto	$25,000 to $35,000

Rivolta, Giacomo	$45,000 to $65,000	Santagiuliana, Giacinto	$50,000 to $70,000
Rocca, Enrico	$60,000 to $80,000	Santucci, Sebastian	$1,500 to $2,000
Rocca, Giuseppe Antonio	$100,00 to $150,000	Sawicki, Carl Nikolaus	$1,500 to $2,000
Rodiani, Giovita	$15,000 to $20,000	Scarampella, Giuseppe	$30,000 to $50,000
Rogeri, Giovanni Battista	$250,000 to $350,000	Scarampella, Paolo	$25,000 to $30,000
Rogeri, Pietro Giacomo	$200,000 to $250,000	Scarampella, Stefano	$60,000 to $80,000
Rombouts, Pieter	$40,000 to $50,000	Schaller, Oswald	$300 to $500
Ronchetti, Domenico	$30,000 to $40,000	Schandl, Anton	$2,000 to $2,500
Roscher, Christain Heinrich Wilhelm	$1,500 to $2,000	Scheverle, Johann	$2,000 to $2,500
		Schlosser	$1,000 to $2,500
		Schmidt	$800 to $1,200
Rossi, Enrico	$30,000 to $45,000	Schneider	$800 to $1,200
Roth, Ernst Heinrich	$3,000 to $6,000	Schonfelder	$2,000 to $2,500
Ruggeri, Franciscus	$250,000 to $350,000	Schonger, Franz	$1,500 to $2,000
Ruggeri, Giacinto Giovanni Battista	$120,000 to $180,000	Schorn, Johann Paul	$1,500 to $2,000
		Schuster	$500 to $800
Ruggeri, Vincenzo	$120,000 to $150,000	Schweitzer, Johann Baptist	$12,000 to $15,000
Ruprecht, Wilhelm	$1,500 to $2,000	Seidel	$1,500 to $2,000
Sacquin	$5,000 to $8,000	Seraphin, Sanctus	$200,000 to $300,000
Saint Paul, Pierre	$10,000 to $15,000	Sgarabotto, Gaetano	$25,000 to $35,000
Salo, Gasparo Da	see Bertolotti	Sgarbi, Antonio	$30,000 to $35,000
Sajot	$2,000 to $2,500	Silvestre, Pierre	$20,000 to $25,000
Salomon, Jean Baptiste	$12,000 to $15,000	Silvestre & Maucotel	$20,000 to $23,000
Salzard	$5,000 to $8,000	Simoutre, Nicolas	$6,000 to $8,000
Santagiuliana, Gaetano	$70,000 to $90,000	Sitt, Anton	$1,000 to $1,500

Skomal, Nikolaus Georg	$1,500 to $2,000
Smith, Thomas	Violins $7,000 to $12,000
	Cellos up to $30,000
Socquet, Louis	$10,000 to $15,000
Soffritti, Ettore	$30,000 to $35,000
Soliani, Angelo	$40,000 to $50,000
Soriot, D.	$1,000 to $1,500
Spidlen, Franz	$12,000 to $15,000
Stadlmann, Johann Joseph	$15,000 to $18,000
Stainer, Jacobus	$85,000 to $120,000
Stainer, Marcus	$20,000 to $25,000
Staininger, Jacob	$500 to $800
Stauffer, Johann Georg	$3,000 to $3,500
Storck, Johannes Friedrich	$4,000 to $5,000
Storioni, Lorenzo	$250,000 to $300,000
Stoss, Martin	$6,000 to $8,000
Stradivari, Antonio	$1,000,000 to $3,500,000
Stradivari, Francesco	$800,000 to $1,100,000
Stradivari, Omobono	$800,000 to $1,100,000
Strnad, Caspar	$4,000 to $5,000
Strobl, Johann	$2,500 to $3,000
Suss, Johann Christian	$800 to $1,500

Szepessy, Bela	$15,000 to $20,000
Tanegia, Carlo Antonio	$25,000 to $30,000
Tassini, Bartolomeo	$65,000 to $85,000
Tecchler, David	Violins: $70,000 to $120,000
	Cellos: $500,000 to $650,000
Tedesco, Leopold II	up to $1,500
Testore, Carlo Antonio	$100,000 to $160,000
Testore, Carlo Giuseppe	$100,000 to $150,000
Testore, Paolo Antonio	$100,000 to $120,000
Thibouville-Lamy, Louis Emile Jerome	$5,000 to $8,000
Thir (Thier), Johann Georg	$10,000 to $20,000
Thir, Andreas	$10,000 to $15,000
Thir, Anton I	$10,000 to $15,000
Thir, Mathias	$7,000 to $10,000
Thomassin, Louis	$3,000 to $4,000
Thouvenal, Henry	$800 to $1,200
Teiffenbrucker, Casper	$800 to $1,200
Teiffenbrunner, Georg	$500 to $800
Tobin, Richard	$15,000 to $25,000
Tononi, Carlo	$150,000 to $200,000
Tononi, Felice	$90,000 to $120,000
Tononi, Giovanni	$90,000 to $120,000

Toppani, Angelo	$35,000 to $45,000
Trucco, Girolamo	$4,000 to $5,000
Ullman, Giorgio	$15,000 to $25,000
Valenzano (Valenciano), Giovanni Maria	$50,000 to $80,000
Vandelli, Giovanni	$8,000 to $10,000
Van Der Slaghmeulen, Johannes Baptist	$4,000 to $5,000
Varotti, Giovanni	$60,000 to $80,000
Vatelot, Marcel	$10,000 to $12,000
Vauchel, Jean	$2,000 to $2,500
Ventapane, Lorenzo	Violins: $80,000 to $100,000
	Cellos: $85,000 to $150,000
Ventapane, Pasquale	$40,000 to $50,000
Ventapane, Vincenzo	$50,000 to $70,000
Varzella, Francesco	$800 to $1,000
Viedenhofer, Bernard	$800 to $1,000
Vignali, Giuseppe	$5,000 to $7,000
Vinaccia, Antonio	$40,000 to $60,000
Vinaccia, Gennaro	$40,000 to $60,000
Vincenzi, Luigi	$30,000 to $40,000
Vogler, Johann Georg	$2,000 to $2,500
Voigt, Arnold	$4,000 to $6,000
Voigt, Carl Hermann	$5,000 to $7,000
Voigt, Johann Georg	$6,000 to $8,000
Voirin, Francois Nicolas	$5,000 to $6,000
Voller, William	$25,000 to $40,000
Vuillaume, Jean Baptiste	$80,000 to $120,000
Vuillaume, Nicolas Francois	$20,000 to $25,000
Vuillaume, Sebastien	$20,000 to $25,000
Wagner, Benedict	$2,000 to $2,500
Wamsley, Peter	$8,000 to $10,000
Weigert, Johann Blasius	$2,000 to $2,500
Weis, Jacob	$2,000 to $2,500
Werner, Franz	$3,000 to $4,000
Widhalm, Leopold	$15,000 to $20,000
Widhalm, (Martin) Leopold	$8,000 to $13,000
Willems, Hendrick	$15,000 to $20,000
Winterling, Georg	$1,000 to $1,500
Withers, George	$1,500 to $3,500
Wutzelhofer, Sebastian	$1,500 to $2,000
Zach, Carl	$800 to $1,200
Zach, Thomas	$1,500 to $2,000
Zacher, Maximilian	$800 to $1,200
Zanoli, Giacomo	$70,000 to $90,000

Zanoli,
  Giovanni
  Battista $80,000 to $100,000
Zanotti (Zanotus),
  Antonio $70,000 to $80,000
Zanti,
  Alessandro $40,000 to $50,000
Zianni,
  Pietro $40,000 to $50,000

Barbieri - 20 - $24,000

Maker	Name	Value
Annarumma,	Vincenzo	$15,000 to $20,000
Arassi,	Enzo	$14,000 to $18,000
Averna,	Enrico	$8,000 to $10,000
Averna,	Gesnaldo	$8,000 to $10,000
Barbieri,	Arnaldo	$7,000 to $9,000
Bedocchi,	Mario	$12,000 to $15,000
Bella Fontana,	Lorenzo	$25,000 to $30,000
Bonora,	Giuseppe	$7,000 to $10,000
Bosi,	Carlo	$7,000 to $10,000
Bottini,	Benvenuto	$10,000 to $12,000
Calace,	Giuseppe	$20,000 to $25,000
Candi,	Cesare	$30,000 to $40,000
Candi,	Oreste	$25,000 to $30,000
Capalbo,	Giovanni	$10,000 to $15,000
Capicchioni,	Marino	$25,000 to $30,000
Carpi,	Oreste	$8,000 to $10,000
Casini,	Lapo	$15,000 to $20,000
Castagnino,	Giuseppe	$15,000 to $25,000
Castellotti, Aldo	di Luigi	$3,000 to $6,000
Celani,	Costantino	$20,000 to $25,000
Chiaraffa,	Guglielmo	$3,000 to $6,000
Contavalli,	Luigi	$20,000 to $25,000
Contino,	Alfredo	$25,000 to $35,000
De Barbieri,	Paolo	$20,000 to $30,000
De Lucca,	Antonio	$12,000 to $15,000
Desposito,	Lorenzo	$4,000 to $6,000
Digiuni,	Luigi	$10,000 to $15,000
Di Leo,	Domenico	$3,000 to $5,000
Di Stefano,	Giuseppe	$7,000 to $10,000
Farotti,	Celestino	$15,000 to $20,000
Ferraris,	Oreste	$3,000 to $6,000
Ferroni,	Fernando	$7,000 to $10,000
Fontanini,	Aristide	$5,000 to $8,000
Gadda,	Gaetano	$30,000 to $40,000
Galimberti,	Luigi	$25,000 to $35,000
Gallinotti,	Pietro	$10,000 to $12,000
Guisquiani,	Raffaello	$3,000 to $6,000
Goti,	Orsolo	$20,000 to $25,000
Guadagnini,	Paolo	$15,000 to $20,000
Guerra,	Evasio	$25,000 to $30,000

Gulino,		Scevcenko,	
Salvatore	$5,000 to $8,000	Vladimir	$15,000 to $25,000
Lombardi,		Sderci	
Colombo	$3,000 to $5,000	Nicolo	
Lepri,		Iginio	$25,000 to $30,000
Giuseppe	$5,000 to $7,000	Sgarabotto,	
Maggiali,		Gaetano	$25,000 to $35,000
Cesare	$8,000 to $9,000	Sgarbi,	
Marconi,		Antonio	$25,000 to $35,000
Lorenzo	up to $5,000	Sisto,	
Martinenghi,		Sisto	$5,000 to $8,000
Marcello	$3,000 to $6,000	Solferini,	
Masetti,		Remo	$4,000 to $6,000
Fratelli	up to $5,000	Stelluto,	
Massara,		Lorenzo	$8,000 to $10,000
Pietro	up to $4,000	Tivoli,	
Mironi,		Fiorini	
Pietro	$3,000 to $5,000	Arrigo	$10,000 to $15,000
Monterumici,		Tramonti,	
Armando	$20,000 to $25,000	Rodolfo	$3,000 to $5,000
Mozzani,		Tua,	
G.	$8,000 to $15,000	Silvio	$5,000 to $7,500
Palumbo,		Ubert,	
Francesco	$3,000 to $5,000	Emilio	$3,000 to $5,000
Parmeggiani,		Utili,	
Romolo	$15,000 to $25,000	Nicola	$10,000 to $20,000
Pedrazzini,		Vachier,	
Giuseppe	$30,000 to $40,000	Galileo	$3,000 to $5,000
Pinheiro,		Valentini,	
Ernesto	$4,000 to $6,000	Arturo	$4,000 to $6,000
Poggini,		Venezia,	
Milton	up to $8,000	Provino	$2,500 to $4,000
Politi,		Vistoli,	
A.	$8,000 to $15,000	Luigi	up to $3,000
Politi,			
Enrico	$15,000 to $25,000		
Puccini,			
Eligio	$3,000 to $6,000		
Radrizzani,			
Angelo	$15,000 to $25,000		
Rocchi, Sesto			
di Erminio	$15,000 to $25,000		
Rovescalli,			
Azzo	$20,000 to $25,000		

Robert Ames

Robert Ames was six years in the employ of William Salchow, Bowmaker, in New York City. While with Mr. Salchow, he produced approximately 200 bows. He also received thorough training in the repair and restoration of fine bows. While associated with Mr. Salchow, he was able to study the finest examples of the French, English, and German bowmakers. He left this position as shop foreman to establish his own business in 1982.

Currently, Mr. Ames is the sole proprietor of his own shop: Robert Ames, Fine Violins and Bows located in Maywood, New Jersey, U.S.A. He is involved in bowmaking, fine repair and restoration, and sales of rare bows and instruments.

His memberships include the American Federation of Violin and Bow Makers and the Violin Society of America. He has won honors at the International Violin and Bow Competition at Hofstra University in Hempstead, New York in 1980 and at Salt Lake City, Utah in 1982.

Robert Ames, Fine Violins and Bows

TELEPHONE: 201-368-3435   FAX: 201-368-3455

WWW.TOURTE.COM

Bows for string instruments hold a unique niche in the music world. They must function on two levels. First and most important, they must serve musicians as tools of the trade by enabling string players to easily produce beautiful music. Toward this end a bow must possess proper strength, a comfortable weight, and a good balance in the hand. These attributes will vary for each musician, but will usually fall into somewhat defined parameters. For example, a good weight for a violin bow is usually around 60 grams although some bows will be very playable at 56 or 64 grams. This weight differential will vary with each player. The strength of a bow is also variable as is the balance. When taken together, these desirable qualities will combine to produce a bow that should enhance a musician's ability to make music. Second, bows are also looked upon by many as collectible items. As such, these delicate wands also represent miniature pieces of art. Collectors of bows look at minute details in the head and also at the frog and button to determine who might possibly have made a particular bow. These details can be subtle, but also very important to a trained eye in determining important information such as country of origin, a particular maker, and also the value of a bow.

The qualities that a musician looks for in a bow may not necessarily be the same qualities that a collector will look for. Even though many times the factors that determine a good bow will be similar for both player and collector. It is also important to know that one does not need to spend large sums of money to acquire a good playing bow, although fine examples of the better makers will always command top prices. There are many thousands of very good bows available in all price ranges that will provide most players with years of satisfactory service. Many bows have been produced by makers who have toiled in obscurity and whose bows were never stamped with their names. These "no name bows" can often prove to be a good value. Do not pass on a bow just because it is unstamped or of an unknown origin. Just remember it should be priced accordingly.

Condition and playability are very much determining factors when selecting a bow. Condition can be determined by careful observation of the bow's parts. Look carefully at the head for cracks and repairs. Also look at the stick for cracks. Check for excessive wear, although often a bow is very worn because it is such a good playing bow that its previous owner used it all the time, thus wearing it down. Whenever I see a worn bow, my first thought is that somebody really loved using this bow. Bows with repairs or excessive wear are not necessarily to be avoided, but overall condition should be factored in when determining a bow's value.

Playability is also very important in determining if a bow will be suitable to the musician and the instrument for music making. Playability is usually determined by the individual musician taking into consideration the three factors mentioned before: weight, strength, and balance. A bow should also have a good "feel" in the hand and the weight, strength, and balance will meld together to contribute toward this comfortable feeling. Bows can often be "customized" to suit a particular player by changing the weight and balance slightly. This should only be done by a competent bow specialist, not an amateur. Musicians will find that each bow will produce a different sound on their instrument. Some of these differences are subtle and some are profound. The quality and type of sound a bow contributes to the instrument should be considered in selecting a suitable bow.

All of this having been said, I believe selecting a bow or even an instrument should be an interesting and rewarding experience. It is possible, when looking for a bow, to become enamored of a particular name or names, to the exclusion of many less well-known, but worthwhile bow makers. Try to keep yourself open to finding the best bow for your needs regardless of name, country of origin, or "new" versus "old". Most string players are familiar with names like Tourte, Peccatte, Sartory, Lamy, Voirin, Tubbs, etc. These makers represent the acme of the bowmaker's art and are sought after because of the high esteem in which they are held. I believe many of these well-known makers were also prolific and were able to produce many bows over a long period of time thereby assuring their reputations by a large output of high quality work. There are also quite a few bowmakers whose names are not as familiar to the string playing community. The reasons are many. These makers may have had a smaller output than many of their colleagues and there are now fewer bows of theirs on the market. There are also makers whose bows were sold through large dealers and therefore not stamped with the maker's name. There are also makers whose names have simply not "caught on" with the string playing community. These makers represent for me some of the best values in well-made bows on the market today. A little research can yield a fine bow that will not "break the bank".

Some makers that I think deserve to be mentioned are listed below although this is by no means a complete list, and I am sure every aficionado will have a few makers they consider to be worthy of inclusion.

Among makers of the French school is a bowmaker who was not only prolific, but also taught many other bowmakers, including the brothers Jules and Victor Fetique. He is Charles Nicholas Bazin, a fine maker whose bows can be likened in style to those of Voirin. The heads are usually delicate and his choice of wood is very good. Others of the French school that pass through my shop and seem to be deserving of a second look are: Andre Chardon, Prosper Colas, Eugene Cuniot-Hury (teacher of E. Ouchard), Louis Gillet (pupil of Sartory), Charles Husson (father and son), Jean Joseph Martin (worked in the Vuillaume shop), Louis Piernot, Justin Poirson (worked for N. Maire and Vuillaume), and Andre Richaume (who worked with Ouchard and Fetique).

Other bowmakers that I consider especially noteworthy are the German makers Ludwig Bausch (his handmade bows are not the mass produced bow that came later), Albert Nurnberger, H.R. Pfretzschner (he worked in the Vuillaume shop in Paris for a short time), August Rau, Otto A. Hoyer (worked for Sartory), Richard Weichold and Fredrich Wunderlich.

There are, I am sure, others that deserve mention, but these are makers whose work, for me, stands out as consistently good and worthy.

I would be remiss if I did not mention the current crop of very talented bowmakers, especially those of the French and American schools. The French, of course, come from a long and honored tradition of bowmaking. The Americans have taken the best of all traditions and are producing some very fine and noteworthy bows. The materials seen in many new bows are as good and often better than that of the old masters. The myth that good pernambuco is no longer available for bowmakers is absolutely false. These new bows are reasonable in price and represent a good value to string players. I feel certain that the bows of these fine bowmakers will be sought after for years to come just as the bows of the great makers of the past have been played and coveted by present generations.

May your hunt for a great bow be interesting and rewarding.

Happy Hunting!

-Robert Ames

Adam,		Eury,	
(Grand-Adam)	$22,000 to $26,000	Nicholas	$22,000 to $26,000
Adam,		Fetique,	
Jean		Jules	$7,000 to $9,000
Dominique	$15,000 to $18,000	Fetique,	
Allen,		Victor	$7,000 to $9,000
Samuel	Rare	Fonclause,	
Audinot,		C.J.	$27,000 to $34,000
Jacques	$3,500 to $4,500	Gaulard	$12,000 to $16,000
Bausch,		Gand &	
Ludwig	$3,500 to $5,000	Bernardel	Depends on Maker
Bazin,		Gerome,	
Charles N.	$5,000 to $6,000	Roger	$3,000 to $4,000
Bazin,		Gillet,	
Francois	$4,000 to $6,000	Louis	$4,000 to $6,000
Bernardel,		Hill, *1960's S/E = 4-5,000*	
Leon	Depends on Maker	W.E.	
Bulthitude,		& Sons	$3,500 to $5,500
Arthur	$2,000 to $3,000	Henry,	
Buthod,		J.	$25,000 to $30,000
Charles	$3,000 to $4,000	Hoyer,	
Caressa &		Otto A.	$3,000 to $4,000
Francais	Depends on Maker	Husson,	
Chardon,		C.C.	
Andre	$6,000 to $7,000	(Father &	
Colas,		Son)	$6,000 to $8,000
Prosper	$6,000 to $7,000	Jombar,	
Cuniot-Hury,		Paul	Depends on Maker
Eugene	Depends on Maker	Kittel,	
Dodd,		N.F.	$26,000 to $34,000
Edward	$8,000 to $10,000	Knopf,	
Dodd,		C.W.	$3,500 to $6,000
James I & II	$8,000 to $10,000	Knopf,	
Dodd,		Heinrich	$4,000 to $5,000
John Kew	$10,000 to $12,000	Knopf,	
	(higher for his best works)	H.R.	$2,500 to $3,000
Dodd,		Laberte,	
Thomas	$8,000 to $10,000	Marc	$2,500 to $3,000

Lafleur, Joseph Rene	$18,000 to $24,000
Lamy I, Alfred	$12,000 to $14,000
Lamy II, Alfred (Camille Hippolyte)	$10,000 to $12,000
Lapierre, Marcel	$3,000 to $4,000
Lenoble, August	$6,000 to $8,000
Lotte, Francois	$2,500 to $3,500
Lupot II, Francois	$22,000 to $26,000
Maire, Nicholas	$26,000 to $32,000
Maline, Guillaume	$26,000 to $32,000
Martin, Jean Joseph	$10,000 to $12,000
Millant, John Jacques	$3,500 to $5,000
Millant, Bernard	$3,500 to $5,000
Morizot, Louis Sr.	$3,500 to $4,500
Morizot, Freres	$2,500 to $3,500
Nurnberger II, Franz	$3,000 to $4,000
Nurnberger-Suess	$2,500 to $3,000
Ouchard, Emile F. (Pere)	$6,000 to $8,000
Ouchard, Emile A. (Fis)	$9,000 to $12,000

Pajeot, Louis Simon (Pere)	$18,000 to $20,000
Pajeot, Etienne	$24,000 to $30,000
Panormo, George Louis	$10,000 to $12,000
Paccatte, Charles	$14,000 to $18,000
Peccatte, Dominique	$50,000 to $75,000 and higher
Peccatte, Francois	$25,000 to $35,000
Persois	$30,000 to $38,000
Piernot, Louis	$5,000 to $7,000
Poirson, Justin	$6,000 to $8000 early period
Pfretzschner I, H.R.	$2,500 to $3,500
Pfretzschner, G.A.	$2,000 to $2,500
Pfretzschner, W.A.	$2,000 to $2,500
Prager, Ed.	$2,000 to $2,500
Prell, Herman	$2,000 to $3,000
Rau, August	$2,500 to $3,500
Richaume, Andre	$6,000 to $8,000
Sartory, Eugene	$12,000 to $15,000
Schuster, Adolph	$2,000 to $3,000
Silvestre & Maucotel	Depends on Maker

Simon, FR	$12,000 to $15,000
Simon, Pierre	$28,000 to $32,000
Thibouville-Lamy	Depends on Maker
Thomassin, Claude	$7,000 to $10,000
Thomassin, Louis	$7,000 to $10,000
Tourte, Francois	Rare
Tourte, Leonard (formerly Louis)	Rare
Tubbs, James	$10,000 to $12,000
Tubbs, Thomas	$8,000 to $10,000
Tubbs, William	$8,000 to $10,000
Van De Meer, Karel	$3,000 to $4,000
Vigneron, Andre	$6,500 to $9,000
Vigneron, J.A.	$8,500 to $11,000
Voigt, Arnold	$2,000 to $2,500
Voirin, F.N.	$12,000 to $16,000
Vuillaume, J.B.	$6,000 to $8,000 or higher depending on maker
Weichold, Richard	$2,500 to $3,500
Wunderlich, Fredrich	$2,500 to $3,500

AFTERWORD, CODA
by Harold Chaitman

In 1973, I wrote a few paragraphs on why violins and other members of the violin family keep and increase their value; these paragraphs can be found on page 193.

These intervening years have seen a proliferation of violin shops in the United States and the American violin making schools have turned out many excellent craftsmen and craftswomen to work in all sections of North America. It remains to be seen if the violin world can support the many restoration workers and makers of instruments; competition has always been difficult.

For some of these violin and bow making artisans it is valid to say as Longinus (that important first century Greek writer on literary aesthetics) has written: "For many men are carried away by the spirit of others as if inspired...,".

"Similarly from the great natures of the men of old there are borne in upon the souls of those who emulate them (as if from sacred caves) what we may describe as effluences, so that even those who seem little likely to be possessed are thereby inspired and succumb to the spell of the others' greatness."

For other violin and bow craftsmen the work will be a job to make something of a living.

One of my first impulses, in writing this afterword, was to disclose much of the double talk and mischief that goes on in the violin business. However, after consideration it might be wise to conclude that only in a work of fiction can these truths be told.

What should be strongly emphasized is that very few individuals are definitely qualified to write certificates for violins, violas, cellos, basses, and their bows and I do not consider myself in this number, even though I have dealt with violin dealers, primarily on the east coast, these past twenty-two years. Perhaps there are a dozen individuals or violin shops in North America qualified to write such certificates and approximately another dozen violin establishments in Europe and the rest of the world qualified to do so.

The aural magic of the violin, viola, cello, and bass is probably more dependent on these instruments and bows than any other musical instrument. Conversely, I recall a distinguished American concert violinist telling me, after I questioned if Mischa Elman's golden tone would be so glowingly warm if he did not play on the Recomièr Stradivarius, that when he, this concert violinist was young — a time going back to approximately 1928 — Mischa Elman visited his high school and after some discussion picked up my friend's inexpensive German violin and played with that ravishing tone for which he was famous. To be sure, Elman's violins were of the Stradivarius and Amati names and Elman's bows were of the Voirin and Lamy brands.

Quality instruments of the violin family have been made throughout Europe and the United States over the last few hundred years. It is unfortunate to consider how many have been relabeled with obscure and not so obscure Italian names; thereby negating the reputation of some talented makers from a different time and place. What is even more tragic is the excessive thinning of the top and back plates to give an immediate liveliness, which ultimately ruins the instrument. Also, improper revarnishing by the unskilled lowers the quality of tone and lowers the monetary value of these tools of the musician's profession.

Because so much is dependent on the tonal enchantment of the string family instrument; it may be considered that two types of artists have evolved. Firstly the player, the musician who delivers the messages of the geniuses of composition; those who can galvanize our emotions from laughter to heartfelt awareness of deep tragedy, from heroic passion to the gentle concern of the lullaby. As well as inducing the sensitive listener to become aware of his or her archetypal self; for great music is the archetypal self in movement. It is not of the utmost importance if a composition is long or short in duration, only if it can speak to our hearts, to our subconscious, and therefore to our personal and collective human memories. For that is the magic of music; this very abstract and very pure art form.

Secondly, let us consider the artistic craftsmen of the violin family and their bows; who through study and long hours at the workbench create these artifacts that can beguile the musician to spend his hard earned money. It has been suggested that the craftsman who does not play upon what he has built is analogous to the baker who cannot taste his cakes and pastries. However, when this violin has a sculpted look with a varnish of opalescent quality resembling more a skin emitted from the body than a layered-on paint job, with fastidious graduations throughout the entire inside, with purfling and scroll of artistic merit, this violin can move us in its silence. And from this state of silence, if this member of the violin family can fulfill its promise of tonal quality than such a violin, viola, cello, bass becomes the painting that can sing and the statue that can dance.

Richmond, Virginia 1999